Gender and Global Justice

Gender and Global Justice

Edited by Alison M. Jaggar

polity

First published in 2014 by Polity Press

Polity Press
65 Bridge Street
Cambridge CB2 1UR, UK

Polity Press
350 Main Street
Malden, MA 02148, USA

ISBN-13: 978-0-7456-6376-0
ISBN-13: 978-0-7456-6377-7(pb)

A catalogue record for this book is available from the British Library.

Typeset in 10.5 on 12 pt Times New Roman
by Toppan Best-set Premedia Limited

The publisher has used its best endeavours to ensure that the URLs for external websites referred to in this book are correct and active at the time of going to press. However, the publisher has no responsibility for the websites and can make no guarantee that a site will remain live or that the content is or will remain appropriate.

For further information on Polity, visit our website: www.politybooks.com

Contents

Acknowledgments

This book has its roots in a workshop on global gender justice held in Oslo in May, 2008, under the auspices of the Centre for the Study of Mind in Nature. The workshop was the first of its kind within the discipline of philosophy. As the organizer of the Oslo workshop, I am extremely grateful for the generous support of the Centre first in hosting the workshop and later in continuing to support my work preparing this book.

My own chapters in the book benefited considerably from comments by the Centre's Christel Fricke and other participants in the workshop. In addition, a number of colleagues and students at the University of Colorado at Boulder gave generous feedback on my chapters. I am indebted to: Eamon Aloyo, Cory Aragon, Lorraine Bayard de Volo, David Boonin, Robert Buffington, Amandine Catala, Anne Costain, Stephen Emedi, Barrett Emerick, Chelsea Haramia, Hye-Ryoung Kang, Deepti Misri, Celeste Montoya, April Shaw, and Scott Wisor.

Many thanks to the wonderful people at Polity, especially editors Emma Hutchinson, who encouraged me to undertake this book, and Sarah Lambert, who was very helpful while Emma was on leave. I also owe thanks to an excellent production team, including Clare Ansell, Susan Beer, Tim Clark, and Glynis Baguley. Annaleigh Curtis created the index with her customary efficiency and speed.

As always, my family has been supportive, especially my partner David Jaggar who has continued to maintain his high vegetarian culinary standards. I can't thank him enough for his constant encouragement over so many decades.

Notes on Contributors

Linda Martín Alcoff is Professor of Philosophy at Hunter College and the Graduate School, CUNY. She is a past President of the American Philosophical Association, Eastern Division. Her writings have focused on social identity and race, epistemology and politics, sexual violence, Foucault, Dussel, and Latino issues in philosophy. Her book, *Visible Identities: Race, Gender and the Self* (Oxford University Press, 2006), won the Frantz Fanon Award for 2009. She is originally from Panama, but lives today happily in Brooklyn. For more information go to www.alcoff.com.

Gillian Brock is Associate Professor of Philosophy at the University of Auckland in New Zealand. Her most recent work has been on global justice and related fields. She is the author of *Global Justice: A Cosmopolitan Account* (Oxford University Press, 2009) and editor or co-editor of *Current Debates in Global Justice, The Political Philosophy of Cosmopolitanism, Necessary Goods: Our Responsibilities to Meet Others' Needs*, and *Global Heath and Global Health Ethics*, and other titles are forthcoming. She has published over 100 peer-reviewed papers in journals such as *Ethics, Canadian Journal of Law and Jurisprudence, American Philosophical Quarterly*, the *Monist*, and the *Journal of Social Philosophy*. She holds editorial positions with a number of journals and book series. She is an Associate Editor for the journal *Politics, Philosophy and Economics*.

Abigail Gosselin is Associate Professor of Philosophy at Regis University in Denver, Colorado. She is the author of *Global Poverty and Individual Responsibility* (Lexington, 2009) as well as articles on human rights, addiction, epistemological limitations of memoirs, and problems with globalizing scientific conceptions of mental disorders. In addition, she has published articles on teaching discernment and teaching ethics from a feminist perspective (co-authored). Her current work examines the epistemological processes by which we develop our understandings of mental disorders and analyzes the justice implications of these conceptualizations.

Alison M. Jaggar is a College Professor of Distinction in Philosophy and Women and Gender Studies at the University of Colorado at Boulder. She is also Research Co-ordinator at the University of Oslo's Centre for the Study of Mind in Nature. She is the author and editor of many books and articles and recipient of many awards and fellowships. Jaggar was a pioneer in feminist philosophy and in recent years she has worked to introduced gender as a category of analysis into the philosophical debate on global justice. In addition, Jaggar is exploring the potential of a naturalized approach to moral epistemology for addressing moral disputes in contexts of inequality and cultural difference.

Hye-Ryoung Kang is Assistant Professor in the Philosophy Department and Faculty Associate in the Women Studies Program at the University of Nevada, Reno. She obtained her PhD in Philosophy and the Graduate Certificate in Women and Gender Studies from the University of Colorado at Boulder. She specializes in social and political philosophy with special emphasis on theories of social justice, human rights, and laws in the global context. Her current research interest is in global justice from a transnational feminist perspective.

Eva Feder Kittay is Distinguished Professor of Philosophy and Senior Fellow, Center for Medical Humanities, Compassionate Care, and Bioethics at Stony Brook University. Her authored books include *Metaphor* (Clarendon Press, 1985) and *Love's Labor* (Routledge, 1999). In her numerous articles, edited books and special issue journals in feminist philosophy, feminist ethics and disability, she has helped to develop these emerging areas of philosophical inquiry and introduced previously neglected topics, such as carework and cognitive disability.

Rachel Silvey is Associate Professor of Geography at the University of Toronto. She received her PhD from the University of Washington, Seattle. Her research interests include gender studies, Indonesia, migration, critical development studies, and transnational Islam. She has published widely on gender and migration in Indonesia in both disciplinary and interdisciplinary journals and collected volumes. She is co-editor (with Isabella Bakker) of *Beyond States and Markets: The Challenges of Social Reproduction* (Routledge, 2008). She has received funding from the National Science Foundation, the Fulbright New Century Scholars Program, and the Social Sciences and Humanities Research Council of Canada.

Scott Wisor received his PhD in philosophy from the University of Colorado at Boulder, and served for three years as a Research Fellow at Australian National University on the project "Measuring Poverty and Gender Disparity." He has published on the resource curse, international trade, social valuation, and global poverty, often from a feminist perspective. His first book is *Measuring Global Poverty: Toward a Pro-Poor Approach* (Palgrave Macmillan, 2011).

Introduction

Gender and Global Justice: Rethinking Some Basic Assumptions of Western Political Philosophy[1]

Alison M. Jaggar

0.1 Philosophical questions of distributive justice

Concerns about the gendered dimensions of global justice have been articulated only recently within the discipline of philosophy. In this introductory essay, I explain how raising such concerns brings into question some of the most basic assumptions of Western political philosophy. I begin by situating reflections on global gender justice in the context of earlier philosophical thought about justice.

Central to justice is the idea of moral balance. Broadly speaking, to be concerned about justice is to be interested in assuring that all claimants should give and receive whatever they are justly due. Normative debate among political philosophers focuses on how the abstract idea of what is justly due should be interpreted substantively and applied in practice.

Western philosophers usually distinguish three main branches of justice, corresponding to three main types of concerns. One branch, retributive justice, addresses questions regarding the appropriate punishment of wrongdoers. A second branch, reparative justice, addresses questions of how to correct or rectify past wrongs. The third branch, distributive justice, addresses questions concerning the fair distribution of the benefits and burdens of participating in a co-operative enterprise. This is the branch that has received most attention from Western philosophers and the essays in this volume mostly fall within this category, although it should be noted that questions of retributive and reparative justice also have gender dimensions and can also be raised in global contexts.

Alternative normative theories of distributive justice are structured as sets of answers to several framing questions. Those questions are, briefly: where, when, who, what, and how?

Where? asks what is the domain or sphere of life within which the moral demands of justice have application.

When? asks what are the social circumstances within which the demands of justice apply.

Who? asks which entities should be regarded as subjects of justice, meaning who or what are entitled to make justice claims deserving of moral consideration.

What? asks which entities should be regarded as objects of justice, meaning which kinds or categories of things should be distributed in a just manner.

Finally, *How?* asks which principles are the most morally appropriate for guiding the allocation of various objects to various subjects in various circumstances.

Any convincing answer to these questions requires a rationale. In other words, it requires addressing the further question, *Why?* Philosophical theories of justice not only offer answers to the central questions of justice but—like all theories—they also explain why they advocate these particular answers.

0.2   Western political philosophy from the sixteenth to mid-twentieth centuries

Between the late sixteenth and the mid-twentieth centuries, Western political philosophers, sometimes termed "modern" political philosophers, developed answers to these questions that were widely accepted by the end of the period.

Where? Modern Western philosophers agreed that the moral demands of justice held only among people who shared a common way of life, and they typically identified the external boundaries of this moral community with the frontiers of the sovereign state. They also identified "internal" limits to the moral demands of justice, drawing these boundaries around areas of supposedly personal life such as religion, household, and family. In these areas, the demands of justice were thought to be inapplicable.

When? Most modern philosophers agreed that the circumstances in which the principles of justice had applicability were those of moderate scarcity. That is to say, they assumed that questions of justice arise only when the necessities of life are not so plentiful that all legitimate claimants can have as much of anything as they want and not so scarce that it is impossible to reach any satisfactory agreement about distributing the available objects.

Who? Modern philosophers tended to regard the legitimate claimants or subjects of justice as those human individuals residing within a particular jurisdiction. Prior to the advent of universal citizenship, even slaves and serfs were thought to be the source of some legitimate justice claims, but foreigners and animals were typically excluded as subjects of justice.

What? The main objects of justice or kinds of things thought appropriate for just distribution were typically taken to be political rights and responsibilities, on the one hand, and economic obligations and access to resources, on the other.

How? Typically assuming certain answers to the questions of where, when, who, and what, Western philosophical debate about justice focused mostly on the question of "how." In other words, it sought to identify morally acceptable criteria to guide just distributions of available goods among legitimate claimants. Popular candidates to ground principles of just distribution have included: equal distribution, distribution according to need, and distribution according to desert.

Why? Underlying much of the thinking of modern Western political philosophers have been basic moral commitments to individual liberty and equality. Throughout the modern period, these values increasingly came to be regarded as default standards. Limits on liberty and departures from equality were both thought to require further justification and this was often presented as the best way of balancing these fundamental values.

0.3   Western political philosophy after World War II

The last half of the twentieth century saw a new flowering of political philosophy, responding to striking changes in the post-war world. The changes included extensive decolonization, the Cold War, and the establishment of social democracy in much of Western Europe. In many countries, new demands for equality were made by women and by the members of previously marginalized or stigmatized communities. These changes inspired philosophers to begin questioning long-accepted assumptions about justice.

0.3.1   Rawls's A Theory of Justice (1971)

John Rawls's *A Theory of Justice* is the pre-eminent work of political philosophy in the second half of the twentieth century. Rawls's theory incorporated much of the new political sensibility of the post-war era, but the world continued to change rapidly over the course of Rawls's career, raising challenges for political philosophy that could be only partially accommodated within the framework established by *A Theory of Justice*. Here I will mention only a few features of Rawls's rich and complex work.

Rawls offers a normative theory of justice which assumes its domain to be a single society, imagined as sovereign and economically self-sufficient. The theory takes justice to be a property that characterizes primarily social institutions rather than individuals' characters or particular relationships. Institutions are relatively stable practices that organize social life. They provide the social context within which people make decisions and structure the options socially available to individuals by assigning costs and benefits to various choices. Rawls's assertion that justice applies primarily to social institutions helps clarify the difference between ethics and political philosophy. Ethics assesses individual conduct and character, as manifested in the choices that people make, whereas political philosophy assesses the design of institutions that together establish the social frameworks within which people make choices. For Rawls, the task of political philosophy is to consider whether the main institutions that regulate everyone's life opportunities distribute social burdens and benefits in ways that are just, or at least more just than feasible alternative arrangements.

At the normative level, *A Theory of Justice* emphasized the interdependence of liberty and equality. Rawls recognized clearly that establishing formal equality did not guarantee that people would be substantively equal, and that the worth of liberty could be diminished by lack of access to economic resources. For Rawls, therefore, citizens in a just society must not only be political equals; their equal claim on the society's economic resources must also be recognized. One of Rawls's boldest principles of economic justice asserted that inequalities in income were justifiable only insofar as they contributed to raising the lowest socio-economic position.

In terms of answering the questions that structure normative theories of justice, Rawls's main innovation consists in his distinctive and remarkably egalitarian answer to the question of *how* the benefits and burdens of social co-operation should be distributed. At the time of its publication the book was hailed as a new beginning in normative political philosophy, following a famous declaration of the death of this field.[2] However, Rawls's theory is better seen as bringing three centuries of Western political philosophy to culmination. It provides the most explicit and developed expression of this tradition, thereby making its assumptions more available to critical scrutiny. Toward the end of the twentieth century, other philosophers began to challenge assumptions largely taken for granted by Rawls and by earlier Western philosophers. These assumptions concerned the *domain*, the *subjects*, and the *objects* of justice.

0.3.2   Late-twentieth-century challenges to long-established assumptions of Western political philosophy

0.3.2.1   Critical thinking about race and ethnicity

Following World War II, concerns over injustice to racialized people arose from several sources. One source was decolonization, especially in Africa and the Indian subcontinent. A second was the African-American struggle for civil rights in the United States, and a third the discrimination experienced by immigrants and students from the erstwhile colonies when they entered Europe and North America. Some of these concerns were soon reflected in Western political philosophy; here I will mention two manifestations.

In their influential little book, *Black Power*, published in 1967, US Black activists Stokely Carmichael and Michael Hamilton distinguished individual from institutional racism. Individual racism consists in personal hatred, contempt, or disregard for people of color. Institutional racism is revealed in social structures that systematically disadvantage people of color. Institutional racism sometimes makes overt reference to race, as in the case of systems such as Jim Crow and apartheid, but it may also be overtly race-neutral. Carmichael and Hamilton show how many seemingly race-neutral institutions in the United States, such as education and housing, often produce systematically less favorable outcomes for people of color. Such disadvantaging can occur even in the absence of overt or felt prejudice on the part of white people associated with the institution in question. Rawls's emphasis that political philosophy is concerned primarily with the justice of institutions may have been influenced by this groundbreaking activist work.

One prominent slogan of the US civil rights movement was "Black is beautiful," which expressed the idea that injustice may be not only political and economic but also cultural and symbolic (Fraser 1997). In the 1980s and 1990s, this idea was the focus of a series of philosophical debates over what came to be called "multiculturalism." The debates considered how cultural "recognition" might be accorded to groups such as racialized, ethnic, sexual, and religious minorities, whose identities had been publicly devalued and stigmatized.

I have selected for mention the institutional and the multicultural aspects of critical race theory because they go beyond demanding that individuals who belong to racialized or marginalized communities should enjoy political and economic rights that are formally equal with those enjoyed by members of the dominant group. Additionally, critical race theory challenges earlier conceptions of both the *subjects* and the *objects* of justice. It suggests that groups as well as individuals may be the sources of justice claims and that these claims may include demands for public recognition and valuation.

0.3.2.2   Western feminism

Western feminist philosophy emerged in the 1970s as an expression of the second wave of the women's liberation movement, which began to rise in the 1960s. Like critical race theorists, feminist theorists also drew on the available resources of Western political philosophy, especially its longstanding commitments to liberty and equality. Yet in pressing the limits of both, feminists too brought into question some of Western philosophy's basic assumptions about justice.

Feminist philosophers began by conceptually distinguishing sex, which they initially (and too simplistically) regarded as a biologically given binary, from gender, which they viewed as a complex set of social norms regulating everyone's lives according to assigned masculine and feminine gender identities. Using the idea that people's social situations differ according to their gender, feminist theorists identified both overt and covert forms of institutional gender injustice. In addition to overtly discriminatory policies, such as those explicitly prohibiting women from certain occupations, covert gender bias existed in many facially gender-neutral institutions of daily life, such as the standard working day structured on the assumption that workers have no care-taking responsibilities (MacKinnon 1987). Feminist theorists articulated their recognition of this type of injustice by asserting that some institutions had a disparate impact on women, not because women had a distinct sexual nature but because their social situations were systematically different from men's.

Just as the critical race theorists had gone beyond demanding liberty and equality for people of color on the same terms as white people, so some feminist philosophers went beyond demanding liberty and equality for women on the same terms as men. They too challenged long-held assumptions about justice. A distinctive insight of second-wave Western feminism was expressed in the slogan "The personal is political," which drew attention to the gendered power inequalities structuring many aspects of personal life. These inequalities, which previously had been regarded as idiosyncratic rather than systemic, included domestic violence, incest, and the expectation that women take primary responsibility for caretaking. Feminist theorists argued that the home should not be excluded from the domain of justice but rather recognized as a site within which the demands of justice held sway (Okin 1989).

Feminists' focus on injustice in personal life expanded previous conceptions both of the site or *domain* of justice and also of its *objects*. Feminist philosophers argued that not only political rights and responsibilities, material resources, and cultural respect should be distributed justly; so too should customary responsibilities for domestic and care work.

0.4   Philosophical work on justice at the global level

Until the mid-twentieth century, political philosophers tended to think that the international sphere could not be a site of justice because it had no sovereign to enforce any agreements made and so could not be a system of social co-operation.[3] Instead, they regarded the international sphere as a potential battleground, in which states must be perpetually prepared for a war of each against all. In other words, political philosophers assumed that the moral demands of justice held only within states, not among them. Following World War II, however, the international scene was radically transformed in ways that undermined this traditional assumption about the *domain* of justice.

Several developments raised the idea that the demands of justice reached beyond state borders, an idea that was institutionalized in the

United Nations Charter model of international relations, replacing the Westphalian model that had existed since the seventeenth century. One aspect of this idea was a cosmopolitan concern for the rights of all human beings everywhere, a concern expressed in the landmark 1948 United Nations Universal Declaration of Human Rights. The Nuremberg and Tokyo war crimes tribunals, as well as other later tribunals, were designed to demonstrate that these rights must be respected universally. In 2002, the International Criminal Court was established as a permanent international tribunal to prosecute individuals for genocide, crimes against humanity, war crimes, and the crime of aggression. Another aspect of the idea that the international realm was a domain of justice was the establishment of international economic institutions designed to promote economic development and regulate global trade. These institutions began with the post-war agreements made at Bretton Woods and culminated in the World Trade Organization. In the latter part of the twentieth century, the idea spread that the world was in some sense a single community, an idea expressed in the popular 1960s expression "global village." In response to these developments, political philosophers began to recognize the international realm as a *domain of justice*—meaning that it was a sphere in which assessments of justice made sense—and some began to speak of a "global basic structure." But who were the *subjects* or claimants of justice in this domain, *what* was to be distributed, and *how* or according to which principles?

In the last quarter of the twentieth century, philosophers working on global justice began to address a wide range of topics to which earlier philosophers had paid little or no attention. Reflections on the topics of just war and human rights have a long philosophical ancestry, but much new work in these areas has challenged the moral authority of the state in unprecedented ways. On the one hand, the authority of states is reinforced by their being charged as guarantors of human rights but, on the other hand, this charge simultaneously limits their authority, since states that fail to discharge this responsibility are often thought to lose their moral legitimacy. Ultimate state sovereignty has been challenged from the perspective of individual citizens, who are now recognized as having the right and even the responsibility to resist violations of human rights on the part of their own governments; from the perspective of groups of citizens, who may wish to establish minority rights or even form their own state (the questions of multiculturalism and secession); and from the perspective of states concerned about calamities in other countries (the question of humanitarian intervention). Morally motivated worries about the limits of state sovereignty have given rise to further questions about legitimate global governance and political freedom. For instance, philosophers are increasingly recognizing the moral urgency as well as the philosophical interest of reflecting critically on the responsibility of states for environmental damage beyond their borders and on international migration. Special attention has been focused on issues of global distributive justice, in part because economic inequalities among countries are glaring and have even increased since 1970.

Recent work on global justice breaks with two long-established philosophical assumptions about justice. It treats the international as well as the national sphere as a *domain* of justice and it asserts that both states and individuals may be *subjects* or claimants of justice. Philosophers concerned with the gendered dimensions of global justice raise even deeper challenges to the assumptions about justice that for centuries have undergirded Western political philosophy.

0.5 Philosophical work on global gender justice

It is sometimes assumed that philosophers working on the gender dimensions of global justice address only a limited range of issues believed to have special relevance to women. Examples of such issues are female seclusion, genital cutting, religiously based systems of law pertaining to marriage and inheritance, and sex trafficking. However, to limit the field of global gender justice to such issues would be to construe it too narrowly. All of the issues addressed by global justice theorists have gendered dimensions and feminist philosophers concerned with global justice take as their task the critical exploration of these dimensions. Thus, philosophical work in global gender justice addresses the gendered dimensions of war, human rights, global governance, political freedom, nationalism, migration, indebtedness, poverty, climate change and more.

Philosophical discussions of topics pertaining to global justice are frequently framed as a conflict between the moral claims of nationalism, on the one hand, and cosmopolitanism, on the other; for instance, this framework structures much of the philosophical debate on global poverty. Nationalist philosophers argue that individuals' nationality is a morally weighty characteristic and that people should be concerned first about meeting the needs of their compatriots; only after those needs are met should citizens of wealthy countries consider assisting impoverished people abroad (Miller 2006). By contrast, cosmopolitan philosophers argue that national identity is morally irrelevant to the injustice of poverty on a global scale (Singer 2002; Pogge

2002). However, framing the discussion of global poverty exclusively as a debate about the moral salience of state boundaries obscures transnational divisions that stretch across national boundaries. One of these divisions is gender. Even though women's situations relative to men's vary widely both among and within different regions of the world, women everywhere tend to suffer more than men of the same ethnicity, class, and even family from poverty, overwork, sexual violence, and political marginalization.

One task undertaken by philosophers concerned with the gender dimensions of global justice has been to trace the ways in which contemporary transnational institutions and recent global policies, most of them facially gender-neutral, have had systematically disparate and often burdensome consequences for specific groups of women in both the global North and the global South. Below, I sketch several examples.

First, the expansion of global trade has resulted in many hitherto well-paid jobs being moved to low-wage areas in the global South. Here, many women have become a new industrial proletariat in labor-intensive export-based industries, especially in much of Asia, where governments have tempted multinational corporate investment with stereotypes of Asian women workers as tractable, hard-working, dexterous—and sexy. Within these industries, wages and working conditions are often very poor and sexual harassment is endemic. At the same time, the offshoring of many erstwhile Northern jobs has had a disproportionate impact on working women in the global North, especially women of color. The replacement jobs available often are contingent or part-time positions in the service sector, typically low-paid and lacking health and retirement benefits.

Second, the expansion of export agriculture and the relaxation of trade rules have allowed wealthy countries to dump heavily subsidized agricultural products on poor countries. Women, who comprise most of the world's farmers, have been disproportionately affected by the decline in small-scale and subsistence agriculture resulting from these developments. More generally, the expansion of global trade has had a devastating effect on the livelihoods of many women in the global South, as small women-run businesses in areas such as food processing and basket making have been wiped out. With the decline of small-scale and subsistence agriculture, many women have been driven off the land and into shantytowns, where they struggle to survive in the informal economy. Women predominate in the informal economy, which is characterized by low wages or incomes, uncertain employment, and poor working conditions. Many women are forced into prostitution, accelerating the AIDS epidemic, and the women who remain landless in the countryside are often forced to work as seasonal, casual, and temporary laborers at lower wages than their male counterparts.

Third, many poor countries are heavily indebted and have been forced to undertake programs of so-called structural adjustment in order to qualify for more loans. A central feature of structural adjustment programs is a reduction in government-funded services for social welfare, such as food subsidies, education, and healthcare. These cutbacks have tended to affect women's economic status even more adversely than men's, because women's socially assigned responsibility for caring for children and other family members makes them more reliant on such programs. Reductions in social services have forced women to create survival strategies for their families by absorbing these reductions with their own unpaid labor. The effect of these strategies has been felt especially in the global South, where more work for women has resulted in higher school dropout rates for girls. Longer hours of domestic work and less education contribute to women's impoverishment by making it harder for them to attain well-paying jobs.

Fourth, arms expenditures have risen sharply since 1990, despite the end of the Cold War, and wars have proliferated. Militarism often affords men certain opportunities, though obviously it harms those who are wars' casualties. Arguably, militarism is disproportionately harmful to women, especially poor women and their children. Women enjoy relatively few benefits from public spending on war industries and they suffer disproportionately when tax revenues are diverted from social into military programs. Although the combatants in war are predominantly male, the majority of the casualties are women and children, who also constitute 80 percent of the millions of refugees dislocated by war. Rape is a traditional weapon of war and military activity is usually associated with organized and sometimes forced prostitution.

Fifth, the integration of the global economy has increased the sexualization of women, partly via a multi-billion dollar pornography industry. Many women have been drawn into some aspect of sex work, including servicing the workers in large plantations, servicing representatives of transnational corporations, servicing troops around military bases, and servicing UN troops and workers. In some parts of Asia and the Caribbean, sex tourism is a mainstay of local economies. Prostitution is of course not new, but globalization has encouraged it by dislocating large populations, disrupting traditional communities, and impoverishing many women, who see few other options for a livelihood.

Finally, the period since World War II has seen a rapid degradation of the non-human environment, including land desertification and pollution of the earth, air, and oceans. Human-caused climate change has become undeniable. Much environmental damage is caused by Northern-controlled industries and especially by military activity. However, poor women pay a disproportionate share of the costs of environmental damage because they are especially vulnerable to disruption of the climate, lack of food, fuel, and water, and because they must give increased care to family members whose health is damaged by toxins.

Once these and other transnational gender disparities are made visible, it is hard not to wonder whether the entire global political and economic order may manifest systematic gender injustice. In order to address this question, philosophers must weigh the benefits and burdens of the prevailing system of global co-operation for groups partially identified by gender. However, normative political philosophers are more than accountants, applying a prefabricated moral calculus; they must also assess the adequacy of whatever measures are used to assess these burdens and benefits. One necessary although certainly not sufficient condition for the adequacy of such measures is that they should not be gender-biased. In other words, the measures should neither overvalue nor undervalue those benefits and burdens that accrue disproportionately to various gendered groups. So philosophers concerned with the gender dimensions of global justice confront a second and more deeply philosophical task, namely, investigating whether elements of gender bias may infect some of the central concepts used in philosophical discussions of global justice.

Existing feminist work provides reason to suspect that many of these concepts are not gender-neutral. For example, it was not until quite recently that war crimes were defined so as to include war rape and sexual torture. It is arguable that the definition of state-sanctioned repression should include family forms in which brides are sold and in which fathers and husbands exert strict control over women's sexuality, dress, speech, and movement, and that slavery should be interpreted to include forced domestic labor. It is also arguable that the definition of genocide should be expanded to include female infanticide, the systematic withholding of food, medical care, and education from girls, and the battery, starvation, mutilation, and even murder of adult women. It is important to ask whether representations of national culture overemphasize masculine achievements or romanticize oppressive gender divisions. Have Western conceptions of citizenship finally been freed from their earlier association with the masculine activities of bearing arms and owning property? Does gender bias infect prevailing systems of international accounting, which have trouble recognizing the contributions and costs of women's unpaid labor? And does gender bias exist in official definitions of poverty (Jaggar 2013)?

This introduction to the topic of global gender justice certainly has not offered a full list of issues that might be addressed by philosophers working in this field, but it mentions some of the areas where philosophical work has begun. Attention to the gender dimensions of global injustice is obviously morally and politically urgent because of the vast extent of transnational gender inequities, which affect almost everyone in the world in ways that differ depending on their gender, nationality, ethnicity, religion, class, and position in the global economic order.[4] Issues of global gender justice are also of great philosophical interest because they raise further challenges to longstanding Western philosophical assumptions about justice. These challenges go beyond recent recognition that the domain of justice includes the sphere of global politics and trade and that states as well as individuals may be subjects of justice claims. In addition, work by philosophers addressing the gender dimensions of global gender justice also includes the following suggestions:

The *domain* of global justice includes households and families, whose arrangements are often affected directly by developments at the global level.

The *subjects* of justice in the global sphere include gendered and sometimes transnational collectivities, including migrant care-workers, sex workers, and women workers on the global assembly line.

The *objects* of global justice include the transnational organization of caretaking contributions and responsibilities.

This introduction has briefly sketched some of the ways in which reflection on the gender dimensions of global justice generates new challenges to political philosophy. Many of these challenges are taken up in the chapters that follow.

0.6   An introduction to the chapters in this volume

In the first chapter, "Transnational Cycles of Gendered Vulnerability: A Prologue to a Theory of Global Gender Justice," Alison Jaggar argues that philosophers considering issues of global justice have failed to address the normative significance of transnational gender disparities. She suggests that these disparities are manifestations of global institutional structures which create systematically gendered vulnerabilities for women and sometimes for men across the world. Jaggar illustrates this by looking at gendered assignments for domestic work and sex work. In Jaggar's view, examining the justice of the structures that create transnational gendered vulnerabilities is a crucial task for philosophers concerned with global justice.

In "Transnational Women's Collectivities and Global Justice," Hye-Ryoung Kang challenges the assumptions of both the nationalist and cosmopolitan models of global justice. Within the nationalist model, the main agents of global justice claims are viewed as nation-states or national collectivities; by contrast, within the cosmopolitan model, individuals, as citizens of the cosmopolitan world, are viewed as agents of global justice claims. Kang argues that neither of these models appropriately reflects the ontological conditions and circumstances of justice produced by current processes of globalization and that neither is able to express the justice claims of women who suffer as a result of the global economy. Kang proposes an alternative transnational feminist model. She argues that processes of globalization have generated transnationalized socio-economic units as ontological conditions of justice, and that, in such conditions, transnational women's collectivities should be recognized as agents of global justice.

Eva Feder Kittay seeks to articulate the moral harm suffered by women migrants who leave their families for extended periods of time to do carework in wealthier countries. In her chapter "The Moral Harm of Migrant Carework: Realizing a Global Right to Care," Kittay locates this harm in the damage done to the migrant women's central relationships, which may be broken in order to allow those in wealthier countries to maintain their own relationships. She ends with a brief discussion of some possible solutions to this injustice.

Continuing the focus on migration, Rachel Silvey's chapter, "Transnational Rights and Wrongs: Moral Geographies of Gender and Migration," examines the challenges that transnational women's labor migration poses to state-centered conceptions of rights. Reviewing global perspectives on gender justice that are being developed by feminist philosophers and transnational migrant rights activists, Silvey argues that these frameworks are contributing to imagining the moral geographies necessary for the protection of women migrants' human rights and welfare. Adequate conceptualizations of justice must focus on the ways in which transnational gendered inequalities are produced—and indeed must be addressed—across "local," "national," and "global" spaces and scales. Such arguments, long commonplace in the discipline of geography, are offered here as an elaboration of the spatial elements of feminist philosophical conceptions of global justice.

Abigail Gosselin's chapter, "Global Gender Injustice and Mental Disorders," analyzes two ways in which global gender injustices contribute to the rising prevalence of two particular mental disorders among many groups of women worldwide. First, socio-economic injustice contributes to high rates of postpartum depression among women who are exploited and burdened by global economic development, and who therefore lack the time and resources needed for self-development and self-determination. Second, hermeneutical injustice contributes to high rates of eating disorders among women who are especially vulnerable to internalizing pervasive global gender norms which uphold narrow and oppressive conceptions of femininity. These narrow conceptions are promoted by global industries that profit from them at the expense of limiting many women's capacities for self-development and self-determination. Gosselin's analysis of the impact of gendered structural injustices on mental health reveals a dimension of global gender injustice that has not previously been addressed in the philosophical literature on global justice.

In her chapter "Discourses of Sexual Violence in a Global Context," Linda Martín Alcoff discusses some of the divergent ways in which sexual violence is described and considers the challenges to global gender justice that are posed by a decentralized and heterogeneous linguistic and social context that determines the meanings of our political concepts. Her discussion focuses on debates over the concepts of consent, victim, and honor. She argues that we need an approach capable of bringing into analysis the diverse normative, political, legal, and social implications of a term. We cannot control the connotations mobilized by a given term, and yet we also cannot ignore what we consider to be mistaken connotations given our goals of social change, of changing minds, attitudes, and practices. Thus, we need an approach to debate that will be attuned to the real world effects of terms in the specific contexts in which they operate, and especially in the global context within which terms may be operationalized in radically different ways.

In "Reforming Our Taxation Arrangements to Promote Global Gender Justice," Gillian Brock examines how reform of the international tax regime could be a very important vehicle for beginning to realize global gender justice, since taxes have important disproportionate effects on women, especially poor women. Brock argues that ensuring that all, including and especially multinationals, pay their fair share of taxes is crucial to ensuring funding of education, job training, and infrastructural development in poor countries. She reviews some recent trends that show the tax burden is shifting from business owners to workers and also from men to women. In the light of this analysis, she discusses the gender implications of some of the most plausible contenders for global taxes, arguing that, insofar as tax arrangements remain unreformed, the basic institutional structure of the global economy is gender-biased as well as unjust in other ways.

In the final chapter of the volume, "Gender Injustice and the Resource Curse: Feminist Assessment and Reform," Scott Wisor considers some gender dimensions of the so-called resource curse: the fact that many countries possessing valuable natural resources, especially mineral resources, are prone to authoritarianism, civil war, and economic mismanagement. Wisor notes that dependence on natural resource exports is often correlated with gender inequality, and contends that the commonly recognized resource curses—of authoritarianism, civil war, and economic mismanagement—result in gender-specific harms. He argues that those who purchase these mineral resources bear some moral responsibility for the foreseeable and avoidable gender injustices that result from the trade. Wisor concludes by considering a range of proposed reforms to address the resource curse and argues that integrating gender into these reforms will help create enabling conditions for local women's movements to move from curse to opportunity and equality.

The studies in this volume break fresh philosophical ground. They address hitherto neglected gender dimensions of familiar topics in global justice theory and also raise entirely new issues. The authors hope that these contributions will inspire a new flowering of work by political philosophers and other scholars on crucial areas within the broad field of global gender justice.

Notes

1 This essay is a revised version of "The philosophical challenges of global gender justice," my introduction to the issue of *Philosophical Topics*, Vol. 37, No. 2.
2 "For the moment, anyway, political philosophy is dead" (Laslett 1956: vii).
3 The main exception to the idea that the international realm was not a site of justice was the body of principle known as just war theory. The principle

of non-intervention established by the 1648 Treaty of Westphalia held that international law did not apply to the domestic affairs of sovereign states.

4 For instance, women's poverty is obviously a major cause of child poverty and women's low wages may also undermine men's wages. However, many people who are not poor derive direct or indirect benefits from women's impoverishment, including the availability of cheap goods and services.

1

Transnational Cycles of Gendered Vulnerability: A Prologue to a Theory of Global Gender Justice

Alison M. Jaggar

1.1 Some troubling worldwide gender disparities

The status of women vis-à-vis men varies widely both among and within different regions of the world. Such variations both provide evidence that women's subordination is not natural or inevitable and also supply data about which kinds of social arrangements tend to promote gender justice. In addition to the variations in status, however, it is also possible to discern transnational patterns of gendered dispari-ties that reveal systematic differences between the lives of men and women whose circumstances are otherwise similar. One pattern is what Saskia Sassen calls the feminization of the global proletariat (Sassen 2002).

Early literature in feminist economics revealed that an enormous volume of goods and services was produced by women's unpaid labor and argued that this labor provided a hidden subsidy both to the market sector and to the state.[1] In the market sector, women's unpaid performance of much socially necessary work caring for household members allowed men's wages to remain lower than would otherwise be required for subsistence. Similarly, the state could avoid making public provision for children, the disabled and the infirm on the assumption that they would be cared for unpaid at home (Benston 1969; Boserup 1970; Waring 1988; Folbre 1994). Today women still do most of the world's unpaid work but many women also have entered the global labor market, where they cluster disproportionately in a relatively few job categories.

Historically, women have produced much of the world's food and clothing either for immediate consumption or for local markets, but today they also produce these goods in extended supply chains for global markets (Oxfam International 2004). Women predominate in manufacturing work in highly competitive labor-intensive export industries, such as transnational electronics assembly, and they constitute the majority of workers in industries involving the care of the body, including nursing and domestic service. Many of those who migrate from poor to wealthy countries to work are women. Some women migrants work in high-skill jobs such as nursing but others work as nannies and maids performing household labor that once was performed in wealthy countries by unpaid women family members (Anderson 2000; Ehrenreich and Hochschild 2002; Hondagneu-Sotelo 2001; Lutz 2002; Parreñas 2001). A large proportion of women migrants are sex workers, especially if entertainment and mail-order marriage are counted as forms of sex work (UNFPA 2006; Sassen 2002: 270).[2]

Women's work is typically low-paid and lacking in labor protections because women often work in circumstances that discourage the formation of labor unions. Women work disproportionately in the informal economy, which by definition is largely unregulated, and in export-processing zones (EPZs) established specifically to escape labor local laws (United Nations 1999; Beneria 2003: 79). Frequently, women perform paid work at home, combining it with the care of children (Beneria 2003: 118). Women migrants often enjoy few labor protections in receiving countries even if they have documents, and women migrants without documents may be trapped by debt bondage and labor trafficking.

Paid work across the world is now feminized in several senses. Not only do women now comprise a larger proportion of the paid labor force than ever before but more of the available jobs are regarded as "women's work." The global labor force is also feminized in the sense that labor-market conditions for many men have deteriorated and become more like the precarious conditions that typically characterized many "women's jobs" (Standing 1999; Elson 2002: 94). Around the world, women frequently receive low pay and endure long hours of work, high pressure, employment insecurity, and sexual harassment.

In addition to the feminization of the global labor force, other transnational gendered disparities include lower rates of political participation by women, lower literacy rates, and more susceptibility to harassment and violence, particularly sexual violence. These disparities, in which women across the world tend to be consistently worse off than men in otherwise similar circumstances, appear evidently unjust. How should political philosophers respond to them?

1.2   Five inadequate philosophical responses to transnational gender disparities

1.2.1   Ignoring them

One response to transnational gender disparities is simply to ignore them. Many recent books on global justice have no index entries on women or gender and many others mention them only in passing. Yet, transnational gender disparities have far-reaching implications. Not only do enormous numbers of women work grueling hours for little reward, making them susceptible to extreme violence and other basic rights violations, but the low wages paid to women also depress many men's earning power. In addition, gender disparities are a main reason why over a billion children suffer extreme poverty, because women everywhere are assigned primary responsibility for caring for children, a responsibility that helps to impoverish both groups.[3] While billions of people are impoverished, however, millions of other men, women, and children may benefit from their poverty through their enjoyment of the cheap goods and services produced by the global poor. Thus, transnational gender disparities affect the lives of almost everyone in the world, not simply poor women; but they affect each of us in different ways depending on our respective locations in various orders of gender, nation, ethnicity, religion, and class. No comprehensive account of global justice can afford to ignore such far-reaching inequalities.

1.2.2   Treating them instrumentally

Scholars in disciplines that address global development have often recognized that women worldwide are disproportionately impoverished and marginalized, but for decades they did not consider the intrinsic injustice of these disparities. Instead, they tended to treat them instrumentally, arguing that women's poverty impeded overall economic growth and promoting so-called empowerment as a means of controlling population growth, achieving sustainable development, and alleviating poverty. Regardless of whether these strategic claims are plausible, their proponents presented the goal of raising women's status merely as instrumental to other desired ends, failing to acknowledge that the disproportionate impoverishment and marginalization of women were issues of justice in their own right.[4]

1.2.3 Treating them as natural

A third inadequate response to global gender disparities is to treat them as natural, in the sense of biologically determined. Many Western philosophers have argued that women suffer from various inherent disabilities but their arguments take a simplistic view both of biological sex differences and of social justice. Although sex is indeed often correlated with differences in physical ability that go beyond differences related directly to biological procreation, biological sex differences in humans can hardly be investigated independently of their gendered contexts, especially when social processes of sex assignment are marked by considerable arbitrariness and coercion (Jaggar 1987; Fausto-Sterling 1985/1992, 1999).[5] In any case, the main point for those concerned about social justice is that the degree to which any characteristic is advantageous or disadvantageous depends on its social context. It is the context that determines whether particular characteristics are assets or weaknesses for those who possess them. Thus the central question for political philosophers is not whether any particular abilities are inherently advantageous but rather how social institutions may be constructed so as to be fair for individuals whose capacities inevitably differ on many dimensions.

1.2.4 Blaming them on non-Western cultures

In the 1990s, some Western philosophers began to address issues of gender justice at the global level but their work focused on the difficulties faced by women in developing countries. Taking the problem to be what Okin (1994) called the plight of poor women in poor countries, these philosophers attributed the problems faced by women in developing countries exclusively to the injustice of non-Western cultures, unrelated either to the subordination of women in Western societies or to global political and economic structures.[6] Because of this assumption, Western philosophers typically treated the issues in terms of "multiculturalism," focusing especially on whether non-Western cultures might legitimately be criticized by those who are not members of the communities in question—particularly, of course, by Westerners.[7] The questions raised by the multiculturalism literature are certainly interesting and important but its tendency to focus on differences among women's situations has diverted philosophers' attention away from the equally striking transnational parallels. Multicultural approaches are unsuited to explaining such parallels if they mistakenly portray cultures as self-contained systems of supposedly traditional values and practices, autonomous and insulated from wider global forces. Such approaches leave transnational gender disparities as inexplicable coincidences. In addition to their empirical inadequacy, these approaches are politically problematic because they tend to disparage non-Western cultures and to rationalize Westerners taking up the missionary role of "educating" or "raising the consciousness" of women in developing countries.

1.2.5 Blaming the victims

Yet another inadequate response to transnational gender disparities is to treat them as no more than the coincidental results of numerous bad decisions made by poor women out of ignorance or false consciousness. This focus directs philosophical attention away from the justice of the social institutions that always structure individuals' decisions. Unlike ethicists, who assess individual choices, political philosophers assess the institutions that make various menus of options socially available while assigning various costs and benefits to those options. Institutions are relatively stable practices that organize social life. When they are just, they provide a fair range of options to all whose lives they regulate; when they are unjust, they unfairly constrain the choices of the members of some social groups.[8] In considering transnational gender disparities it is certainly important to remember that poor women make decisions, but focusing exclusively on those decisions neglects crucial questions about the justice of the institutions and structure of incentives and disincentives which create the menu of available options among which the women must decide.

1.2.6 Gendering global justice theory

Each of these five responses in one way or another disregards or dismisses questions about the justice of transnational gendered disparities, leaving the latter as an unacknowledged elephant in the room of global justice theory. In the remainder of this chapter, I attempt to bring into sharper focus some questions regarding the justice of the disparities.

Many theories of justice exist each of which assigns different degrees of moral significance to disparate outcomes. Distributional egalitarian theories accord them the most significance, contending that inegalitarian outcomes require special justification, but even these theories do not regard disparate outcomes as unjust if some moral justification can be provided for them or if they are for some reason inevitable. Some theories of justice do not regard disparate outcomes as unjust if they are "deserved" for reasons such as bad choices or lack of effort. Other, relational, theories consider that the proper objects of moral assessment are not the distributive outcomes *per se* but rather the relations that hold among individuals or groups. According to these theories, disparate outcomes are unjust if they are maintained by oppressive social relations such as violence, marginalization, or exploitation. For all theories, it is impossible to assess the justice or injustice of distributional disparities without knowing their causes.

This chapter does not offer a particular moral analysis of the global gender disparities I have sketched. Instead, it offers an explanatory model for understanding the causes of many gender disparities and therefore should be seen as a prologue to a theory of global gender justice. I argue that many global gender disparities are best viewed as elements in transnational cycles of gendered vulnerability, an explanatory model which presents various disparities as connected causally both with each other and with some basic features of the global order.

In most areas of inquiry, finding the right answers depends on asking the right questions. I suggest that the model of transnational cycles of gendered vulnerability helps political philosophers identify some of the right questions about global gender justice. The model highlights some of the gendered and raced dimensions of the global situation that appear morally problematic but which have been largely overlooked by global justice theorists. It also sketches a causal account of these disparities that emphasizes the causal significance of transnational political and economic structures, though it presents the various causal factors as interactive and dynamic. In light of this model, I propose that political philosophers go beyond treating gender disparities in particular locations as self-contained phenomena. Instead, many gender disparities are better viewed as manifestations of underlying institutional structures which create systematically gendered vulnerabilities for women and also for men across the world. I contend that the gendered dimensions of these transnational structures deserve systematic attention from philosophers concerned with global justice.

1.3　Transnational cycles of gendered vulnerability

1.3.1　The basic idea

In 1989, Susan Moller Okin developed the idea of a gendered cycle of vulnerability by marriage. She argued that the institution of gender-structured marriage, in which husbands are the main providers and women are unpaid caretakers, rendered women in societies such as the twentieth-century United States vulnerable to poverty and abuse. Okin explained that the expectation that girls would marry and be supported by their husbands meant that they were often unprepared to support themselves, and their poor job qualifications made them economically dependent on their husbands. This in turn made it difficult for them to leave unsatisfactory marriages and forced them to tolerate inequality and even violence. Thus Okin argued that "a cycle of power relations and decisions pervades both family and workplace, each reinforcing the inequalities between the sexes that already exist within the other" (Okin 1989: 4).

Okin drew on the work of Robert Goodin to argue that "any dependency or vulnerability is arguably created, shaped or sustained, at least by existing social arrangements. None is wholly natural" (Goodin 1985: 191). Of course, all human beings are naturally vulnerable to injury, disease, and aging as well as to random misfortune. Bad things happen not only to good people but also to rich and famous people. However, rich people have more resources than poor people to deal with biological frailty and random contingencies, and are less vulnerable to these hazards. Okin argues that many of the bad things that happen to women occur not because of any inherent female weakness or individual misfortune but rather because women suffer from a distinctive vulnerability that is socially created by the institution of gender-structured marriage. Okin acknowledges that marriage may be a good strategic decision for many women and that some marriages may even be egalitarian, but she regards the creation of this gendered vulnerability as a systemic injustice. Even though fortunate or exceptional individuals may find ways of escaping or even benefiting from the gender structure of marriage, the gender socialization and sex-typing of jobs associated with the institution make women as a class systematically vulnerable. For Okin, this vulnerability is not an inevitable fact of life but rather an injustice to women as a group.

Okin's analysis is problematic because the supposedly typical US woman she describes is actually a woman who enjoys certain privileges of race, class, and sexuality. The family life that Okin identifies as "traditional" in fact characterizes mainly middle- and upper-class life in the United States, though better-off sectors of the working class also aspire to it. Such a family is not at all traditional for other large sectors of US society. Most working-class women have always worked for pay—in factories, in fields, in the homes of others, or doing piecework on consignment in their own homes—and they continue to be brought up with this expectation, particularly in African American, Latino and Asian American communities (Amott and Matthaei 1991).[9] Okin has also been charged with privileging the heterosexual nuclear family (Kymlicka 1991: 84).

Despite the limitations of Okin's account, Iris Marion Young has argued that its basic structural logic can be used to understand the situations of many women in some less developed societies of Asia, Africa, Latin America, and the Middle East as well as in Western countries (Young 2009). Young finds the explanatory model of a gendered cycle of vulnerability especially helpful for understanding the lives of urban women or women who migrate from rural to urban areas, even though their situation differs in a number of significant ways from the situation of Western women.[10]

Young asserts that such women's gendered vulnerability is founded on the family division of labor that assigns women primary responsibility for looking after the household, children, and other family members who need care. In less developed as well as more developed societies, women's primary responsibility for domestic carework makes them dependent on husbands for material support and this, in turn, renders them vulnerable to domination and abuse. When wives seek paid employment, they often wish to combine this with carrying out their family responsibilities, and this makes them vulnerable to exploitation. Thus Young argues that "the gender division of labor in the family that operates as a strong and enforced norm among many newly urbanized women produces and reproduces a vulnerability to domination and exploitation in wage employment" (Young 2009: 230). She notes that women raising children alone are especially vulnerable to poverty because it is difficult for one adult both to care for children and household and to earn enough to provide a decent standard of living. Moreover, single mothers are often socially stigmatized, which makes their lives even more difficult. Like Okin, Young observes that the cycle is reproduced in the socialization of both girls and boys, perpetuating women's specifically gendered vulnerabilities in less developed societies.

Young, again like Okin, argues that the gendered cycle of vulnerability by marriage is maintained by law and public policy. She notes that public gender dynamics, which expect men to concentrate on public activities, make it difficult for them to contribute to domestic work and childcare even if they want to do so, and asserts that the implicit or explicit reliance of public institutions on unpaid work performed at home often enlarges the total amount of unpaid work that must be done. Young follows earlier feminist economists in arguing that both state institutions and many private enterprises in less developed countries benefit from the gendered division of family labor because it helps them to avoid internalizing the costs of social reproduction. Therefore, both states and businesses adopt policies that perpetuate the gendered cycle of vulnerability.

1.3.2   Domestic work in a transnational context

The recognition that inequalities in one area of life tend to be linked causally with inequalities in other areas is not new. The distinct contribution made by feminist theorists like Okin and Young lies in revealing the ways in which gender assignments are a crucial causal factor in creating cycles of vulnerability that are specifically gendered. I suggest that this basic idea may be helpful in understanding not only women's liability to exploitation and abuse within more and less developed countries but also in understanding patterns of gendered inequality that stretch across borders and regions.

Domestic work as we know it today has not always existed, even though cooking and caring for children have always been necessary. Instead, housework is a relatively modern phenomenon that emerged with the sharpening division between paid and unpaid labor and the move of paid labor out of the home (Strasser 1982). As Young notes, modern domestic labor appears along with urbanization in developing countries. Because housework developed as a specifically feminine occupation, social radicals of the late nineteenth and early twentieth centuries dreamed of liberating women by making it a social responsibility. However, those dreams have not been realized and today housework remains largely privatized and feminized, though the specific tasks that it includes shift constantly according to changing expectations regarding the care of families.

At the beginning of the twenty-first century, many women's domestic burdens are even greater than those borne by their mothers because states worldwide have retreated from their responsibility for citizen welfare. This retreat is linked with the integration of the global economy and the increasing influence of international institutions, such as the World Bank, the International Monetary Fund, and especially the World Trade Organization. In response to the collapse of the Soviet bloc and intensified global economic competition, many countries in both the erstwhile First and Second Worlds have reduced their provision of social services. In the erstwhile Third World, indebted countries have been required to privatize public resources, to cut social spending, and to re-orient their economies toward exports in order to earn foreign currency. Thus many poor states have reduced provisions for social security and welfare, such as food subsidies, the supply of utilities including street paving, water, sanitation, electricity, and police protection, and the availability of such services as healthcare, education, childcare, and eldercare. Women are especially dependent on these goods because they typically bear primary responsibility for the well-being of their families, and women also compensate for the lack of them with their own unpaid work and the work of their daughters. Although the cuts in social welfare provisions are not explicitly directed against women, they are predicated on the assumption that women's unpaid labor will compensate for them and they increase women's gendered vulnerability. Thus, although the cycles of gendered vulnerability by marriage that Okin and Young describe are located within national spaces, they are intensified by international structures and policies.

In addition, a related cycle of gendered vulnerability now extends across transnational spaces. One part of this cycle is the global domestic work industry, in which millions of women cross borders and oceans to seek employment as maids and nannies in private homes. Transnational developments generate both the demand for this labor and its supply. The supply is stimulated by the scarcity of good jobs for both men and women in poor countries and by many poor countries' consequent reliance on remittances from citizens working abroad. In Western Europe, domestic workers include women teachers, students, lawyers, doctors, and nurses who cannot find professional employment in their own East European countries (Lutz 2002: 95). "Maids" are currently said to be the Philippines' most important export product (Lutz 2002: 92) and Sassen (2002: 271) reports the Philippine government's efforts to encourage the migration of Philippine women to the US, the Middle East, and Japan. Silvey (this volume) describes the flow of documented women migrants from Indonesia to perform domestic work abroad. Much of the demand for domestic labor in wealthy countries is created by the fact that public provisions for childcare and eldercare remain inadequate even as more women work outside the home and as male family members continue to resist domestic responsibilities. The shortfall in care in wealthy countries is often made up with immigrant women's cheap domestic labor.

The global domestic work industry resembles local cycles of gendered vulnerability by marriage both in that it is predicated on the assignment of domestic work to women and in that it is causally influenced by many of the same policies, designed by many of the same transnational actors, which intensify local cycles. However, in many ways the global "maid trade" is more similar to traditional domestic service than to marriage. The work is paid rather than unpaid and the worker is not married to her employer—except arguably in the case of mail-order brides. In addition, the racial/ethnic identities of migrant domestic workers and their employers are likely to differ from each other, whereas wives usually come from the same racial/ethnic group as their husbands. Migrant domestic workers often have considerable linguistic and cultural differences from their employers and they are often drawn from groups that are racially stigmatized in the receiving country. All these factors affect the social meanings assigned in the receiving country to the work done by migrant domestic workers. Despite the complex, sensitive, and socially important nature of this work and despite the fact that migrant domestic workers often come from their own country's educated middle class, their work is more likely to be regarded as low-wage, unskilled labor than as a loving sacrifice (Huh 2008).

Can the global domestic work industry be seen as extending local cycles of gendered vulnerability to a transnational scale? I think the answer is a qualified yes. As a group, migrant domestic workers are extremely vulnerable, especially those without work visas and those who live in their employers' homes. Employers often take advantage of their vulnerability to force them to work long hours, to withhold pay, to subject them to violence and sexual abuse, and sometimes to hold them in conditions close to slavery (Anderson 2000, esp. ch. 8; Zarembka 2002). For such migrants, the global domestic work industry appears to be a new link in a cycle of gendered vulnerability that now stretches across the globe. Their performance of this labor also typically increases the domestic burdens carried by female members of migrant women's families, who must take on the work of caring for the children that migrants have left behind. This may reinforce the gendered vulnerability of migrant women's mothers, sisters, and daughters.

The gendered vulnerability of domestic workers allows them to be not only dominated but also exploited. Just as national economies have always relied covertly on women's unpaid domestic labor, today the global economy relies overtly on the low-paid domestic labor of women migrants. In more developed countries this labor subsidizes the costs of social reproduction, and in many less developed countries it provides a needed flow of remittances. Thus women's cheap or unpaid domestic labor underwrites the entire global economy by subsidizing the indispensable tasks of cleaning and care and especially by producing the next generation of the global labor force.

As soon as the transnational gendering of domestic work and domestic workers is recognized, the recognition needs immediate qualification. It is important to note links and parallels among the situations of many women transnationally but it is equally important to notice vital differences among their situations. Gender does not have a single unequivocal meaning, women are far from being a homogeneous group, and their gendered vulnerabilities are not all the same. Although domestic work is done mostly by women and coded as feminine, different women do it under very different conditions. In many places, women of moderate circumstances do most of the unpaid domestic work for their own families but better-off women can often buy out of this gendered responsibility by hiring poorer women. When the women hired are from the same country, they usually come from the lower classes and are often migrants from the countryside to the city. By contrast, international migrant domestic workers typically are not among the poorest women in their own countries, though their countries are poor. Indeed, international migrants may hire poorer women compatriots to fulfill "their own" domestic responsibilities. Thus although women across the world are made vulnerable by their gendered responsibility for domestic labor, this gendered vulnerability varies in kind and degree according to the women's class, race, and national origin.[11] The global "maid trade" reveals a neglected aspect of global gender injustice, but it equally illustrates that gender issues, including global gender issues, always have class, ethnic, and national dimensions.

1.3.3   Sex work in a transnational context

The gendered vulnerabilities faced by many women across the world are not caused only by their assignment of responsibility for domestic work. In the concluding section of her essay, Young points to the need to investigate the ways in which heterosexual norms, desires, and expectations additionally create specifically gendered vulnerabilities for women in both the developed and developing worlds. Young's suggestion may be extended to show how these norms also make women vulnerable at the transnational level.

Gender is central to the sex trade, which is one of the largest global industries. Gendered constructions of sexuality create the meanings of the services traded and determine how individuals are able to partici- pate in the trade. The vast majority of those who supply direct sexual services are women and girls, although many men and boys are also suppliers. By contrast, the vast majority of those who consume sexual services are men and so are most, though certainly not all, of those engaged in transporting sex workers and establishing the institutional infrastructure for the trade. The commodification of sexuality raises its own ethical questions but here I point instead toward questions about the gender justice of the global sex industry's institutional structure.

Conditions for sex workers vary widely. Some are self-employed and mix occasional sex work with other paid occupations, while others work in conditions of extreme confinement. Regardless of their cir- cumstances, the rewards of sex work tend to be small for most direct service providers. It is true that some high-priced escorts and call-girls win financial rewards that far surpass anything they could hope to earn in other fields, and that for many more ordinary women sex work, including marriage, creates welcome opportunities for extra income, for migration, and even for a new family. However, many sex workers, especially migrant sex workers, find themselves trapped in situations of extreme abuse, including rape and other forms of sexual violence and physical punishments. "They are severely underpaid and their wages are often withheld. They are prevented from using protection methods to prevent against HIV, and they typically have no right to medical treatment" (Sassen 2002: 269). Mail-order brides are also frequently subjected to violence, regardless of nationality of origin (Sassen 2002: 273). Exit from sex work is often extremely difficult so that participation in the sex industry, perhaps even more than marriage and paid domestic work, often intensifies gendered vulnerabilities.

Although the direct providers of sexual services typically receive small recompense, their work provides immense rewards for others. I set aside here the question of whether individual consumers of sexual services "get what they pay for" to look instead at some other beneficiaries of the sex industry. Sassen reports that trafficking in women for the sex industry is highly profitable for those running the trade. "The UN estimates that 4 million people were trafficked in 1998, producing a profit of USD7 billion for criminal groups" (Sassen 2002: 267). Many families and countries rely heavily on the remittances sent home by migrant workers abroad, a considerable proportion of which come from sex work (*New York Times*, March 17, 2008), and increasing numbers of poor countries depend on the tourism industry, with its concomitant entertainment and sex work. Thus the rewards of the global sex industry seem to accrue disproportionately to those (mainly men) who organize sex work rather than to those (mainly women) who perform the services directly. Despite the opportunities it provides for individual women, the structure of the global sex industry seems disadvantageous to women as a group.

Just as one can ask why women do most of the world's domestic work, one can also ask why they enter the global sex industry on such unfavorable terms. There is nothing particularly natural about women "pleasuring" men in exchange for money. Women may buy sexual services when they are in a position to do so and men and boys may supply sexual services to women as well as to men (Phillips 1999). Most sex work is chosen in some sense but the extent to which sex workers' choices can be regarded as free depends on the situation. Some women choose sex work as a way of earning a little extra money, while others are deceived, coerced, or seeking to satisfy addictions. Some women enter sex work voluntarily, as they move from rural to urban areas, while others are pressed into sex work by their parents or tricked by being told that a different job awaits them. Some sex workers migrate voluntarily but some are "trafficked" in the sense of coerced to cross state boundaries (Sassen 2002: 266).

It is easier to understand why so many women's decisions converge on sex work when the decisions are seen in the context of interlocking cycles of gendered sexual vulnerability. These include transnational as well as national norms of gendered sexuality, gendered inequalities of access to economic resources, and transnational as well as national policies and institutions that encourage the emergence of a gender-structured global sex industry. Dominant norms of masculine and feminine sexual desirability are spread across the world by media such as the internet, through entertainment, advertising, and pornography, and they often eroticize gendered power inequalities, which are usually further complicated by eroticizing inequalities of age, race, class, and nation. Simultaneously, transnational media promote gender-structured marriage as an institution that will guarantee happiness, social status, sexual satisfaction, and economic security for both men and women. Women and men both seek trophy spouses but women seek husbands who are good providers while men seek wives who are attractive and deferential (Hughes 2000, 2004). Exposure to these ubiquitous images and fantasies molds the sexuality of both girls and boys, influencing their sense of their own and others' desirability. They normalize the idea of women pleasing men and prepare girls and boys to participate in the global sex market as workers and as consumers respectively. Women's participation in sex work reinforces conceptions of women as primarily sexual beings. Gendered norms of sexual desirability circulate in a world where men's access to economic resources is often greater than women's. Men are more likely to have some disposable income and to feel more entitled than women to spend money on themselves rather than on their families. Buying sexual services may provide not only physical pleasure but also an otherwise rare opportunity to dominate another person. Meanwhile, as we have seen, women's opportunities for employment are limited and among them sex work or one of its variants may be the best option.[12]

Like the gendered vulnerability caused by women's responsibility for domestic work, the gendered vulnerability created by asymmetric constructions of masculine and feminine sexuality is exploited and reinforced by transnational institutions and policies. Not only do poor countries often send workers abroad for the sake of remittances, but destination countries for migrants may intensify women's vulnerability by treating sex work differently from other forms of work.[13] Similarly, the mail-order bride industry would not be possible without the privileging of marriage in international immigration law. Furthermore, many poor countries have been encouraged by the IMF and the World Bank to view tourism as a development strategy, and have received loans for this purpose. Sassen writes: "At some point it becomes clear that the sex trade itself can become a development strategy in areas with high unemployment and poverty and where governments are desperate for revenue and foreign currency" (Sassen 2002: 270).

1.3.4   Possible additional links in cycles of gendered vulnerability

The idea of transnational cycles of gendered vulnerability helps to make intelligible some striking transnational gender disparities. Recognizing the gendered vulnerability created by women's internationally assigned responsibility for domestic work helps explain why women worldwide tend to be impoverished relative to men even as they work far longer hours, and why they are especially at risk of violence and other rights abuses. Factoring gendered sexuality into the cycle can illuminate otherwise unexplained aspects of the situation, such as: why so much of women's work is sexual and why so many of the supposedly non-sexual jobs that women do have a sexual dimension; why so much sexual harassment exists in workplaces; why the incidence of HIV infection among women is increasing; why sexual violence is so widespread and why women are so often targeted sexually in wars. A fuller understanding of these and other disparities would likely be obtained by investigating how the cycles interact with each other and how they are linked with other aspects of the contemporary global order, such as increasing militarism and environmental degradation.

1.4   What is the philosophical value added by introducing the idea of transnational cycles of gendered vulnerability into global justice theory?

In earlier work, I have argued that transnational gender disparities deserve more attention from political philosophers than they have received so far (Jaggar 2002a). Here I have suggested that these disparities should be seen as components in transnational cycles of gendered vulnerability. This suggestion is intended to focus attention on the ways in which these disparities are systematically and predictably maintained and intensified by gendered global institutions. I especially wish to encourage questions about the justice of a global order in which domestic and sex work, widely considered to be the world's dirtiest and most demeaning jobs, are assigned primarily to unpaid and underpaid women.

Seeing global gender disparities as systematically produced and reproduced by gendered cycles of vulnerability raises moral questions about the justice of the resulting disparities but it does not offer any specific diagnosis of their injustice. As noted earlier, many theories of justice exist, each with its distinctive vocabulary and norms. Some speak of disproportion in the benefits and burdens of social participation, or of systematic inequality in life chances, or of denying capabilities or under-fulfilling human rights; some speak of exploitation, Marxist or non-Marxist, or of domination or oppression. Young asserts that the moral significance of the cycle of gendered vulnerability in less developed countries lies less with the inequality of its outcomes than with its systematic production of vulnerabilities to abuse and exploitation (Young 2009: 228). Thinking in terms of transnational cycles of gendered vulnerability does not imply a commitment to one of these normative theories. However, it does help us to ask the right questions about transnational gendered disparities because it provides an alternative to several misleading or mistaken ways of thinking about them.

Most obviously, the model of transnational cycles of gendered vulnerability begins from the assumption that gendered disparities matter morally and that treating them instrumentally is morally unacceptable. The model offers an alternative to the view that women are in any way naturally disposed to dirty or demeaning labor, working double days, or providing sexual services. It does not explain the diverse historical origins of these gendered divisions of labor but it does explain how they are currently maintained transnationally. It shows how gendered expectations on the parts of both women and men are reproduced and how gendered divisions of labor are reinforced by global as well as national institutions.

The model also provides a plausible alternative to the supposition that most gendered disparities result exclusively from local causes, such as the supposed backwardness of local cultures. While gender inequalities have long existed in most societies, today most are re-shaped by developments in the global economy and by policies imposed by transnational actors (Jaggar 2005a). When these transnational causal influences are identified, cross-national parallels become intelligible instead of remaining as unexplained coincidences.

In addition, seeing gender disparities as manifestations of transnational cycles of gendered vulnerability provides an alternative to the implausible view that they are the happenstance consequences of innumerable unrelated choices made by ignorant women. Poor women are no more prone than anyone else to irrationality or "false consciousness." Just as gendered divisions of family labor are shaped by transnational as well as national institutions and policies, so are gendered divisions of labor at the transnational level. The model of transnational cycles of gendered vulnerability shows that poor women are frequently placed in situations where they have few options and where those options may be structured to provide few gains and often even to be "no win." In such situations, it is often rational for women to accept low-paid domestic and sex work as well as unpaid responsibilities. The model also shows how exploiting women may provide many men's best opportunity for making even small gains. It reveals that decisions that are rational for individual men and women lead predictably to outcomes that leave women far worse off than similarly

situated men. The patterned outcomes of these decisions further reinforce stereotypically gendered expectations and strengthen gender-
unjust institutions.

The cycles of gendered vulnerability model provides an alternative
to blaming men, which has occasionally occurred in the feminist literature. Far from placing exclusive blame on men, most of whom are also
relatively powerless, the model creates space for revealing the costs as
well as the benefits of current gender arrangements to many men, who
face their own gendered vulnerabilities. For instance, men tend to have
higher suicide rates than women and also higher rates of premature
death due to violence, accidents, coronary heart disease, and drug and
alcohol abuse (Moeller-Leimkuhler 2003).

Overall, the model of transnational gendered vulnerabilities highlights the causal interplay among gender-biased local and transcultural
norms, gendered inequalities in access to economic resources, and
inequalities among countries in wealth and power that leave poor
individuals, families, and countries desperate to exploit any available
resources, human or otherwise. It acknowledges that everyone is vulnerable to bad choices, bad luck, and biological frailty but it shows
how gendered institutions mean that these factors have very disparate
impacts on men's and women's lives respectively. Nor is everyone
equally vulnerable to deprivation, exploitation, abuse, exhaustion, and
sexual violence. Instead, gendered institutions make many women,
especially poorer women in less developed countries, systematically
and unequally vulnerable both to natural calamities and to social
domination.

Political philosophers should give priority to addressing vulnerabilities that are socially caused and so likely preventable. The idea of
transnational cycles of gendered vulnerability focuses on global institutions as they intersect with local institutions and these intersections
are the proper objects of analysis for those concerned with global
justice. By focusing especially on vulnerabilities created by possible
gender bias in global institutions, the idea provides a conceptual tool
for investigating global gender justice.

Some may worry that talking about gendered vulnerability dispar-
ages women's autonomy and agency, implying that women are natural
victims who need special protection from a nanny super-state. To
make this objection is to forget that gendered vulnerabilities are by
definition socially created. Feminists concerned with gender justice do
not seek institutions that constrain autonomy or provide special privileges for women or any other group. Instead, we wish to construct
institutional arrangements at transnational as well as local levels that

do not systematically restrict the life choices of members of some social groups, especially but not only groups of women, or render those groups systematically vulnerable to domination and exploitation.

The model of transnational cycles of gendered vulnerability provides a useful tool not only for beginning to assess global gender disparities but also for focusing inquiry about who is responsible for addressing them. On the one hand, by showing that patterns of global gender disparity are neither coincidental nor inevitable, the model encourages us to avoid dismissing questions of responsibility. On the other hand, it encourages us to avoid misattributions of responsibility either through victim-blaming or through conspiracy theories. Understanding women's vulnerability as produced by social structures does not mean that all of these structures are deliberately planned or even foreseeable. Most social institutions and structures combine elements of planning with elements of unplanned evolution. They are created by multiple agents, who are responsible in different proportions and ways, in multiple spheres, and at multiple levels (Young 2006).

Whether or in what way particular disparities are unjust depends not only on their causes but also on the possibilities and costs of creating alternative ways of structuring the social world.[14] If large-scale gender disparities are indeed manifestations of transnational cycles of gendered vulnerability, it is unlikely that they can be remedied piecemeal, one region or one country at a time, because local efforts may be subverted by global developments. It is especially difficult for poorer countries to address them because they have limited economic and political autonomy. However, the cycles are created by human institutions and so are open to human intervention. When transnational and local cycles interact, they may reinforce some gendered vulnerabilities but they may also provide opportunities for resisting them. For example, although the global domestic work industry props up gender-structured marriage in receiving countries, it can undermine oppressive forms of marriage in sending countries. Some migrant domestic workers are able to take home sufficient savings to gain more respect in their communities of origin and to enable them to renegotiate their family and work options (Huh 2008). In addition, both domestic and sex workers are forming associations to negotiate for better work situations in the receiving countries (Kempadoo 2005). And in both poor and rich countries women are refusing birth and viewing marriage as a less attractive option. The point is not that existing institutional arrangements provide opportunities for some individuals to better their lives but rather that they provide opportunities for people to begin changing oppressive norms and practices. Thus although the model of transnational cycles of gendered vulnerability discourages the idea that any simple strategy for global gender justice exists, it does encourage the optimistic idea that other worlds are possible!

Acknowledgments

This chapter was written originally for a workshop on global gender justice hosted in Oslo by the Centre for the Study of Mind in Nature. I wish to thank the director of the Center, Christel Fricke, and the other participants in the workshop for their very helpful comments. In addition, a number of colleagues and students at the University of Colorado at Boulder gave generous feedback. I am indebted to: Eamon Aloyo, Cory Aragon, Lorraine Bayard de Volo, David Boonin, Robert Buffington, Amandine Catala, Anne Costain, Stephen Emedi, Barrett Emerick, Chelsea Haramia, Heri-Young Kang, Deepti Misri, Celeste Montoya, April Shaw, and Scott Wisor. Finally, Thomas Pogge provided valuable comments on a late draft.

Notes

1 The absence of records and the lack of any accepted accounting system make it impossible to provide more than the roughest estimate of the value of women's household labor, but studies in many countries indicate that its value might range between one-third and one-half of measured GNP (Beneria 2003: 117).

2 The sex trade is one of the largest global industries, estimated to have a turnover of $5–7,000 billion, greater than the combined military budget for the whole world (Monzini 2005). Subscription-only channels playing pornographic content are a prominent feature of the television industry and the internet is riddled with pornographic websites. The global demand for "mail-order" brides is exploding. In addition, sex work permeates the tourism and related entertainment industries, which are now among the world's largest industries (Judd and Fainstein 1999).

3 One UNICEF report estimates that over 1 billion children suffer the severe effects of poverty. See http://www.unicef.org/media/media_15082.html (accessed November 29, 2012).

4 The World Bank has received much feminist criticism on this account and has finally checked this tendency in its *World Development Report 2012*. This Report's main message is: "Gender equality is a core development objective in its own right. It is also smart economics" (World Bank 2011: xv).

5 For instance, men tend to be able to run faster than women and to have greater upper-body muscular strength. By contrast, women are often stronger than men on other physical dimensions such as surviving starvation, exposure, disease, and fatigue; overall, women tend to have greater endurance and longer lives. However, these tendencies are subject to wide individual variations, they are often exaggerated by social practices, and they are not correlated with important differences in mental abilities.

6 This direction may have been set by Amartya Sen's groundbreaking work attributing the absence of 100 million women to male-dominant values characterizing many Asian cultures (Sen 1990). It is an example of the approach that Thomas Pogge calls "explanatory nationalism" (Pogge 2002: 110–17).

7 For critical discussion of this literature, see Jaggar 2005a.

8 For instance, in many societies racist institutions govern crucial aspects of people's lives. They systematically restrict the life chances of individuals who are assigned to devalued racial categories and render them disproportionately vulnerable to violence, impoverishment, and political marginalization.

9 Patricia Hill Collins, along with many other Black feminists, denies that contemporary African American girls confront a choice between "either domesticity and motherhood or career" (Collins 1990: 124).

10 Young notes that the public norms in many less developed countries do not affirm women's equality with men and acknowledges that many husbands in these countries have difficulty earning sufficient income to support a family. Young also recognizes that, in many less developed contexts, women who enter paid employment are motivated less by the prospect of developing their creative potential than by the need to contribute to the survival of their families and perhaps to improve their prospects by paying for schooling.

11 The different ways in which women are made vulnerable by their gendered assignment for domestic work also makes their children vulnerable in different ways. When the responsibilities of childcare are privatized, questions of justice always arise for the children of working parents, but these questions become more acute when parents are working overseas and gone for years at a time, creating a "care deficit" for families in sending countries (Parreñas 2002; Kittay, this volume).

12 For example, in the republics of the former Soviet Union, where the implementation of market policies led to unemployment rates as high as 70 percent and 80 percent among women (Sassen 2002: 268), many women enter sex work and dream of marriage to a foreign man who will provide protection and economic security.

13 Some specifically forbid prostitution for foreign women, which increases their dependence on criminal gangs. "If [sex-workers] seek police help they may be taken into detention because they are in violation of immigration laws; if they have been provided with false documents they are subject to criminal charges." Other receiving countries such as the Netherlands and

Switzerland tolerate foreign women engaging in sex work more than in other forms of work. "According to the International Organization for Migration (IOM) data, the number of migrant women prostitutes in many EU countries is far higher than that for nationals (for example, 75 per cent in Germany and 80 per cent in the case of Milan, Italy)" (Sassen 2002: 269).

14 This means that improvement in poor women's situation is not enough to make it just; for example, even if absolute poverty is decreasing, the gender gap may be widening. Conversely, a narrowing gap may be due to a deterioration in men's circumstances.

2

Transnational Women's Collectivities and Global Justice

Hye-Ryoung Kang

2.1 Introduction

As globalization has proceeded, its benefits and burdens have been unevenly distributed between genders as well as among nations. Given that the global circumstances of justice are new, a crucial question comes to the fore: Have new types of agents of global justice claims emerged, agents whose claims have so far been neglected by philosophers?

Currently, two competing theoretical models of global justice dominate philosophical thinking: nationalism and cosmopolitanism. Within the social ontology of the nationalist model, the main agents of global justice claims are viewed as nation-states or national collectivities. By contrast, within the social ontology of the cosmopolitan model, it is individuals, as citizens of the cosmopolitan world, who are viewed as the agents of global justice claims. In this chapter, I shall argue that neither of these models appropriately reflects the ontological conditions and circumstances of justice which have been engendered by current processes of globalization and, therefore, that neither effectively captures the justice claims of women who suffer as a result of the global economy. As an alternative, I propose a transnational feminist model. I argue that on this model the processes of globalization have generated transnationalized socio-economic units as ontological conditions of justice. In such conditions, transnational women's collectivities are viewed as agents of global justice; they have justice claims as collectivities *in themselves* engendered by ontological conditions. They also make and act for their justice claims as collectivities *for themselves*, formed by an epistemic awareness of their situation, as well as advocating for the justice claims of others mobilized by political solidarity, whose burdens are related to their benefits in the context of globalization.

I shall begin with a sketch of the circumstances of many women in the globalized world. Then, I shall provide a feminist critique of nationalism and cosmopolitanism and propose women's transnational collectivities as agents of global justice claims. Although these collectivities differ internally in geography, nation, language, and culture, their similar or related locations in the process of globalization provide a basis for reaching an overlapping consensus on global justice claims. Finally, I shall argue that addressing the claims of these collectivities can be compatible with the concerns of nationalism and cosmopolitanism.

2.2   Background assumptions

2.2.1   Globalization as a sphere of global justice

In this chapter, I adopt a non-idealized structural contextualist approach. The contextualist approach implies that theories of justice are context-relevant, in particular, in three significant non-ideal conditions: first, the circumstances of justice, i.e., those situations which make justice necessary; second, the spheres of justice in which the circumstances of justice arise; and finally, social relationships between the members in the spheres of justice, i.e., between those among whom burdens and benefits are distributed. Given the ways in which theories of justice are context-dependent, until we have identified the context in which justice issues arise, we cannot determine who should be the agents of justice claims, who has a responsibility to whom and why, or which principles should apply to the circumstances of justice. Given this approach, I need to begin by sketching the spheres of global justice which provide the specific context for the current project.

Ongoing philosophical discussions on the topic of global justice have made little distinction between the sphere of international justice and that of global justice. However, I contend that the trend of current globalization is making more visible a distinctive sphere of global justice that cannot be adequately accounted for by the term "international justice."

"Globalization" has been defined in various ways. Here the term will be used, following Alison Jaggar, to refer to "the rapidly accelerating integration of many local and national economies into a single global market" and to "the political and cultural (even military) corollaries of this process" (Jaggar 2001: 298). Globalization, in this broad sense, is not new. Yet newer, more pressing issues of global justice begin to arise when a neo-liberal version of globalization begins to predominate. The contemporary neo-liberal version of globalization is theoretically supported by neo-liberalism and institutionally regulated by financial and political organizations such as the World Trade Organization (WTO), the International Monetary Fund (IMF), and the World Bank, whose policies are concretized as "free" trade, privatization, deregulation, and structural adjustment (Jaggar 2001: 298–300).

Given the institutionalized nature of globalization, discourse about the justice of global institutions and structures should be different from discourse about the justice of relationships among nations, just as Rawls argues that justice principles for institutions should be distinguished from justice principles for individuals and their actions in a domestic society (Rawls 1971: 54). There are two grounds on which I see globalization and its institutions as a sphere of global justice.

First, by playing roles analogous to, though not the same as, those of the basic structures of nation-states, institutions of globalization affect the distribution of goods across borders. For example, as the most powerful legislative and judicial body in the world, the World Trade Organization deals with the rules of trade in goods, services, and intellectual property on a global level. By August 2012, the WTO had 157 member countries and regulated more than 97 percent of world trade.[1] The integration of national economies into a global market has produced a fairly unified socio-economic unit in which the production, exchange, circulation, and consumption of goods occur at a global level, and in which supply chains stretch from fruit and vegetable farms in Latin America and Africa and garment factories in South Asia and China to the supermarket shelves and clothing racks of shopping centers in developed countries. A context of global justice obtains when the WTO agreements in effect determine the distribution of advantages and disadvantages for those people—as consumers, producers, investors, and traders—involved in global supply chains.

Second, the institutions of neo-liberal globalization also affect people's life prospects indirectly by reshaping the basic socio-economic structures of nation-states. For example, the IMF's structural adjustment programs have resulted in the socio-economic restructuring of more than 60 debtor countries, which, in turn, has profoundly affected people's life chances and prospects. The IMF programs contribute to reshaping the basic structure of nation-states by reducing government expenditure, especially on social welfare, by privatizing state enterprises and deregulating other industries, opening up the possibility of sale to foreign investors, and by removing protection from domestic markets (Jaggar 2002b: 2).[2] The reality of the globalized world as an emerging sphere of global justice raises a question about which types of agents of global justice have emerged in the circumstances of justice.

2.2.2 Women in the sphere of global justice

Neo-liberal globalization has engendered new circumstances of global justice in which the benefits and burdens of globalization are systematically unfairly distributed not only among nations but also between genders. Many factors indicate that neo-liberal globalization has disproportionate effects on the lives of women compared to men, particularly women in the global South. All existing global gender inequalities may not be issues of global justice, but I highlight three aspects of the disproportionate burden that are relevant for justice in the process of globalization: the feminization of the global labor force; the deterioration of the feminized global labor force; and the procedural unfairness in the decision-making processes of global institutions.

First, the "feminization of the global labor force" refers to the fact that global production has increasingly relied on cheap female labor over the past 30 years. According to International Labor Organization (ILO) reports, there was a dramatic increase in workers in export processing zones (EPZs) worldwide. The number of countries using EPZs increased from 25 in 1975 to 130 countries in 2006, employing 66 million people in 3,500 EPZs, in most of which 70 to 80 percent of the workers were women.[3] Women constitute the majority of workers at one end of the global supply chain, picking and packing fruit, sewing garments, cutting flowers. On the other hand, there were over 80 million migrant workers in 2002, often doing "the dirty, dangerous and difficult jobs" under conditions far inferior to those available to nationals in host countries (ILO 2004a). Despite their increased burden, women are still concentrated in low-paid service sector or agricultural work, and they are generally paid the lowest, insufficient as a living wage. Out of the total number of 550 million estimated working poor who live below the poverty line, around 330 million are women (ILO 2004b). Some might say that bad jobs with bad wages and bad conditions are better than no jobs at all. But the question relevant to distributive justice would be whether they are getting fair shares of what they produce under such impoverished conditions, rather than whether their incomes are slightly better than they would be without this work.

Second, though globalization does provide jobs for many poor, vulnerable women, these jobs are characterized by impoverished working conditions in which not only minimum wage standards but also labor standards covering hours worked and workplace safety are often violated. For example, three teenage girls from Bangladesh— Lisa Rahman, Mahamuda Akter, and Sk Nazma—testify that, in order to meet deadlines, they are forced to work for 16 hours a day, seven days a week, with one day off a month, and that they need permission to use the filthy bathroom, and are totally denied freedom of association. They wish that their unhealthy, demeaning, long-hour working conditions could be improved, their wages raised from 14 cents to 34 cents an hour in order to be able to live with "a little dignity," and their legal rights respected.[4] When women who work in such conditions feel that "we have buried our dreams. Our only concern for the future is to make sure that the same thing doesn't happen to our children" (Oxfam 2004), this should be treated as a justice issue in the same way that, as political philosophers have emphasized, poverty causes some people to "feel inferiority and shame at the way they must live" (Beitz 1994: 124–5; Rawls 1999: 114–15).

Finally, the majority of the women of the global South lack both legal rights and a voice in the decision-making processes determining their life prospects. An Oxfam report states that over the past 20 years the legal rights of transnational corporate entities have been deepened and extended dramatically, while the legal rights of poor people working for transnational corporate entities have been dramatically weakened (Oxfam 2004). In addition, women make up only 5.5 percent of the World Bank Governors, and 2.2 percent of high-level positions in the IMF. Out of the 159 trade policy experts selected in 1998 for the WTO roster of dispute, which settles trade-related disagreements, only 12 experts were women (United Nations Development Fund for Women 2002: 26).[5] The situation is even worse for women of the global South, given that among the IMF's 186 member-countries, the US has 16.8 percent of votes while the total share of the 45 sub-Saharan African countries is a mere 4.8 percent (IMF 2012). No democratic process exists whereby poor women whose lives are influenced by decisions taken at the global level might participate in the decision-making process. This type of disparity raises the justice question of the "procedural unfairness" of current dominant global institutions, involving both the "unwarranted exclusion from a decision-making process in whose outcomes an individual has an interest" and an "asymmetry in the terms of participation in a process not justified by its aims."[6]

Taken together, these statistics illustrate that many women in developing countries are affected in distinct ways by the new economic global order. However, questions about the justice of these patterns of benefits and burdens are obscured when agents of global justice claims are viewed either as national collectivities or as individual citizens of a cosmopolitan world.

2.3   Agents of justice claims in nationalism and cosmopolitanism

2.3.1   National collectivities in nationalism

According to nationalists, the main agents of justice claims are national collectivities (Miller 1995, 1999; Walzer 1983, 1994). This position is supported by three related concepts: communitarian social ontology, the communitarian moral reasoning for distributive justice, and the concept of nationality as the largest community.

Communitarian social ontology: In political communities, "language, history, and culture come together to produce a collective consciousness" (Walzer 1983: 28). Thus, in communitarian social ontology, individuals are viewed as being embedded in and constituted by their language, history, and culture. The members in a community collectively participate in shaping their shared understanding of social goods and goals.

Communitarian moral reasoning for distributive justice: Distributive justice must be considered within a bounded political community, and the standards for distributing social goods are derived from the understandings of the social goods shared by the members as a collectivity of a community. In communitarian moral reasoning, it is to the shared understanding of the members situated within a political community, not to the understanding of "rational agents ignorant of their own social standing," nor to that of philosophers alone, that we must appeal when we make our argument on distributive justice. In this sense, the situated, collective members of community are viewed as the main agents shaping, pursuing, and revising social criticism and justice for their community.

Nationality as the largest community: The largest political communities in which common meanings for distributive justice can be established are nations. This claim is supported in three ways.

(1) "National identities tend to create strong bonds of solidarity among those who share them, bonds that are strong enough to override individual differences of religion, ethnicity and so forth" (Miller 1995: 18). Given this, shared understandings about the value of resources or about the basis of justice claims can be easily achieved within national communities, whereas we cannot imagine a global community as our setting for the sphere of justice with understandings shared by all members.

(2) Being members of a national community in a particular territory is a way to realize political self-determination as an expression of group autonomy by deciding collectively on matters that concern one's own community primarily.

(3) Distributive justice issues among different groups of people arise when the groups in question belong to "a single universe of distribution whose overall justice we can meaningfully assess" (Miller 1999: 5). However, such a universe of distribution does not obtain in the global context.

Given these three conceptions, national collectivities are the largest and main agents of political self-determination and distributive justice. It follows that there can be neither spheres of transnational distributive justice nor transnational claimants of distributive justice.

I agree that self-determination is necessary for revealing injustice and exploring fair relationships between nations or states, and I also endorse the moral significance of national identity and citizenship. However, I argue that this recognition does not entail that no further issues exist regarding transnational distributive justice and that no further transnational agents of distributive justice may exist.

My first concern is that nationalist models fail to capture many significant features of the global economy, which both creates a single unified system of distribution across borders and shapes patterns of distribution within borders. Persons across borders within this global economy are affected by these patterns of distribution, which also affect their relative share of advantages and disadvantages of distribution—as consumers, producers, investors, and traders. The existence of these patterns makes it sensible to ask whether, taking into account differences in purchasing power, it is just and/or fair for Bangladeshi workers to receive 5 cents for each shirt which is subsequently sold for $17.99 in developed countries (Hayden and Kernaghan 2002).

This leads me to a second concern in two ways. The supposedly "shared understandings" of national collectivities often fail to reflect the concerns of the marginalized within nations, in particular, of the poor women within nations. Because of this, I contend that the realization of self-determination of national collectivities often does not include the realization of self-determination of women within nations. As Heng (1997) points out, states and nations have often benefited economically from women's cheap labor. In most cases, states and nations (through the shared understanding of national collectivities) have allied themselves with transnational corporations in reducing poor women to cheap labor, in the name of national economic growth. Thus, it is questionable whether women's justice issues and concerns, for example in the EPZs, can be captured by reliance on the notion of shared understandings within national collectives.

In contrast, a sense of shared understanding of distribution may often be formed among people across borders. Although precise *meanings of the good* may be relative to a specific shared language, culture, and history as nationalists argue, it seems to me that understandings of *how to distribute goods* are often influenced more strongly by people's shared material interests and locations in political economy, than by their shared national culture and history. Poor women workers and farmers at one end of global supply chains, in spite of their differences in nationality, culture, language, and geographical location, may have an often greater shared understanding about the standards of distribution of goods and the concepts of human rights than they share with their compatriots of the same language and culture. An example of this can be seen in the work the Korean Women Workers Association United (KWWAU) did to assist a group of Honduran women workers who were hired in Honduras by a Korean manufacturer. The KWWAU urged the firm to improve the women's working conditions and to provide a wage increase and health benefits.[7]

In sum, by neglecting the ways in which global economic institutions shape the patterns of distribution, the nationalist model of justice renders invisible issues of injustice across borders which are generated by transnational economic or political institutions, such as multinational corporations and the IMF, and which disproportionately affect poor women workers and farmers.

2.3.2 Individuals as world citizens in cosmopolitanism

Contrary to the nationalist model, the cosmopolitan model of global justice recognizes moral obligations to individuals across national boundaries. This claim is supported by appeal to three related principles of liberal moral reasoning and social ontology—individualism, universalism, and impartiality, which are regarded as defining characteristics of cosmopolitanism by most cosmopolitan justice theorists (Barry 1998; Pogge 1992; Nussbaum 1996; Jones 1999).

(1) Individualism: The ultimate units of concern are human beings or persons, rather than family lines, tribes, ethnic, cultural, or religious communities, nations, or states.

(2) Universalism: Cosmopolitanism does not recognize any categories of people as having less or more moral weight.

(3) Impartiality: To count people as moral equals is to treat nationality, ethnicity, religion, class, race, and gender as morally irrelevant.

Following these principles, cosmopolitanism claims that individual human beings—citizens of the cosmopolitan world as a single human community—are the appropriate objects of moral concern and the agents of global justice claims.

Individualism and universalism have been interpreted in many different ways. I endorse the ideal that no individual should be excluded from moral concern because of their class, race, gender, nationality, etc. I also agree with individualism in the sense that persons, not groups, have ultimate intrinsic value, and that the ultimate concern is the well-being of individuals, so policies should be judged by their ultimate impact on the individual human beings who constitute a group, rather than by their impact on the group as a whole.

However, if the theses of individualism and impartiality mean viewing and treating agents of justice claims as abstract human beings stripped of their nationality, gender, class, etc., and of their locations in the spheres of justice within which the claims of justice are made, then my worry is that such an individualistic ontology fails to accurately capture patterns of injustice within the global system in the current non-ideal conditions, in which the injustice suffered by individuals is inseparable from their identities and political and economic locations. In such types of gendered and/or racialized circumstances of justice, treating individuals' ethnicity, class, race, and gender as morally irrelevant can result in neglecting injustice, rather than achieving moral equity.

For example, on a cosmopolitan view, the justice claims made by the three teenage girls from Bangladesh are often viewed as the claims of individual human beings abstracted as "the global poor" or "the distant needy," who are detached from the circumstances of justice and social relationships between those among whom burdens and benefits are systematically distributed. Yet such an abstract view leaves out morally salient features relevant to grasping certain key issues, such as whether and why these claims are legitimate, who bears moral responsibility and why, and what are the appropriate remedies to these injustices. As a result, cosmopolitanism is inadequate to capture the justice claims of the most disadvantaged in the process of globalization.

First, as shown in Singer's interactional cosmopolitanism, the cosmopolitan view of agents of justice claims as abstracted individual human beings, or as the distant needy, often leads to support for affirmative remedies rather than transformative and structural remedies. For example, the leading suggestions for poverty reduction involve the transfer of resources or aid from rich countries to poor ones, and/or the use of international pressure on corrupt governments to change their ways or renounce their power, as indicated in many works on cosmopolitanism (Singer 1972; Barry 1998; Rawls 1999; Nussbaum 2000; Beitz 1979). Yet such solutions ignore the underlying problems; as long as the transnational corporations and retailers of developed countries are able to manipulate and coerce developing countries into offering the most competitive (i.e., lowest) wages, getting governments like that of Bangladesh to improve workers' conditions will only result in the movement of transnational retailers to other countries providing cheaper labor, thus increasing the possibility for exploitation of another group of girls under even harsher conditions. On the other hand, if we view working poor women as agents of collective justice claims, we are better able to develop sustainable and transformative remedies such as legally requiring retailers or transnational companies to put "decent work"[8] or "fair trade" labels on their merchandise or to question the fairness of the entire global political economic system as it is currently structured and operated.[9]

Second, viewing justice claims as those of individual human beings often neglects the systematic or patterned group injustices that have arisen in the globalization process. Differently from interactional cosmopolitanism, Pogge's (2004) institutional cosmopolitanism focuses on institutional injustice and its remedies, but it too views agents of justice claims as abstract human beings in a way that often overlooks the relation between the impoverished conditions of 66 million workers in EPZs and their identity as women and workers. When some women workers are collectively and disproportionately disadvantaged in the process of globalization on the basis of their gender and class, their conditions can be better improved by the implementation of their specified collective rights as both women and workers. Without realization of their rights as women and workers, their human rights will also not be protected.

Finally, it might be said that such gender issues can be addressed in terms of a gender-sensitive cosmopolitanism such as Nussbaum's (1996, 2000). But women's issues in Nussbaum's cosmopolitanism are viewed as being mainly due to factors of male-dominated local politics, cultures, and practices, or of undeveloped economies, on which basis it is claimed that domestic violence, rape, child marriage, etc., are the main barriers to women's capability, and that women's issues in developing countries can be solved by educating the women who have adaptive preferences or by giving guidance to those local governments which are insensitive to equal gender capabilities (Nussbaum 2000). In so doing, however, gender-sensitive cosmopolitanism often obscures the systematic relationship between women in the transnationalized sphere of globalization—for example, the connection between women as beneficiaries of globalization and women as burdened by globalization. We in developed countries are wearing the clothes and shoes made by those living in impoverished conditions. As a result, we may forget that our responsibility is not simply grounded in some sense of shared humanity in a cosmopolitan world, but rather arises from the direct or indirect relation between their burdens and our benefits in a shared political economy. Thus, viewing the justice claims of global women workers as those of unlucky women in developing countries does not enable us to distinguish between what we owe to, for example, the Indonesian women victims of tsunamis or of local culture and what we owe to the Indonesian women workers making our clothes in impoverished conditions.

The view I am proposing is based on a transnational justice ontology which recognizes that current significant injustice has been systematically created among collectivities who are differently situated in the transnationalized social and economic spheres by global factors. Given this, the justice claims of some individuals in the current global context can be more adequately addressed by considering them as the justice claims of the relevant transnational collectivities—which are becoming more appropriate social ontological subjects in the global economy—

rather than by reducing them to the justice claims of individual humans stripped of their gender, race, class, etc., in a cosmopolitan world, or to the justice claims of national collectivities.

2.4   Transnational women's collectivities: having, making, and advocating justice claims

The ontology of the distributive justice model I am proposing contends that the agents of justice claims should be considered within a sphere of justice in which the relative share of benefits and burdens of the relevant people are decided, and in which people are related to each other through their share of benefits and burdens. The integration of national economies into a global market has produced a transnational socio-economic unit as a sphere of global justice, in which the production, exchange, circulation, and consumption of goods occur at a global level. This kind of transnationalized unit creates a transnational scope for distributive justice as well as a new type of transnational social relations as an ontological condition. Given that its benefits and burdens have been disproportionately distributed between genders and, as a result, many women are collectively and similarly situated in the transnationalized spheres of justice, I argue that transnational women's collectivities are best viewed as agents of global justice, agents who have justice claims as collectivities in themselves, who make and act for their justice claims as collectivities for themselves, and who also advocate for the justice claims of others, whose burdens are related to their benefits.

Transnational collectivities differ from national collectivities in that they are formed *across* borders. Furthermore, insofar as they are women's *collectivities*, they differ from individual human beings across borders. The Central American Network of Women in Solidarity with Maquila Workers is one example of a transnational women's collectivity.[10] In what follows, I shall provide a more detailed explanation of the concept of transnational women's collectivities as agents of justice claims. In doing so, I will argue that this concept better addresses the justice concerns raised by both cosmopolitanism and nationalism.

2.4.1   Why collectivities, not individuals?

Cosmopolitan theorists argue that only individual persons, not collective groups, have intrinsic value, and that the ultimate concern from the standpoint of justice is the well-being of individuals,[11] not that of whole groups. Given this, a supporter of cosmopolitanism may be skeptical of the concept of collectivities as agents of justice claims. In this section, against this skepticism, I will argue that cosmopolitanism's concern with individual well-being is better addressed by employing the concept of collectivities, more specifically through the concept of individuals in collectivities, rather than that of individuals without collectivities. Collectivities provide a better space for individuals to articulate their rights or well-being, and also contribute to their empowerment.

First, collectivities often provide both informal and formal spaces in which similarly situated, vulnerable individuals can participate in free, dialogical discourse about their justice claims. By discussing their experiences with one another, individuals in collectivities are better positioned to raise awareness about the deprivation of their rights and are more likely to conceptualize these as justice claims. Jaggar argues that a collective project is epistemologically indispensable for the subaltern woman to overcome her silence: "they should collaborate with other subaltern women in developing a public language for their shared experiences," and they must "become part of a group that constitutes itself as a class for itself as well as in itself" (Jaggar 1998: 13).[12] This point can be seen in the Central American Network of Women in Solidarity's statement of purpose:

> Given the situation of discrimination and super-exploitation in which women maquila workers live as a result of the process of globalization of the regional economy and given the lack of proper space and conditions that permit them to make demands and proposals and stake claims regarding their rights as women and as workers; we have come together in order to analyze, generate and contribute by means of this organization a space which could serve this purpose. (Quoted in Mendez 2002: 126)

Second, collectivities provide a space for making more visible the justice claims of vulnerable individuals, as well as for empowering these individuals. When vulnerable individuals are separated, they are less likely to recognize that their rights are being violated; and even in cases where they do recognize their situation as unfavorable, vulnerable individuals may take these conditions for granted, as inevitable or with "adaptive preferences" (Nussbaum 2000). In other words, separate or isolated individuals are more likely to accept unfavorable conditions with resignation, or ascribe them to their own bad luck.

Although these voices do break the silence, it is often difficult for a thousand *isolated* voices of vulnerable individuals to be heard, especially given the full range of geographical locations, races, and classes that these justice claims embody. By contrast, the voices of a collectivity, consisting of a hundred vulnerable individuals, are often easier to hear. For example, prior to 1995, the voices of the *individual* workers of Tijuana's maquiladoras were silenced and inaudible to most of the world. However, these voices have been amplified and gained a larger audience since the formation of the Maquiladora Solidarity Network, which makes justice claims as a collective agent.

One may argue that just as the shared understanding of national collectivities does not reflect the claims of oppressed minority groups within those collectivities, the strength of collectivities as agents of justice claims may come at a cost to the autonomy and self-determination of the more powerless individuals within those collectivities. However, women's transnational collectivities as agents of global justice claims are different from national collectivities in at least two ways: The power disparities among their members are small, and their membership is voluntary.

First, memberships in national or ethnic collectivities are formed on the basis of a shared identity and often involve vast disparities in power between members. In contrast, transnational women's collectivities are constructed, not on the basis of a shared female identity, but because of the shared disadvantages and conditions of powerlessness that arise due to the ways women are more exploited and vulnerable in the process of globalization—which, in effect, give rise to overlapping justice claims. Although members of collectivities are disadvantaged in the context of globalization, because they are disadvantaged in similar ways and to similar degrees, power differences between them are relatively small. Individuals in such collectivities are in a better position to speak their thoughts freely and to be "authentic" (Jaggar 1998: 14). Thus, the justice claims that arise within these collectivities reflect the justice claims of individuals.

Second, because membership in national collectivities is involuntary, it is often practically impossible for members to choose to relinquish their nationality, even if they find that the justice claims of their national collectivities are oppressive. However, members of collectivities making global justice claims are free to leave or to not participate if they disagree with the way the claims are being formulated. As long as membership in collectivities is voluntary, it is unlikely that these collectivities will be detrimental to the autonomy of their individual members.

2.4.2   Why transnational, not national?

Nationalists, on the other hand, may be concerned that transnational collectivities are detrimental to the values of national self-determination and sovereignty. In this section, I will argue that the concept of transnational women's collectivities as agents of justice claims is not incompatible with maintaining the integrity of nation-states.

First, the view of transnational women's collectivities as agents for justice claims does not collapse into the view expressed by Virginia Woolf that "as women, we have no country; as women, we want no country; and as women, our country is the whole world" (Woolf 1938: 109). Rather, I claim that transnational women's collectivities should be those that are situated, but critically situated, in their national and geopolitical locations. This critical situatedness is a result of the ways in which the process of globalization indirectly affects the lives of women by reshaping the basic structures of nation-states, thereby engendering circumstances and issues of justice that vary with different contexts, and take the form of intersected "scattered hegemonies" (Grewal and Kaplan 1994). Given this, critical scrutiny of the locations of women's collectivities in both a national and a global context is necessary in order to detect patterns of global injustice.

Second, as far as the underprivileged in the global context are also the underprivileged within national contexts, the empowerment of *transnational* collectivities will improve the situation of many underprivileged citizens *within* nations. The empowerment of the underprivileged within nations may even contribute to democratization from below, given their positions as internal critics who are familiar with and influenced by policies within nations. For example, Korean women workers, who struggled for their rights as workers in export free trade zones, raised their own awareness of their civic and political rights, causing them to play a more remarkable role than any other actors in the democratization movements of South Korea and in ending the long-time cycle of military governments (Nam 2002).

The question then arises, "How are locally and nationally situated transnational collectivities possible?" The idea of transversal practice (Yuval-Davis 1997b), which is characterized by a process of both rooting and shifting, is what makes these collectivities possible. According to transversal politics, each individual participant (or collectivity) roots herself in her own concrete and material political reality, and at the same time tries to shift her awareness in order to understand women who have different material political realities (Yuval-Davis

1997b). When we apply this transversal politics to transnational women's collectivities, the collectivities are able to become somewhat more "rooted" in that they are concerned with their own local and national contexts of struggle. At the same time, they shift their focus by contextualizing their particular experience within larger global contexts, as well as by connecting with others who may be similarly or differently located in the global context. As Yuval-Davis (1997b) conceives of it, the process of shifting should not involve self-decentering (i.e., losing one's own rooting and set of values), nor should it homogenize the other. The collectivity of Coalition for Justice, for example, is composed of labor, environmental, community, and women's groups in Mexico, the US, and Canada. In spite of different nationalities and locations, their justice claims are more effective when the members critically question the impacts of labor policies of their respective countries' transnational companies and the impacts of the foreign policies of their own governments on Mexican workers.

Finally, the concept of transnational women's collectivities as agents of justice claims can be compatible with the nationalist claim that we owe more extensive special obligations to compatriots than to outsiders (Miller 1995: 48–83). If the nationalist claim for the special obligation to compatriots is true, then it must be extended to the claim that we also have more special extensive obligations to redress any injustices done to outsiders by our compatriots or government than by other governments. Such an extended special obligation is compatible with the perspectives of transnational women's collectivities. Thus, women's collectivities can be transnationally collaborated by working also within their own nations to contest and change their unjust intra- and international policies, which contribute to global injustice.

2.4.3   Why women's collectivities, not other collectivities?

A final concern may stem from the worry of non-feminist transnational justice theorists that global justice is not simply an issue of women, and that focusing on women's collectivities is exclusive. This worry, however, seems misguided. Rather, given the fact that globalization has distinct and especially serious consequences for poor women,[13] focusing on women's transnational collectivities can allow for more inclusive accounts.

First, it allows us to include special justice claims of women's collectivities that cannot be captured by the claims of other transnational collectivities and that have often been neglected. The ILO reports that women workers' matters deserve more attention, not only because the majority of workers in export processing zones are women, but also because they experience the living and working conditions differently from men (ILO 1998: 31–7). The split of the Association of Women in Solidarity from the Syndical Federation of Food and Agroindustry in Guatemala is only one of many examples that show why autonomous women's collectivities are often necessary in order to raise particular justice claims of and for women workers, and not simply of workers (Mendez 2002: 128).

Second, the most disadvantaged of the disadvantaged often encompass the most various types of justice claims. The justice claims of women workers within the global economy involve several intersected axes of justice claims of other collectivities. As is shown in the term, "racialized feminization of global labor" (Lowe 1996), focusing on the justice claims of women workers often requires more inclusive perspectives, not simply perspectives of gender justice but also those of racial and class justice in the global context.

For these reasons, I focus on transnational women's collectivities, but this does not mean denying other types of transnational collectivities in principle. The conceptual model of women's transnational collectivities can be extended to include other types of transnational collectivities, whose justice claims overlap within the context of injustice due to globalization. Transnational farmers' collectivities may serve as an example of those whose justice claims related to the agenda of the WTO in Cancun, 2003. However, in interactions between transnational women's collectivities and other collectivities, the process of the shifting of transversal practice, without self-decentering or homogenizing the other, is again required. In this case, the transnational feminist justice paradigm can be expanded into a transnational justice paradigm without changing its core background assumptions, categories, and concepts.

2.4.4   What are transnational women's collectivities, and do how they work?

The concept of transnational women's collectivities refers to agents for justice claims in the process of globalization, not to agents for identity politics or for communitarian politics. Therefore, such collectivities are not identified by any shared essential identities or ways of life among their members, but by their socio-economic locations and/or their justice claims as mediated by their locations. More specifically, they are identified from their locations in the process of globalization, described as the integration of many local and national economies into a single global market. Thus, transnational women's collectivities arise not out of some shared identity as women or as members of some particular race. The collectivities arise, rather, because neo-liberal globalization has engendered circumstances of justice in which the benefits and burdens of globalization are systematically unfairly distributed between genders, between the global South and North, as well as among nations. This creates a situation in which the justice claims of women across borders overlap.

Second, insofar as all women are not similarly situated in the context of globalization, the existence of "women's transnational collectivities" would not imply a single universalized global women's agency. To the contrary, such collectivities are multiple and fluid. Because the structures of globalization operate at macro levels and its impacts appear in various forms intersected with local factors, these collectivities arise in accordance with their specific justice claims in multiple sites across borders.

Women's collectivities have raised diverse justice claims from their specific locations. Some focus on women workers' rights in export processing zones and free trade zones (e.g., the Central American Network of Women in Solidarity with Maquila Workers); others on immigrant women workers (e.g., the Asian Women's Immigrant Advocates); some on the effects on women of the structural adjustment policies of the IMF and World Bank (e.g., women's groups in sub-Saharan Africa); some on sweatshop issues (e.g., Feminists Against Sweatshops); some on the issues of damage to the environment done by transnational companies and World Bank dam projects; and others on women's security from global militarism (e.g., East Asia-US-Puerto Rico Women's Network against Militarism). Also, justice claims are related to globalization to a greater or lesser extent. Some collectivities raise global justice claims as one part of their project, while others raise global justice claims as their whole project.[14]

Three questions about how to individuate the transnational collectivities may be raised. First, given that there are no globally shared justice claims or a unified single agency, one may wonder why the collectivities can be called agents for global justice. In other words, on what basis do we call such different collectivities "transnational women's collectivities as agents of global justice"? My reply is that though their justice claims are different and there may be no unitary, shared consensus among the diversity of those claims, an overlapping consensus does in fact exist insofar as their claims all center on the unjust aspects of neo-liberal globalization. Thus, each justice claim is raised relative to the same process of neo-liberal globalization, though in different ways and to different degrees.

Second, women's transnational collectivities have, in fact, raised such claims in various ways, as collectivities in themselves and for themselves: some in advocacy, speaking for others who have different socio-economic locations and whose burdens are related to their benefits; others in their own names, speaking for themselves. Also, transnational collectivities often consist of members who have different socio-economic locations: some advantaged, others disadvantaged. For example, the Coalition for Justice in the Maquiladoras is composed of members in Mexico, the United States, and Canada with special emphasis on defending the rights of women in the Maquiladoras. On what grounds, then, can members of a collectivity, in spite of their different locations, have and make shared claims to justice on the basis of a shared understanding?

Though the US and Canadian members of the Coalition for Justice have a different socio-economic location from that of the maquiladora workers, globalization, and in particular NAFTA (North American Free Trade Agreement), brings them into the same political economy as a sphere of justice with the maquiladora workers. Given this, the responsibility for making the political economy more just, and for building fairer relations among its members, enables people to work together. Thus, people with different locations in the same political economy can participate in collectivities with the same or overlapping goals as insiders of that economy.

Finally, these collectivities exist on various levels—local, national, regional, and transnational. Though some of them may be linked in networks (e.g., Women's International Coalition for Economic Justice), there may be no center among them. Given this, another question may arise: In spite of such decentralized localness, what makes us call such localized collectivities "transnational" collectivities? My reply is that although the justice claims of a collectivity are raised geographically in local areas, if those claims are raised in relation to the process of globalization, then they can be considered to have arisen in politically transnationalized spheres of justice.

2.5 Conclusion

In this chapter I have suggested that we begin to employ a concept of transnational women's collectivities as agents of global justice claims.

These collectivities are different from national collectivities in that they are formed across borders; and they differ from collectivities of abstract *individual human beings* across borders in that they are *women's collectivities*. They diverge from a single universalized global women's agency, in which distinctions of class, race, nationality, or sexuality are erased. Rather, the collectivities I am proposing are situated in their class, race, nationality, or sexuality on the basis of which global injustice has been committed. The concept of transnational women's collectivities as agents of global justice claims is one part of a larger transnational feminist justice framework, which can work with other cohering background assumptions.

Since it may be objected that my model is not universal, I would like to conclude by identifying the scope of applicability of this framework. The concept of transnational women's collectivities outlined here applies not to agents of identity politics, but to agents of claims to structural justice. Furthermore, this concept is not presented as addressing justice issues that may arise in all ages, in all possible, or even in all our actual, worlds. For example, it may not be suitable for capturing the justice claims of those distant needy whose poverty is not related to global factors; for such concerns, cosmopolitanism may well work better than this framework. It is plausible that we should help the distant needy across borders, even though their unfavorable situations are not related to global structural factors. My account is also not suitable for addressing international justice issues between nations. Here, nationalism surely will work better than this framework in ensuring that self-determination and the sovereignty of the nation should be protected from attack or intervention by other nations. Rather, my model is intended to illuminate global justice issues in non-ideal conditions arising from current neo-liberal globalization, issues which cannot be adequately captured by the dominant philosophical frameworks of nationalism or cosmopolitanism, nor by a global feminism based on the notion of global sisterhood.

I do not think that limiting the scope of the framework in this way implies a weakness. Insofar as we live in an age with multiple types of injustice, being equipped with multiple justice paradigms can only be a strength in addressing justice issues more adequately.

Acknowledgments

The writing of this chapter was supported by an International Women Fellowship from the American Association of University Women.

Earlier versions were presented at the Pacific Division Meeting of the American Philosophical Association and at the Feminist Ethics and Social Theory Conference. I am grateful to Alison Jaggar for valuable suggestions; to Theresa Tobin, Abigail Gosselin, and Audra King for discussing the issues with me; and to two anonymous referees for helpful comments on earlier drafts.

Notes

1 See the World Trade Organization website, in particular, "What is the WTO?," available at http://www.wto.org/english/thewto_e/whatis_e/whatis_e.htm (accessed September 1, 2012).

2 According to Ambrose, after user fees were introduced, in Kenya there was a 52% reduction in outpatient visits; in Papua New Guinea, a decline of about 30% in attendance at rural clinics; in Tanzania, a drop in school attendance of 53.4%; in Nicaragua, about 25% of primary school children were not enrolled; and in Niger, as a result of the structural adjustment program between 1986 and 1988, there was a sharp decline in what were already very low primary school enrollment rates from 28% in 1983 to 20% in 1988 (Ambrose 2001: 104).

3 According to the ILO, export processing zones are defined as "industrial zones with special incentives set up to attract foreign investors, in which imported materials undergo some degree of processing before being exported again" (ILO 1998). For the various statistics on employers in EPZs, see ILO 2008.

4 Meet them at http://www.globallabourrights.org/campaigns?id=0007 (accessed September 1, 2012). For similar reports of serious conditions of women workers, see Oxfam 2004; International Confederation of Free Trade Unions 2004; and Ingeborg 2010.

5 At the level of the board of directors, the primary decision-making body at both organizations, the World Bank has only two women directors, while at the IMF there are no women with director status.

6 I have borrowed the concept of "procedural unfairness" from Charles Beitz (see Beitz 2001: 107).

7 For the Korean Women Workers Associations United, see http://kwwa.tistory.com/category/OUR%20ARCHIVE (accessed April 26, 2013).

8 "Decent work" was defined by ILO as productive work in which rights are protected, which generates an adequate income, and which comes with adequate social protection (ILO 1999).

9 Structural changes can contribute to assisting the global poor more effectively than interactional assistance. Thus, according to an Oxfam report, if poor countries were each to increase their share of world exports by 1 percent, the resulting gains in income could lift 128 million people out of poverty (Watkins 2002: 5). If we can find a way to let farmers sell their

coffee, bananas, and other products at a few more cents, millions of their children may be able to go school instead of doing child labor. It would also eliminate the concern that benefits of the transfer from the rich countries might go into the hands of corrupt despots, rather than to the poor.

10 There are more than 4,000 maquila factories in Mexico, most of which are owned by transnational corporations. Coalition for Justice is composed of more than 100 organizations from religious, labor, environmental, community, and women's groups in Mexico, the US, and Canada who work to improve the working conditions and living standards for maquila workers. The Central American Network of Women in Solidarity with Maquila Workers is a network made up of autonomous women's organizations from Guatemala, Honduras, Nicaragua, and El Salvador aiming to improve the lives and working conditions of women garment assembly workers. See Mendez 2002: 121–41.

11 This may be differently defined in terms of human rights, capabilities or anything else, according to cosmopolitan theorists.

12 For an example of discourse using these types of collectivities, see the model of feminist practical moral discourse with discursive equality and openness espoused by Jaggar (1995).

13 For globalization as a gendered process, see Moghadam 2005; United Nations Development Fund for Women 2002; ILO 2004a.

14 For more various examples of women's transnational movements, networks, and their organization, see Moghadam 2005.

3

The Moral Harm of Migrant Carework: Realizing a Global Right to Care

Eva Feder Kittay

3.1 The purpose and scope of the inquiry

"Migrant labor" evokes images of men leaving villages to work on oil rigs or at seasonal jobs while women stay home to tend to families. That picture is no longer accurate. More than half of those who migrate with the intent of sending home remittances are now women, many of whom leave their families—aging parents, spouse, and children—behind. In the receiving countries, these women frequently occupy paid positions in the domestic sphere where they provide direct care to children, frail elderly or those chronically ill or disabled (INSTRAW 2008).[1] Wealthier nations employ the migrants to solve a "care crisis," presumably brought about by changing demographics and women's increased full-time labor participation in the labor force. Sending countries, in turn, have come to depend heavily on migrant women's remittances to bring in needed capital (Parreñas 2005: 22–3).[2] But the absent female workers leave the sending countries with a "care deficit" (Schutte 2002: 138–59).

The migration of women care laborers constitutes a global movement of caring labor, circulating as if it were a scarce resource, from those parts of the world where there is a need for cash to those parts of the world where there is both a demand for caregivers and a willingness to pay for their services. In an essay suggestively entitled "Love and Gold" Arlie Hochschild describes the situation of a college-educated Filipina schoolteacher who left her five children in the Philippines for a job as a live-in domestic caring for a young child. Although she opted for migration and chose to do carework in Los Angeles, the teacher, Vicky Diaz, spoke of her depression, saying "the only thing you can do is to give all your love to the child [in your care]. In my absence from my children the best I could do in my situation is to give all my love to the child" (Hochschild and Ehrenreich 2002: 22).[3] Hochschild glosses the bestowal of Diaz's love and care on the children in Los Angeles that would otherwise go to her children in the Philippines as a "global heart transplant" in a global "care chain."

To speak of this global transaction as a "heart transplant" starkly represents the view that something critical and irreplaceable to an organism is extracted to serve another's need. The idea that there is a moral harm is clear. Yet the nature of the moral harm needs an articulation, as migrant labor is a practice that can be defended in light of the facts that these women are not overtly coerced to migrate, their children (for whom they send back remittances) tend to do better materially and have more opportunities than children of comparable families without income from remittances, and the GNP of sending countries goes up as a consequence of these remittances. The women themselves may also benefit from the migration by being able to leave abusive spouses, and by developing a greater sense of agency. In other words, it is arguable that all (i.e., the children, the mother, the sending nation) who might be thought to be harmed in this transaction, when considered separately, gain significantly from the transaction.

Beginning with the idea that the "global heart transplant" (GHT) is morally problematic, I set out to clarify the harms in question and the moral resources needed to identify these harms. I focus on the micro-relationships between individuals whose important relationships are now transnational, although there is an important story to tell about the macro-relationships between nations and the mid-level relationships between both sending and receiving countries and the migrant worker. The argument effectively is that traditional theories consider the impact of the GHT on each party considered as an *independent* entity. It is not that traditional theories have nothing to tell us about the harms. It is rather that in each case one can find responses that seem to counterbalance the harm with significant goods. However, when we posit a sufficiently broad and nuanced right to care, we see that there is an important harm to the migrant women's central relationships. These are not easily addressed using the traditional theories from which challenges and defenses are drawn. And this harm affects individuals not as individual citizens of particular nations but as families, which, separated by space and time, function as "transnational families."

Using conceptions of "self" and "harm" derived from an ethic of care—that the self is relational and that among the most serious harms people experience are the fracturing of central relationships—we can diagnose the harm of the GHT more adequately. Given these conceptions and the realities of women's migration, I set out to develop a right to give and receive care, a right that is at best imperfectly realized by these women, even as their own work facilitates the more perfect realization of this right on the part of those employing them. Because caring relationships and the right to nurture these (a right to give care) are so critical to one's self-respect, especially for women who are expected and who expect themselves to care for those who depend on them, the injury to the migrant careworker is also an injury to her self-respect, which Rawls identifies as the most important of social goods. However, this deployment of the concept requires that we understand the "self" in self-respect to be relational, that is, a self that views broken relationships as the worst of harms. But a fully developed right to care also understands the distribution of such goods as requiring a global framework. The right to care sketched here transcends national boundaries and requires transnational institutions as guarantors of these rights. I conclude with some brief remarks about what a resolution to the moral quandary of migrant carework will involve.

What we are calling the GHT is characterized by a set of conditions. These include *commodified carework*, *migration between economically disparate nations*, and *fixed gender roles*.

Commodified carework: The work the migrant women assume is *carework*. The carework is frequently done in a domestic setting, a setting which itself presents some moral hazards (Tronto 2002). Yet not all this carework is done in private homes.[4] When done in nursing homes and daycare facilities, it still partakes of the uncomfortable transmutations of "love" into "gold" highlighted by Hochschild.

Migration across economically disparate nations: The migration is transnational from poorer to wealthier nations. The migrants earn wages, which though low by the standards of wealthier receiving nations, are lucrative compared to what they can garner at home (even in higher-status work). Additionally 1) the migration is not permanent, that is, all or most of the family remain in the country of origin, and the migrating worker intends to return to her home country; 2) the absences are extended, lasting ten years or more because the distances are great and the cost of travel is high. Many prefer to use the money they earn to send back to their families instead of using it for transport back and forth.

Gender in fixed roles: We are talking about *women—women in traditional gender roles of caregiver in and outside the family*. It is these women who sending nations have traditionally depended on for the care of children, the ill or disabled, and the elderly, that is, the "inevitably dependent" (see Fineman 1995; Kittay 1999). Although they forgo engaging in intimate daily care with their dependents, they understand themselves to be acting as good mothers and daughters, caring by providing material benefits and finding responsible people to do the daily care. If these women defy the traditional gender roles in their countries of origin, they nonetheless enact the traditional gender role of caregiver in receiving countries by "pouring" (Parrenãs 2001: 181), as they say, love into their charges.

Many questions have been raised about the practice of migrant labor. An economy normally has to consider the costs of reproducing its labor force, but here receiving nations are absolved of the costs of raising, sustaining and educating the next generation. Nancy Folbre asks whether such practices are sustainable (2002: 185–205); that is, whether the sending nations will be able to manage their own care crisis and whether the supply of such transnational careworkers will therefore continue.

Others have asked whether the use of migrant labor to do carework is not in conflict with feminist ideals of shared responsibility for carework (Tronto 2002). Still others have emphasized the exploitation, daily humiliations, and violence many migrant laborers endure (see, among others, Rollins 1987; Chang 2000).[5] Elsewhere I, and others, have made the case that it is precisely women's increased workplace opportunities that have contributed to the demand for hired careworkers, making this issue especially important for feminists (see Eckenwiler 2009; Kittay et al. 2005; Kittay 2008; Weir 2008). Each of these discussions focuses on some of the conditions outlined above. But the GHT involves all three. We will take up each in turn.

3.2 The commodification of caregiving

Central to the inquiry is the propriety of treating caring labor as a commodity like any other. Carework that is bought and sold is nothing new, but certain new features arise when it is considered within a globalized economy.

Care, when worthy of the name, generally involves an emotional bond between the caregiver and another individual. As Folbre (2003) points out, this bond frequently serves as the "intrinsic motivation" beyond the material compensation that commonly motivates work. Thus even when the carework is paid for, we are not simply transmuting love into gold. Whence comes this intrinsic motivation when the carework does not emerge from intimate bonds but is initiated in a material transaction? From the work of care itself, that is, from the bond formed in the process of devoting time and attention to ensure the welfare of another, and from the perceived response from the cared-for that such attention returns.[6] Surely, this can feel very similar to—and to a third party may look very much like—the bond between a familial caregiver and her dependents.

In the national context, a nanny, for instance, returns home each evening to nurture her own child, thus renewing their relationship. But as the separation grows lengthier, because of the employer's demands or the distance imposed by geography, the bond motivating family caregiving increasingly appears—to her dependents, to outside observers, and to the woman herself—to be displaced, hijacked from the familial to the commercial relationship.

In the transnational context the absences are of necessity lengthy, because of both distance and cost, impeding the restoration of intimacy that feeds the familial affective bond. The women attempt to maintain closeness through telephone, email, and letters, but these cannot fully replace the embodied, that is, fleshly, contacts that signal intimacy. Therefore it seems as if the *work* of care *and* the *love* so often tied to informal carework make the transnational journey together, that the familial affective bond is effectively expropriated. It appears that, as Mary Zimmerman puts it: "there is an emerging global hierarchy of emotional care and love, depriving poorer nations and further enriching wealthier ones." That there can be a hierarchy of this sort seems *particularly* unjust—an injustice that goes beyond a material injustice. But why?

One difficulty in articulating why lies in the usual language of justice. This language is largely voluntaristic. If adults voluntarily consent to an arrangement wherein each benefits, then there appears to be nothing unjust in that arrangement. The movement of labor and care are not *overtly coerced*, and there are real benefits to the sending nations as well as the receiving nations, the employed as well as the employer. As one defender of globalization, Jagdish Bhagwati, puts it:

The migrant female worker is better off in the new world of attachments and autonomy: the migrants' children are happy being looked after by their grandmothers, who are also happy to be looking after the children; and the employer mothers, when they find good nannies, are also happy and they can work without the emotionally wrenching sense that they are neglecting their children. (Bhagwati 2004: 78)

So why worry?

While this rosy picture presents a skewed view, there is *some* truth here. Women would not volunteer to leave their children for ten years or more if there were no advantages that accrued to them and their families. One World Bank report cites studies indicating that these migrations lower the poverty levels of sending nations, that the children of migrant families stay in school longer and are healthier, and girls especially are impacted in a positive way (World Bank 2005: 1).

Still, even traditional moral concepts indicate that the practice is morally problematic. It is normally a parent's responsibility to see to it that a child has hands-on daily care and has the material provisions needed to provide that care. Traditionally these responsibilities have been defined by gendered familial roles. When parents (however the responsibilities are divided) cannot provide both, when one is sacrificed for the sake of the other, parents face a Sophie's choice, one in which either option means forgoing an important good; yet one must choose. The dilemma is encountered whenever there is no institutional support and the income prospects of all available familial providers are insufficient.

For the migrant woman, it is nonetheless a choice; poor as the alternatives are, they do not involve starvation or total destitution (Parrenãs 2001). The money that she can earn is far greater than any position available to her in her native land. She may be excited about the prospect of new possibilities. She might be leaving behind an unhappy or abusive marriage. She may prefer to do carework so that she can at least have an emotional connection to another, similar to the sort she had to abandon. She may feel that her children will be better looked after by her own mother than they would be if cheap childcare arrangements in the new land would have to suffice. She might feel that she can save her own child the humiliations that she will experience as a migrant. She may see how the children of her neighbors have better opportunities because their mother left and is sending home remittances and want such opportunities for her own children (Parrenãs 2001).

Although the woman certainly appears to be making autonomous choices, these could be seen as cases of adaptive preference formation. In many ways it looks as if the woman is acting against her own best interests, for mothers generally do not make choices to leave their small children for extended periods of time (not only for the sake of their child but also because they themselves do not want this sort of separation). The classic case of adaptive preference formation is the woman who claims she wants to eat leftovers and prefers that her husband eat first. Similarly, the migrant woman, rather than remain with her family and demand better pay, chooses to leave; rather than stay at home and work out her marriage problems, opts to migrate; rather than saving her affectionate labor for those who are most meaningful in her life, bonds with another's child. As these choices appear to diminish the woman's own flourishing, they are suspect. While the choices are not coerced nor necessarily a consequence of desperation, they are nonetheless constrained by adverse conditions—ones, as we will see below, in which globalization figures as both a cause and a response. Under more just conditions and under conditions that do not offer the transnational opportunities, she is likely to choose to give daily attention and care to her dependents and have an income sufficient for them to live well (Khader 2008). As we will see below, there are reasons to believe that there are economic benefits to be had by all parties involved. Yet even if we grant the benefits of this migration, it doesn't mean that the remedies do not come at significant cost.

The cost that we are considering is the commodification of the *affective component* of care. I do not here want to argue that care should not be something we pay for—or rather I do not want to argue that carework is not something for which one should get paid—indeed I have argued that all carework should be recompensed and Bhagwati may be right when he suggests that the price of carework will increase as more seek to hire careworkers.[7] But caring labor has properties that resist commodification. First is the intrinsic motivation requirement. Because the motivation for the caring tends to derive from affective bonds more than from extrinsic rewards, it is more likely that the carer will do the caring for relatively low extrinsic rewards, thus keeping the market price of the care labor relatively low, lower than its actual social value. Furthermore, tradable commodities are tradable largely because they are fungible. But in the case of care, it matters who cares and for whom they care. And not only does it matter—it matters a lot. This is a point to which I shall return below.

This last argument against the commodification of care would be definitive if it were not the case that care can sometimes be fungible.

The nurse or hospital orderly who comes in one day may be different from one who comes in the next. If the mechanisms for the transmission of important information are in place and if the standard of care is kept high, the caregiving need not be compromised. Still, such professionalized care shares little with that of the migrant careworker who lacks the same status, pay, and access to her own familial attachments.

3.3 The moral significance of transnational carework

The Sophie's choice, as I have dubbed the choice to migrate for remittances, is the consequence of "background *injustice*"—that is, unjust global and national basic institutions.[8] What is morally problematic with the "GHT" therefore begins with the context in which it occurs.

Forces of globalization that include inequities in global trade agreements, monetary policies, neo-colonial practices, and structural adjustment policies have eviscerated public services in developing countries, thereby endangering women's economic well-being, impoverishing the middle class, and deepening the poverty of the poor. In the Philippines, which has been extensively studied, there is a 70 percent poverty rate. Both men and women have poor employment prospects. Because overseas employment tends to be more easily available and more lucrative (because less seasonal) for women, it is the women who choose to migrate in order to provide private education in the face of a deteriorating public education system and to earn enough for nourishing fare rather than sugared fried bread.

The concerns raised here can be analyzed on three levels:

Macro-level concerns—the extraction of care-resource: Parreñas (2005), using the analogy of colonial exploitation of the natural resources of colonized lands, has referred to the care chain hierarchy as "care-resource extraction." Care that is more highly valued leaves, and care that remains is less highly valued: care is compensated at a lower value the further down the chain we go. That is, a migrant woman who receives 400 dollars a week working as a nanny is likely to pay her own domestic about 50 dollars a week.

The metaphor of "extraction" gains credibility when we take into account the fact that, as a rule, sending nations have had to reduce education and welfare provision (forms of care in a larger sense) to restructure and refinance their debts. This restructuring has additional adverse effects on women's caregiving responsibilities (Schutte 2002) and becomes an important factor driving many to migrate in order to earn income sufficient to purchase private services rather than depend on deteriorating public services. In this way, the worth of care is "extracted" in three strokes. First, the sending nations use money which would otherwise go into social services, providing forms of care, to pay off foreign debt. Care is not here directly extracted, but the worth of that care (the money that would be used to provide the care-related services) is sent from the poorer to the wealthier parts of the world. Second, the women who would otherwise provide care leave their dependents to care for dependents in wealthy nations, resulting in a direct extraction of care. Finally, as remittances not only increase the earning of the migrants' families, but also inject valuable wealth into the local economy, the wealth can be taxed and used by the government to pay off foreign debt. Once again the worth of the care (the income it has generated this time) is extracted from the poorer nations and sent back to the wealthy nations.[9]

Mid-level concerns—costs of migrating with families and immigration policies: There are two sets of concerns. First, as reproduction costs are higher in receiving nations, workers simultaneously find migrant work profitable and are discouraged from bringing along their families. Receiving nations get the benefit of the laborer's labor without having to pay the reproductive costs of maintaining her family.[10] *Second*, harsh immigration and re-entry policies discourage family reunification, making it difficult for workers to return home frequently (even if it were economically viable). Calls for respecting the human rights of migrants have urged more lenient immigration policies, an end to raids, and the granting of basic welfare provisions to migrants (NGO Committee on Migration 2008).

Micro-level concerns—potential for exploitative wages and work hours of migrant careworkers: Lacking good language skills, worker protections, citizen rights or ties to friends and family, the migrants are especially vulnerable to abuse and exploitation. It is this interpersonal relationship between employer and employee that many feminists have targeted for criticism.

The above concerns need to be evaluated in light of the advantages that accrue to the women, their families, and their nations. Advocates of globalization claim that the answer to the ills of globalization is more globalization. While the global dimensions of migration offer multiple sites for injustice, migration for remittances has also been called the largest anti-poverty program in the world.[11] As we will see below, the benefits to the families in sending countries are especially felt by the girls, because the marginal utility is more likely to accrue to them. Furthermore, a migrant woman's ability to work unencumbered by family responsibility and to provide a very substantial portion of her family's income may bring about an increase in her agency, especially if she comes from a strongly patriarchal and traditional society.[12] If Amartya Sen is correct in claiming that the increased agency of women, which is a source of increased freedom for the women concerned, is a powerful positive force in development, then such increases in women's agency, as well as remittances sent home, contribute to a nation's development.

One might therefore argue that exploitation in the macro and micro situations of sending nations and migrant women is offset on the macro level by the economic importance of the income produced by migration for the development of developing nations and on the micro-level by the increased agency of the migrating women. Thus, while the wealth inequality that creates the push and pull that drives the migration of careworkers from poor nations to wealthy ones is, in itself, morally condemnable, it may be that the migrations themselves are active in redressing this very inequality. Furthermore, the migrant women themselves may derive a benefit of increased agency precisely by being released from their daily care responsibilities in their home countries. If so, then the global dimension may serve in several ways to mitigate the moral wrongs in the situation of the migrant women, even if it is also responsible for many of those wrongs. Clearly it is a daunting bit of moral mathematics to weigh the benefits and harms. Nonetheless, for all moral harms articulated in the traditional language of justice, there are significant countervailing benefits that can be held up as mitigating (if not canceling) those harms.

3.4 The gender question

The persuasiveness of the above argument may be undercut by gender considerations. Gender issues have been pervasive in our discussion already, for, after all, we are speaking of women's migrations. In addition, it is women who are expected to care for and are held responsible for the welfare of their families; it is women who suffer most when social services are cut, when daycare is curtailed, when hospitals discharge patients early, and when schools decline; it is women who are sought to do low-paying carework. Were we to live in a world in which we have gender justice, where the entire burden of dependency care would not fall on women's shoulders, and where such work was valued with high status and high pay, assuming carework would be taking on a coveted position, not a move of desperation.

We asked above if the migrant's agency is enhanced given that these women broke with traditional gender roles when they migrated and left their families behind. Tellingly, studies appear to indicate that gender roles in at least one sending nation, the Philippines, are reinforced, not subverted, by the migration of mothers, and that children want fathers, not mothers, to migrate (see Parreñas 2001). Unabated patriarchal attitudes in the sending nations help shape expectations that leave children feeling more abandoned by their migrant mothers, and allow fathers to avoid assuming the carework of absent mothers. In the receiving nations, gendered workplace rules are the reason that women, when they migrate, return at less frequent intervals than men. The fact that migrants are women is often viewed as an advantage to an employer insofar as they can exploit socially ingrained values of submissiveness. The women are vulnerable to sexual exploitation, especially when they work in the intimate space of the private home. There can be little doubt that the fact that the workers are women increases the possibilities of exploitation and abuse of migrants.

Yet for many of the reasons we have already mentioned, it is not necessarily an unalloyed evil for all the women involved, although all suffer from the lost intimacy with their children. Women coming from strictly patriarchal nations into ones that have a modicum of gender equality can acquire a new sense of self-worth. Many of the women express real pride in what they alone can provide for their families. Coming to and working in a foreign land can be an enriching experience for them, no less than for citizens of wealthy nations. Although the relationship between the "madam" and the "maid" is often problematic (and notice that many a "maid" is a "madam" in her own land), sometimes the women who hire the migrant women can have a positive impact.

As I mentioned previously, the benefit accrued to the children of migrant women is especially felt by the girls, thus sowing seeds for increased gender equality in the future of sending nations. Ghazala Mansuri's results on educational benefits provided by remittances are especially noteworthy: "Enrollment rates increase by 54 percent (from 0.35 to 0.54) for girls but only by 7 percent (from 0.73 to 0.78) for boys." Again, "The decline in dropout rates is also substantially larger for girls: 55 percent (from 0.56 to 0.25), compared with a decline for boys of 44 percent (from 0.25 to 0.14)" (cited in Özden and Schiff 2007: 6).

There are many more gender tales to tell than I have space for. But with respect to the harms that more directly affect the individuals involved, we can conclude that while gender injustice accounts for some harms, opportunities for gains in gender equality are also made possible for the women and their daughters. These gender factors cannot, again, fully explain the particular moral opprobrium expressed by the idea of "a global heart transplant."

There is still another gendered aspect we should mention, one which relates to the nature of the care labor. Some have argued that the practice of caregiving gives rise to distinct ethical values and a subjectivity that conceives of the self as always in relationship. As carers have traditionally been women, it is likely that women are more disposed than men to view themselves in relational terms. We shall explore the importance of this notion for the GHT in the next two sections.

3.5   The harm of the GHT and the "relational self"

Traditional theories of justice, what Nancy Fraser (2008) has called "normal justice," treat relations among citizens and the relations between a state and its citizens. But the harm we encounter in the case of the GHT is not inflicted on citizens qua citizens. Migrant laborers are not citizens of the receiving nations, nor is there overt coercion in sending nations that obligates them to make the journey.

A theory of global justice[13] meant to govern relations between nations allows us to diagnose injustices between sending and receiving nations. We have seen that although there are identifiable harms that may be said to be suffered by sending nations, and the practice of global migration takes place in the context of unjust conditions, it is also arguable that the benefits sending nations receive outweigh the harms and serve as a positive response to the background injustices that are (partially) responsible for the economic disparities between nations.

A cosmopolitan theory that identifies global harms to individuals qua individuals might do better than the two previous models, and the sort of gender injustices that migrant women are vulnerable to may fall into this category. But, once again, there are arguably countervailing benefits to be gained by the women and their children, especially the girls.

But we also need a diagnosis of the moral harms to the individuals as persons whose lives and critical relationships span national boundaries.[14] Perhaps a theory of justice is not well suited to such a task—those of which we have spoken are not. An ethic of care can be helpful because it understands the self not as an independent entity, but as formed through and sustained by relationships.

Care ethics' emphasis on relationality, I argue here, helps clarify the special harm of the GHT: the threat to core relationships—relationships that are pivotal to identity. We occupy some relationships by virtue of critical social or institutional roles: mother, daughter, parent, child, teacher, etc. But the particular individuals who occupy these roles give specificity to our emerging selves. The pivotal relationships in our lives are often those in which affection and caring are the norm.

What is lost in the migration of the mother for extended periods of time? Kin or domestics can execute the necessary daily care more or less satisfactorily, and the mothers normally continue to love their children—in fact their work is undertaken in the service of their love for their children. Yet children receiving physical daily care from kin, domestics, and fathers are receiving these intimacies from someone other than the individual with whom they first formed this caring relationship and, not insignificantly, with whom they expected to form such a relationship.

If care ethicists are correct in their understanding of the self as relational—that is, an understanding of a self-identity that incorporates one's relationships into the construction of identity rather than standing apart from identity—then such a relational self will incorporate those close dependency relations into its very identity. After all, the very preservation and development of self, as well as self-understanding, depends on this other. Surely then, whomsoever you relate to in these crucial ways—*that* individual—is incorporated into your own self-identity. If you are the vulnerable dependent, it is *this* individual and her relationship to you that forms the very ground of your being—at least that is how a young dependent would experience it, and for an ill or ailing person it is only someone with whom she has such a relation that offers real solace during a vulnerable time. Such bonding makes the boundaries of the self porous. When physical, day-to-day contact between the people who stand in such relationships is blocked, there is a danger that the cathectic potential for an essential relationship goes unrealized. The mothers speak of not recognizing their children, of the children not recognizing them.

When the mothers take on carework the cathexis occurs in relation to another non-familial dependent. The energy is released by "pouring" the love into another child—her charge. Given the relational constitution of self, and the motivational structure of care, the care expected of a hired caregiver occupies a phantom space in this geography of relationships. The expression "pouring one's love into . . ." is reserved for the relationship with the ward and is not used when speaking of their own dependents. Perhaps the idea of "pouring love into" another is an image that captures the less than fully relational nature of that love (Parreñas 2001: 122, 183). While the relationship to the charge may in some way lessen the harm to the woman migrant, as it provides an object for cathectic energy, it is not a relationship that she can genuinely invest in fully. It is rather a temporary bond.

Again, it is not that someone other than a person motivated by love cannot perform the tasks that make up the repertoire of caring activities—they can, and, under good circumstances, can do it effectively and with kindness and affection. But when a relationship forged through dependency is disrupted and different actors are substituted, a relational conception of the self would predict a disturbance in one's self-understanding as well as a rupture in the relationship that cannot always be mended. Thus, on the one hand, identity-forming relationships which should not be fractured become so; on the other, the meeting of dependency needs that forge such identity-forming relationships are ersatz relationships—formed only to be broken. In her empirical work on women, Carol Gilligan found that what her subjects wanted most was to avoid broken relationships. Migrant mothers make the attempt to sustain their relationships with their own children, but relationships forged in intimacy are difficult to maintain across a distance, especially for a dependent child whose ways of knowing and relating to her mother reside in the intimacies of daily care and emotional sustenance. When mothers leave for a foreign land they risk fracturing centrally important relationships. When they take on carework, they become vulnerable to investing too much in relationships that are ultimately meant to be broken. The GHT results in a compound fracture—a specific harm of this sort of arrangement—a harm that is inextricably related to the nature of care and the relationships it promotes. If the fractured relationships are harmful not only to the dependents but to the migrating women as well, should we not say that there ought to be a right to care—to give it and to receive it? If so, can we then return to the more conventional language of rights to delineate the harm of the GHT? We can, but the right will have a relational twist.

3.6   Human rights and the right to care

Caregiving is Janus-faced. While it can be burdensome (a responsibility to be discharged), it can also be among our most meaningful and rewarding work (a right to be exercised). While different cultural attitudes and circumstances influence these views, even those who seek to avoid caregiving may feel bereft when actively deprived of the opportunity to care for loved ones; similarly those who embrace a life of caregiving will see the work as too burdensome at times. Furthermore, while we happily give care to those we care about, care *demanded* of us by others can seem to be sheer toil. Given the complexities of care, how should we view the choices made by migrant careworkers? In leaving their families behind, are they shedding a burden or forgoing a benefit? In assuming caregiving for a stranger are they recouping some of the benefit of caring or are they redoubling the burdensome nature of caregiving? And how should we view the situation of the children and other dependents? Do they experience the material advantages they accrue as a form of care that is an adequate replacement for the hands-on care they would have otherwise received? Is the fact that their mother's or daughter's income comes from caring for another a source of comfort or salt in a wound?

Perhaps it is the burdensome nature of care for the caregiver that has obscured the extent to which we want the ability to care for those who are close to us as a protected right (or freedom or capability necessary for flourishing). While the UN Declaration of Human Rights never stipulated either a right to care or a right to be cared for by family members, Principle 6 of the Declaration of the Rights of Children does posit a right of a child to be cared for and, in the earliest years, to be cared for by the mother. It states:

> [The child] shall, wherever possible, grow up in the care and under the responsibility of his [*sic*] parents [not mother], and, in any case, in an atmosphere of affection and of moral and material security; a child of tender years shall not, save in exceptional circumstances, be separated from his mother. (United Nations 1959)

Similarly it would seem that all frail elderly have a right to decent care and treatment. But is it a right to be cared for by a specific individual? Must the care be delivered in one's own home? Will any passable level of care discharge the right to receive care? Does the obligation that is the correlate to the right fall only on family members, or does the state owe anything either to the one with the right to be cared for or the one who has a right to give care? While no UN Declaration specifies a right to care for the elderly as such, Article 25 of the Declaration of Human Rights states:

> Everyone has the right to a standard of living adequate for the health and well-being of himself and of his family, including food, clothing, housing and medical care and necessary social services, and the right to security in the event of unemployment, sickness, disability, widowhood, old age or other lack of livelihood in circumstances beyond his control. (United Nations 1948)

This does seem to indicate that care for our well-being is owed to us as a right during our old age, even though it doesn't state explicitly who is responsible for assuring this right.

A serious difficulty arises, however, when we try to define what counts as care. Much depends on our definition. Fischer and Tronto have given a particularly inclusive conception of caring as "a species of activity that includes everything that we do to maintain, continue, and repair our 'world' so that we can live in it as well as possible" (Fischer and Tronto 1990: 40). This is too inclusive to be helpful here. To capture the sense of care we want we must parse the concept.[15]

Diemut Bubeck adopts a definition of "caring for" that emphasizes the idea that care requires "face to face interactions" (1995: 131). We have also pointed out that much caregiving is non-fungible. As a first approximation, therefore, we could say that a right to care for and be cared for needs to have two features:

First try:

I. The recognition and protection of the non-fungible nature of caring.
II. The protection of the importance of face-to-face care.

The GHT can then be viewed as violating a right to care for and be cared for, since the caregivers have to substitute another person who does the face-to-face care for those about whom they care. At the same time, their role as caregiver to those they most care about is really not fungible. However, while we want a right to give care to protect the importance of non-fungible, face-to-face care, such a right can only protect the *choice* to engage in such caregiving—otherwise it would be a coercive demand, not a right, for the caregiver. The migrant mothers, we have said, have chosen not to do so.

Furthermore, it is not clear that all dependents have a right to demand such care from specific others. Formulating a right to care in this way suggests falsely that the children are being neglected when in fact they generally do have their basic care needs met. Equally importantly, it suggests that the mothers are not engaged in caring for their children, which is not how they themselves view what they are doing. Sociologists Pierrette Hondagneu-Sotelo and Ernestine Avila interviewed transnational mothers from Mexico and Central America and noted that these women believed that their role as breadwinner *expanded*, rather than *replaced*, their caregiving roles.[16] Women interviewed in many different studies have reported that they regret not being with their children, watching them grow up, being involved with the intimate details of their lives, helping them with their daily activities, and so forth. But it is the absence of adequate resources, not distance as such, that they see as the greatest obstacle to properly caring for their families. Only through their work abroad can they send home sufficient money to enable their children to have, both objectively and in their view, better lives—lives in which they receive the care their mothers want for them.

Importantly, these mothers do what they do for the sake of their children. This significance of this motivation is incorporated by Steven Darwall in his definition of caring: caring for someone means desiring what is good for the person *for his own sake* (Darwall 2002: 7). While a set of contested practices constitute what it is to care *for* another, this attitudinal aspect is central to any notion of caring *about*, though it is not as stringent as the non-fungible condition in our first definition.

Let us try again to define caring, but loosening the face-to-face condition and the non-fungible condition: caring is *attending to those interests of another that the person in need of care cannot reasonably be expected to satisfy on his or her own, and to attend to these interests for the sake of the one in need of care.* To say that care requires attending to the interests of another for the sake of the other is one way to characterize Folbre's concept of the intrinsic motivation characteristic of carework. Thus we may *attend to x's need n* because we want to promote x's welfare for x's own sake. But *why* do we want to promote x's welfare for x's own sake? This *second-order* motivation has three possible sources:

(1) I have acquired the *virtue* of acting to attend to another's interests for that person's sake. This is the virtue that a good nurse has acquired. Acting in this way does not require any pre-existing personal relationship with the person in need.

(2) I may have such a strong bond with the person in question that this person's welfare is as or more important to me than is my own

welfare. When another's welfare is constitutive of our own well-being we tend to call such a bond "love." This is the motivation characteristic of a parent, a spouse, a child acting on behalf of an ailing parent, or a friend attending to the needs of a treasured friend.

(3) I may believe that the duty I have voluntarily assumed obligates me to attend to another for their own sake. A doctor or lawyer may exemplify this more delimited form of intrinsic motivation. So may a person hired to care for a dependent.

Looking at care from the second-order motivational perspective allows us to see that it is possible both to give and receive care without the affective bond characterized by 2—that is, a child or ailing relative can receive more than perfunctory care even when it is not given by one who loves them. But it may nonetheless be the case that we want to say that a child, if not a friend, spouse or ailing relative, should be able to claim 2.

Furthermore, the motivational considerations above suggest that if there is a *right* to give care it must be the sort of care that has the motivational structure of 2 (which retains the non-fungible aspect, though less stringently). This is because rights are not invoked to protect the cultivation and exercise of a virtue, and nor is the relevant right to care limited to obligations that are voluntarily assumed. Let us then reformulate our right to care to reflect these considerations.

Second try:
A right to care will consist of two parts, each of which has a number of conditions:

I. The right to give care:
    A. Protects the expression and manifestation of an attitude of care by allowing one to engage in the practices of care toward certain *particular* persons; these are persons
        i. who are dependent on another to meet essential needs to survive and thrive, needs which they cannot meet themselves, and
        ii. whose welfare the carer cares about for the sake of the cared-for and because the carer's sense of well-being is greatly diminished when these persons are not well-cared-for.
II. The right to receive care is just the right to be a recipient of the caregiving protected in I above.

Under this definition, mothers who try to ensure that their children are well cared for by working abroad in order to send home remittances, all the while sacrificing or deferring their own desire to be with their children, may be said to be *caring for* their children, and so their children are being cared for by them. But in that case, transnational migration violates neither the right of a dependent to receive care nor the right of the woman who leaves her dependents behind to give care. Perhaps something important is missing from this conception of a right to care.

Robin West has argued that we have a right to care that she calls a "doulia right" (2002: 98). Doulia (after the postpartum carer, a *doula* who cares for the mother so that she can care for her newborn baby) is a principle that claims that some third party, often the state, must support those doing "dependency work," so that the dependency worker does not have to sacrifice her own well-being in order to discharge her duties to her dependents (see Kittay 1999, Chapter 2). "Dependency work" is care limited to meeting the needs of one who is in a condition of inevitable dependency. Dependency work also delimits certain practices of care, namely those devoted to meeting needs that are a direct consequence of the dependency and that are, for the most part, hands-on: dressing, feeding, fundamental aspects of healthcare, instruction, and socialization, as well as the emotional needs that accompany this state of need. We can acknowledge that procuring the necessities that are a precondition for meeting those needs is also part of caring, but it is not the hands-on care that the term "dependency work" delimits. Doulia is a concept that captures the support a dependency worker requires of a "provider" to provision both the dependent and the dependency worker, allowing both to survive and thrive.

Our earlier formulation of a right to care failed to distinguish these moments of care. We need a clause about the need for a carer to be supported in her caring for dependents. The second part of Article 25 in the UN Declaration of Human Rights can be seen to affirm such a right for mothers when it states: "Motherhood and childhood are entitled to special care and assistance." We could interpret this clause to say that a right to care needs to include or be backed by a right to the material means to carry out such care. Let us try again.

Third try:

I. The right to give care
   A. Protects the expression and manifestation of an attitude of care by allowing one to engage in the practices of care toward certain *particular* persons; these are persons

i. who are dependent on another to meet essential needs to survive and thrive, needs which they cannot meet themselves, and

ii. whose welfare the carer cares about for the sake of the cared-for and because the carer's sense of well-being is greatly diminished when these persons are not well cared for.

B. includes *doulia rights* defined as rights to resources that enable one to engage in the practice of dependency work with provisions adequate to meet the needs of the dependent and without depleting the resources of the dependency worker or otherwise making it impossible for the dependency worker to meet her/his own urgent needs.

II. The right to receive care includes

A. a right to be cared for when we are unable to meet our own essential needs and

B. a right to be cared for by one who cares for us in the sense specified in IA.

This formulation of care does not preclude activities such as procuring the economic means for the dependent to survive and thrive. Migrant mothers are not denied a right to care in the sense of IA, where practices of care include procuring the means for benefiting the dependent. But these women could be said to lack doulia rights precisely because they are not supported in their efforts to do the hands-on dependency work for the dependents most close to them. In some respects their dependents may be cared for by them, but not in other important respects.

This formulation of a right to care still leaves many questions unanswered: Who is authorized to define care practices for the purposes of fashioning "a right to care"? And what public entity is to secure these rights? Sending nations lack the resources for such provisioning, which is why the women are motivated to migrate in the first place. Do the receiving nations have duties correlative to these rights? Does this formulation help identify the specificity of the harm of the GHT? Finally: whence come such rights? That we may have rights to receive certain goods and services essential to our ability to survive and function is not in question if we accept something like the UN Declaration of Human Rights. That we have a right to a family is also already in the UN Declaration and does not require the formulation of a specific right to care. But while IAi or IIB might be inferred from passages in the UN charters, one justification for interpreting the clauses of the charters in such a way is found in a care ethics which has gone global.

For the relational account of the self and the notion of harm as the failure to maintain critical relationships give us a right to care that incorporates the importance of both clauses IAii and IIB. It also undergirds the need for doulia, without which maintaining these critical relationships is either not possible or is deeply damaging to at least one of the parties in the relationship.[17]

3.7 Conclusion

When a woman cannot exercise her right to care in the full sense we delineated above, and she is engaged in caregiving for another, it seems as if her heart leaves home to service another. Yet as suggestive as the phrase "global heart transplant" is, there is really not even a metaphorical "heart" transplant. We know that the migrating women do what they do for their dependents' sake and attempt to maintain as close a contact as possible. They do not transfer their love. But neither appearances nor expectations are inconsequential. How does the mother who can contact her child only by phone convince that child that as she takes care of another she is not transplanting her love? How does the family receiving the remunerated care understand and distinguish motivations? How does the mother herself keep all the motivational structures clearly delineated? And how is she to maintain her own understanding of her ethical self, her sense of self-respect?

John Rawls famously argued that the most important of social goods is self-respect. It is the social means by which we recognize our equal inherent worth. In a just society the quest for self-respect ought not be a zero-sum game. But in "the global heart transplant" one individual sustains her self-respect as a carer (or as someone who discharges her responsibilities to care) at the expense of another.

This chapter has attempted to give voice to the specificity of the harm inherent in the global migration of those who give care for dependents. Some of the harms can be mitigated with better working conditions, better immigration policies, and specific provisions to make it easier and financially viable for careworkers to return home on a regular basis. But it still will not address all the harm of the length of absences which are unavoidable in transnational families and which are at the source of the difficulty of maintaining relationships of intimacy. Boosting welfare provisions in wealthy states, including increasing the pay for careworkers, although these should be done, also will not necessarily help the women who migrate. If carework is not available because native workers are attracted to the higher pay of carework in a state that pays well for carework, we can still expect that the push of poverty will induce many women to make the voyage abroad. Even if they do not do carework, the migrants' right to care would remain partial. Bolstering welfare provisions in sending as well as receiving nations would help with the pull as well as the push that drives the migration of careworkers. Yet unless we rectify the vast economic disparities that motivate migration such increases are unlikely.

Additionally, *all* inequities in carework require a more equitable division of labor between genders. Finally, all inequities in care labor require recognizing the ways in which the intrinsic motivation of carework works against the market forces. We therefore need to ensure that carework is well remunerated whether its motivation is based on familial responsibilities or professional obligations, and that we do not allow market forces alone to adjust the pay of careworkers. Another essay is needed to review the recommendations that have been offered to redress the injustices we find in the global trade in carework. Here we will be satisfied if we have correctly diagnosed the harms.

Notes

1 Also see Parreñas 2005: 22. The receiving nations have come to depend on this female labor. Cf. Eckenwiler (2009) for a study on migrations of healthcare workers.

2 Also see Stilwell et al. 2003: 8.

3 The quotation is from one of the interviews in the excellent study by Parreñas, *Servants of Globalization* (2001: 87).

4 "The [care] chains bring together multiple modalities of care in a diversity of spaces which include the market, the household and public or private non-profit institutions" (Penson 2007: 2).

5 See also *Long Island Care at Home, Ltd., et al. Petitioners v. Evelyn Coke*, 551 U.S. 06-593 (2007).

6 See Darwall (2002) for a discussion of the close connection between care and welfare. Also see Fischer and Tronto (1990) for the idea that response from the cared-for is necessary to complete the act of care. I would rather say that the carer "perceives" a response, because it is not always clear that the cared-for is capable of responding, but the carer nonetheless has a subjective experience of responsiveness.

7 He writes "The social value of childcare . . . becomes more manifest as mothers seek it from others instead of providing it themselves freely at home because of their traditional roles" (Bhagwati 2004: 78).

8 See John Rawls's discussion of background justice in Rawls 2001a: 50–1.

9 There is still another form of care extraction which I will not discuss here. The poorer nations train nurses and other healthcare professionals, yet they do not enjoy the fruits of that investment, but instead are left with serious shortages because care professionals tend to migrate to nations where they can earn higher wages (see Dugger 2006; Bettio et al. 2006).

10 Cf. Nancy Folbre's fantasy island, CorpoNations, where there are no dependents and no dependency responsibilities (Folbre 2002: 185–208).

11 "Remittances sent home by migrants to developing countries are equivalent to more than three times the size of official development assistance and can have profound implications for development and human welfare. Remittances can contribute to lowering poverty and building human and financial capital for the poor." See World Bank Group News and Broadcast, "Migration and Remittances," http://web.worldbank.org/WBSITE/ EXTERNAL/NEWS/0,,contentMDK:20648762~pagePK:64257043~piP K:437376~theSitePK:4607,00.html (accessed May 13, 2013).

12 For an argument that women's freedom means not having to make such a choice, see Weir 2008.

13 Such as that offered by John Rawls (2001b).

14 For a fuller exploration of an ethics of care for the question of transnational caring see Kittay 2008.

15 Cf. Fischer and Tronto's four phases of care (1990: 49).

16 See Hondagneu-Sotelo and Avila 2006: 259. Their findings replicate those of Parreñas, whose work stands behind most of the empirical claims made here.

17 For a thorough discussion of this last point see Kittay 1999.

4
Transnational Rights and Wrongs: Moral Geographies of Gender and Migration

Rachel Silvey

4.1 Introduction

The rise of women's transnational labor migration has prompted new questions about the scope and limits of migrants' rights and the boundaries of state jurisdiction (Cholewinski 1997; Taran 2000). While conflicts between international human rights norms and state sovereignty are far from new, the issues become particularly thorny when citizens from one nation-state are recruited by another as temporary contract laborers (Piper 2005). In this situation, how does one determine for example whether a sending state or a host state should be held responsible for addressing the employment grievances of foreign workers? Or, when formal labor or human rights laws differ between the sending and receiving states, how and where can migrant rights advocates gain legal traction on behalf of the rights claims of migrants? To complicate matters further, when migrants work abroad in a widely unregulated sector such as domestic labor, what sorts of moral geographies can they invoke in their efforts to have their basic labor rights recognized and protected? I enter these conversations here through the example of transnational women migrants' struggles in Indonesia, and ask what these struggles reveal about both newly emerging and longstanding maps of gender (in)justice.

This chapter focuses on understanding what the geographies of migrants' gender justice claims can offer to the frameworks put forward by feminist theorists of global gender justice. Over the last decade, feminist scholars have worked actively to identify priorities for theorists of global gender justice (Elson 2002; Jaggar 2002a). Alison Jaggar argues that gender justice is "not best addressed in terms of moral universalism versus cultural relativism." Rather, as she points out, "one may endorse universal or at least global values and still be reluctant to focus one's philosophical attention on local practices in the global South" (Jaggar 2002a: 230). This is a crucial theme for thinking about migrants' rights because while the rights abuses frequently experienced by migrant workers are both local and immediate, the historic and systemic roots of those abuses—and thus what enables them to persist in the present—are never reducible to local cultural practice nor separable from global processes and inequalities. Thus, in order to develop insight into the where and how of strengthening migrant women's rights, it is necessary to imagine and enact a geography of connection and interrelation across places and times.

The politics and possibilities associated with cross-place connections and collaborations have been a major concern of feminist geographers (for an overview of feminist geography, see Nelson and Seager 2005; on transnational feminist praxis, see Swarr and Nagar 2010). In general, feminist geographic work is aligned with the priorities laid out by Jaggar (2002a). However, geographers place more emphasis on three additional points. First, we underscore the observation that so-called local practices are in fact forged in complex relation to "global" political-economic dynamics, such that conceptually it is more fruitful to see these scales as intertwined than as separate. Relatedly, we emphasize the socially constructed nature of space and scale, and are concerned with identifying the implications of particular scalar analytics (e.g., the global impacting the local) for social policy and everyday lives. Second, we highlight the existence of concentrations of wealth within the "global South" and pockets of extreme poverty within the "global North," and this focus guides us to reject maps of global inequality that are drawn along the lines of North and South. Third, we place importance on anti-essentialist interpretations of identity in relation to location, and this commitment leads us to ask who indeed a "Western" scholar might be in the contemporary age of diaspora and which governments are indeed "our own" in transnational times.

Questions such as these—about how space and place shape (and are shaped by) material inequalities, and which spatial metaphors to use in mapping one's political location and analytical priorities—have long been at the center of conversations in the discipline of geography (Massey 1993; Katz 2001a). I offer a discussion of these geographic insights—again, through the example of Indonesian migrant rights activists' engagements with international human rights discourse—as an elaboration of the spatial elements of feminist philosophical conceptions of global justice.

4.2 Transnational migration and gender justice

Migration scholars and policy makers have tended in recent years to analyze migration primarily in terms of what it has to offer to economies in the way of income earned, remittances to the place of origin, or the productive labor that migrants' departures may withdraw from their home country's economy (i.e., the "brain drain"). International "interagency task forces," involving the UK's Department for International Development (DFID), the World Bank, the United Nations' International Labor Organization (ILO) (e.g., 2000) and the Organization for Economic Cooperation and Development (OECD) (e.g., 2004), have targeted migrants' remittances as a development issue, and they have promoted economistic approaches to the circulation, investment, and "productive" use of migrants' earnings. Such approaches generally acknowledge the gender justice dimensions of the contemporary migration economy, but they place primary emphasis on women's migration as a "pathway out of poverty" (World Bank 2007) or a "passage to hope" (UNFPA 2006) rather than on the rights of migrant workers in need of recognition and protection (Silvey 2009).[1]

In contrast to economistic approaches to migration, feminist migration scholarship is primarily concerned with questions of exploitation and justice (e.g., Parreñas 2001). In many countries, low-income migrant women workers are permitted entry into national territory as temporary contract laborers in large and growing numbers worldwide (UNFPA 2006). They are generally not permitted by host countries to bring along members of their families, nor in most cases to become citizens of host countries after completing their contracts.[2] Such patterns of unequal citizenship continue a long "legacy of people of colour being admitted to some countries only through coercive systems of labour that do not recognize family rights" (Arat-Koc 2006: 76). The economies of host countries benefit from the low cost of the labor of individual migrants as workers, and they further benefit from the "offshoring" of the labor and resources that go into the social reproduction of migrant workers and their family members. Through transnational migration, the labor and capital invested in migrants' and their families' own healthcare, education, childcare, and eldercare are "transferred to a different location and state" (Arat-Koc 2006: 88), constituting a direct and clearly gendered development subsidy from poor to wealthy countries.

Feminist political economists have focused on the necessity of socially reproductive labor for the ongoing production of goods, services, and capital. Of particular interest to geographers is the requirement that such labor, the "fleshy, messy, indeterminate stuff of everyday life" (Katz 2001b: 711), be carried out in local proximity to the bodies that require care or the domestic spaces that require cleaning.[3] The international migration of low-income domestic and care labor has provided *in situ* support for the bodies, homes, families, and national economies of employers, and meanwhile in migrant-sending countries it has produced care deficits and strained migrants' family relationships (Parreñas 2005; Pratt 2012).[4] Such transfers of support and labor are transnational manifestations of the inequalities of nation, race, class, and gender that characterize the global labor market. The unequal transfers both reflect and reinforce the intersecting injustices that exist across local, national, and global scales.

Transnational labor migration thus poses a series of challenges to state-centered conceptions of justice and rights. Most fundamentally it involves the employment of a non-citizen abroad, often with limited or no protective legislation in the host state (Piper 2005).[5] The issues facing international migrants thus raise more complicated issues for theories of justice than those facing internal migrants in their home countries. Beyond state borders, states lose the legal enforcement mechanism that is a central assumption of Westphalian conceptions of the state (for a discussion, see Bagchi 2008). For women migrants from postcolonial states, the situation is further complicated. First, like women everywhere, their rights vis-à-vis the nation-state have been historically subordinated to those of the ideal-typical citizens implicitly and often explicitly assumed to be male (Yuval-Davis 1997a). Differences in the distribution of rights along gender lines within states are thus of critical importance for conceptualizing gender justice within and beyond nation-state borders. Second, the Westphalian state ideal is modeled on practices observed within North Atlantic states, and it conceives of the nation-state's territorial boundaries as sovereign. However, of course histories of colonial and neo-imperial control over the flows of capital, resources, and migration across borders reflect the inequality of the global political economy (Chowdhry and Nair 2002). The inequalities between nations leave migrant women from low-income postcolonial countries with especially limited state support and protection, reduced employment options, and worsened working conditions both at home and abroad.

According to Jaggar, "to address women's global inequalities, most Western feminist philosophers should follow the lead of many theorists in the global South, who use the language of rights and sometimes empowerment to analyze the complicated interactions between local practices and global structures" (2002a: 230). For gender and transnational migration studies, her argument leads scholars to reject those explanations of migrant abuse and exploitation that are focused primarily on local culture, religion, or tradition. Instead, it directs Western scholars in particular "to examine critically the ways in which our own countries are implicated in the impoverishment and political marginalization of women in the global South" (Jaggar 2002a: 230). Moreover, in concert with a growing body of work on transnational feminist collaboration, such an approach "should provide [both] a self-critique and means for critically understanding globalism" (Swarr and Nagar 2010: 22). It redirects attention away from a sole emphasis on the vulnerable Third World Woman as subject/object of inquiry and shifts energy toward critically self-reflexive, collaborative approaches to research (Swarr and Nagar 2010).

A transnational feminist approach to research on migrant domestic workers refuses a primary focus, for example, on the abuses that migrants face or the individual inhumanity of their employers. It calls instead for greater attention to how, for example, the experience of Indonesian women workers in Saudi homes is intimately interlinked with the political economy of petro-finance and the global military-industrial complex (see Enloe 1989, 2000, on gender and militarization). How has feminist writing been unwittingly complicit in the problems it aims to address, and how might it be better oriented toward collaboration with the efforts of migrant rights advocates, for example, within Indonesia and elsewhere (Swarr and Nagar 2010)? These are the political and analytical directions in which transnational feminist research is moving, and although these agendas differ nominally from the overt and immediate priorities of migrant rights advocates in Indonesia, activists are providing clues to help scholars overcome the distance between ideals of justice and practices of justice promotion.

4.3   Indonesian overseas migrants: transnational feminist approaches

Migrant rights activists in Indonesia have focused since at least the mid-1980s on the women's human rights issues at stake for Indonesian overseas workers (Tagaroa and Sofia 2002), and they continue to do so at the time of writing (Human Rights Watch 2012). Their activism has grown alongside the numbers of contract workers employed abroad. Indonesian overseas contract workers are a relatively recent phenomenon; the government only began in 1983 to actively promote international labor migration as a development strategy (Robinson 1991). That year, 47,000 fully documented workers left Indonesia for employment in Saudi Arabia, a number that has increased every year thereafter except during the economic crisis of 1997–98, and in 2011 when a temporary ban was imposed on women's migration to Saudi by the Indonesian government. Of the states receiving migrant workers from Indonesia since the 1980s, Saudi Arabia has received the largest number (Hugo 1995: 280, Hugo 2007; BNP2TKI 2012), and the majority of these have been women employed as domestic laborers (*pembantu rumah tangga*, PRT, or household helpers).

Human and labor rights advocates have paid a great deal of attention to the problems facing migrant domestic labor in general, giving special attention to Saudi Arabia (Human Rights Watch 2004b, 2010). Human Rights Watch has reported that Saudi Arabia is "a country whose hereditary, unelected rulers continue to choose secrecy over transparency at the expense of justice . . . without respect for the rule of law . . ." (2004b: 4) and where migrants in general face gross labor exploitation and multiple forms of abuse at the hands of their employers as well as the Saudi government (2004b: 5). In response, critics of human rights discourse (e.g., Risse and Ropp 1999) have pointed out that Saudi Arabia is far from unique in its exploitation and abuse of migrant laborers. Secondly, the focus on the Saudi government as distinctly in need of political pressure from international human rights advocates is troubling because it risks reinforcing an Orientalist view of the Saudi Kingdom as a peculiarly brutal regime (and a place where "white women need to save brown women from brown men") (Spivak, paraphrased in Jaggar 2002a: 352).[6]

Such a view of the Saudi government, decontextualized from the global political economy, is dangerously incomplete (see Jaggar 2005b). A more thorough and accurate rendering of the forces permitting and promoting violence of multiple kinds, including human rights abuses around the world, would take serious account of the geopolitical history of oil corporations (e.g., Aramco, the Arab-American Oil Company) and US military involvement in Southeast Asia and the Middle East (Chomsky 2002). While feminist scholarship on migrant domestic labor tends to analyze corporate and military interventions as background and context (most fully elaborated for migrants from the Philippines [e.g., Parreñas 2001; Pratt 2004], and Mexico [e.g., Hondagneu-Sotelo 2001; Wright 2006]), there remains a need for more detailed research that develops the connections between the cultural politics of gendered immigrant labor processes (Lowe 1996), and the political economies of production and violence tied to these processes in different parts of the world (Marchand and Runyan 2011).

Migrant rights activists in Indonesia share a "global" view of the sources of human rights violations faced by migrants. Indeed, as one migrant rights advocate in Indonesia put it, "We do not see the governments abroad as the sole or primary culprits in the abuse of Indonesian migrants. Rather, governments are players in the international systems of exploitation that culminate in the abuse of Indonesian women abroad" (Wahyu Susilo, personal interview with author, 2008). Increasingly widespread information about particularly serious cases of abuse abroad has prompted activists and the news media to concentrate public attention on the plight of women migrants (Robinson 2000; Human Rights Watch 2010). Within Indonesia, in the 1980s, *Solidaritas Perempuan* (Women's Solidarity), and more recently Migrant Care, have been among the most active non-governmental organizations (NGOs) working long-term on behalf of overseas workers' rights. They, alongside Human Rights Watch (2004a, 2010), have consistently reported that migrants face multiple forms of exploitation, including underpayment and non-payment of wages, overwork, sexual harassment, sexual abuse, torture, and rape, as well as unfair treatment and extortion before, during, and on the way home from sojourns abroad. The newspapers and Human Rights Watch reports are often illustrated with graphic images of migrants' injured bodies and detailed stories about murders, suicides, and stolen incomes.

Since the fall of President Suharto in 1998, after 32 years of authoritarian rule in Indonesia, space for public advocacy has expanded, and funding for NGOs from international sources has multiplied (Robinson and Bessell 2002). In this context, migrant domestic workers' issues have become a topic of concern to a rapidly growing number of organizations, including Migrant Care, Caram Asia, Migrant Rights International, and Human Rights Watch (Piper 2005). According to Michelle Ford, there are "at least 70 migrant labour NGOs in Indonesia" alone (2004: 104), many of which are at least nominally concerned with overseas migrant workers' issues. In addition, the ILO, UNIFEM, and the UN Special Rapporteur for the Human Rights of Migrants have recently focused on the rights issues that are specific to migrant domestic workers (UNSRHRM 2001), as have the CEDAW and CERD Committees (Satterthwaite 2005). The growing international attention to women migrant domestic workers has been a source of optimism for some advocates of migrants' rights within Indonesia, who see the international concern as long overdue.

Several international human rights conventions have been particular sources of inspiration for Indonesian migrant rights activists. In 1990, the United Nations drafted the International Convention on the Protection of the Rights of All Migrant Workers and Members of Their Families (ICMR). The ICMR finally came into force in September 2003 after reaching the required minimum number of ratifications. It was the first international convention to address migrants, including non-nationals. It defined a "migrant worker" as "a person who is to be engaged, is engaged or has been engaged in a remunerated activity in a State of which he or she is not a national" (UNHCR 1990, Resolution 45/158, Article 2). The convention is radically transnational in scope in that it applies

> during the entire migration process of migrant workers and members of their families, which comprises preparation for migration, departure, transit and the entire period of stay and remunerated activity in the State of employment as well as return to the State of origin or the State of habitual residence. (UNHCR 1990, Resolution 45/158, Article 1).

Such an expansive definition of transnational rights, according to migrant rights advocates in Indonesia, is clearly a distant ideal, but it is one toward which they have long been pushing their own government. On April 12, 2012, the tireless work of advocates finally paid off in the formal legal arena: the Indonesian government ratified the ICMR, obliging itself to "harmonize" its national laws with the standards set forth in the convention (Human Rights Watch 2012).

Most recently, on June 16, 2011, the ILO adopted a "landmark treaty to protect domestic workers" (Human Rights Watch 2011). The Convention on Decent Work for Domestic Workers (No. 189) and its associated Recommendation (No. 201) was the first international agreement to set standards for domestic laborers. It has been celebrated by national and international migrant rights groups as a "historic step" (ILO 2012), representative of the successful culmination of decades of feminist labor organizing and campaigning. The ILO and the supporters of the convention see it as "the instrument needed to transform the employment relations of some 100 million domestic workers, from one based on exploitation, to one based on rights" (ILO 2012). They are aware that "the fight for domestic workers' rights is far from over," and they are focusing now on the challenges of getting governments to ratify and implement the convention (ILO 2012). Eighteen months after the ILO's adoption of the convention, only three countries (Uruguay, the Philippines, and Mauritius) have ratified the convention, and no country has yet begun to enforce the recommendations. Nonetheless, activists within Indonesia and elsewhere are already mobilizing the convention in their efforts to pressure governments to strengthen existing laws and protections for migrant domestic workers (Human Rights Watch 2011). These trends constitute an emerging internationalism of migrants' rights ideals and a move toward the global regulation of migration, reflected also in the ILO's older conventions (Nos. 144 and 97) that apply specifically to migrant workers.

The Domestic Workers' Convention represents a strengthening and expansion of the scope of human and labor rights into new gendered territory. Prior to the convention's adoption, the existing instruments did not include any clauses that dealt explicitly with women or domestic laborers, making it especially difficult for migrant rights advocates to deploy UN protocol in the service of women migrants' particular rights struggles (Piper 2005). However, as Satterthwaite has argued, migrant rights advocates had been able nevertheless to use existing human rights treaties as a starting point in their efforts to protect women migrants. As she puts it:

> Despite the international human rights system's significant limits, it provides advocates with a language and a practice through which to engage states . . . International human rights law should be seen as a crucial tool to capture the attention of both sending and receiving countries. (Satterthwaite 2005: 4)

The Women's Convention thus provides an advance in the instruments available to domestic workers with which to claim rights. The extensive debate and dialogue (for a discussion, see Hune 1991, cited in Satterthwaite 2005) that has gone into the development of these documents lends support to Alison Jaggar's argument that

> an enormous amount of reflection . . . is occurring already and that those who are reflecting do not necessarily lack a moral compass . . . A variety of existing moral traditions makes available a wide range of candidates to serve as standards for assessing the processes of contemporary globalization . . . Among the available traditions, the secular and universalistic discourse of human rights currently receives the widest assent. (Jaggar 2002a: 232)

Indeed, activists within Indonesia have framed labor rights and migrant rights as human rights issues (Ford 2004). KOPBUMI (*Konsorsium Pembela Buruh Migran Indonesia*, the Consortium of Indonesian Migrant Workers' Advocates), the "network of approximately 70 NGOs which deal with migrant workers in 14 provinces," has been explicitly involved in campaigns concentrating on the ratification of the United Nations' ICMR, among other issues (Ford 2004: 109), and are currently actively engaged in pressuring the government to ratify the Convention on Decent Work for Domestic Workers (Human Rights Watch 2010).

Activists at Migrant Care and KOPBUMI are aware, along with scholars and legal practitioners, of the limitations of the systems available to protect human rights in practice. However, rather than viewing the gap between UN conventions and state practices as a barrier to advocacy, activists at KOPBUMI highlight the UN standards in order to pressure states to be more "responsive to the gendered, racialized, and class-specific impacts of economic globalization on women who cross borders to find work" (Satterthwaite 2005: 4). They have built transnational alliances with the international migrants rights groups (Ford 2004), and Migrant Care, based in Jakarta, has collaborated effectively with Human Rights Watch, based in New York (Human Rights Watch 2012). From a geographic perspective, the "global," "national," and "local" work of migrant rights activists involves the deliberate, strategic deployment of specific scales for particular political purposes. The work of activists, and their ability to work across scales, thus also reveals a model of the geographies of justice from which scholars can learn.

4.4   Domestic gender justice is global gender justice: rethinking the scales of "global" justice

Taking a cue from the cartographies being forged by migrant rights activists, what can geographers add to the development of feminist understandings of global justice? As a discipline, geography takes space, place, and scale as primary defining themes. So, for feminist geographers interested in global justice, a core question is how various scales, including the global, the national, the household, and the body, are constructed. What are the spaces within which gender justice and injustice are produced and reproduced? How are particular places enmeshed in global systems and structures of gendered power? How do "global" ideals of gender justice reverberate and refract across scales, between, for example, national scale policies, UN conventions, international human rights organizations, migrant rights NGOs, and local scale practices?

Many efforts to grapple with such questions within geography have revolved around critiques of the social construction of scale and the need to link scales of analysis (Hyndman and Walton-Roberts 2000; Marston 2000; Mountz and Hyndman 2006). Rather than taking scale as ontologically *a priori*, geographers unpack the political and gendered dimensions of discourses of spatial scales. We ask how spatial scales are defined by specific social actors and institutions and with what sorts of material effects. This work "is important precisely because such assumptions define research questions, shape government policies, and generate common frames of reference" (Hyndman and Walton-Roberts 2000: 246). Rather than presume that there is a "global" scale of justice that exists in the world, critical geographers interrogate how the "global" is defined and situated and what sorts of implications its deployment as a concept holds for multiple forms of inequality. Particular groups of activists, including Indonesian migrant rights activists, have claimed the banner of the "global" in support of migrants' issues, yet their subordinated locations within both national government bodies and so-called global institutions, such as the UN, leave them with only limited power to make "global" or even national-level changes in policy or practice. Migrant rights leaders have examined the limits and effects of invoking the global and national scales as metaphors for their causes, and they have also worked actively within political institutions that represent these scales to push for policy change aimed at affecting the daily lives of migrant women.

From the perspective of migrant rights advocates in Indonesia, the intentional invocation of migrants' issues as international human rights concerns has been one of the most powerful tools for pushing the Indonesian government to act on behalf of migrants. Yet, along with feminist migration scholarship, the work of Migrant Care has demonstrated the socially differentiated and gendered hierarchies of belonging that characterize the "international" human rights arena for both citizens and temporary migrants (see also Huang and Yeoh 1996). Yeoh and Huang, among many others, have pointed out that migrant workers' relegation to domestic space "signals the lack of a foothold on . . . potentially more inclusive notions of citizenship and civil society" (Yeoh and Huang 1999: 1164). This work joins a distinguished lineage of feminist scholarship that has emphasized the role that masculinist conceptions of the nation have played in the production of gender injustice (Yuval-Davis 1997a). By corollary it also serves as a reminder that in order to contribute to gender justice, it will be necessary not only to expand spaces of participation and belonging within nations or the global economy, but also to expand historically exclusive definitions of the nation, national belonging, and citizenship.

In addition to work on the global scale and the scale of the nation, feminist migration research has continued to rework the scale of the household (Lawson 1998). In the case of "immigrant domestic workers and their employers, networks of caring labor interlace the home and the world" (Mattingly 2001: 384). The migrant "household" thus imbricates migrants as individuals, members of their families in origin countries, and "local" and "global" labor markets. An approach to gender justice that incorporates this insight would thus require recognition of the interconnected, inseparable nature of scales. It extrapolates from the classic feminist insight about the personal as political to make the point that domestic gender justice is global gender justice. For migrant domestic workers, justice depends not only on their treatment by nation-states or global human rights bodies, nor only on their household and employment relations, but on the ways in which their rights, entitlements, and power are produced within and across these interconnected scales.

Understanding the "particular and the concrete specificity of [the] daily experience" (Pratt and Yeoh 2003: 160) of migrant workers requires that analysts adopt a notion of the "local" that takes seriously the relational dynamics of "global"/"local" geographies. It demands that we attend to the ways in which quotidian practices of immigration and labor control reproduce "global" gender inequality through the regulation of bodies and borders. It focuses our attention on the interconnected, mutually constitutive nature of the *scales*—the body, the household, the nation-state—at play in the making of migrant experiences and inequalities. Put another way, "Macro-processes do not have an umbrella-like impact, but they do impel the confrontation of similar issues of migration among workers in similar economic locations. Parallels therefore do not emerge out of some ontological similarity in institutions globally" (Parreñas 2001: 247). The parallels in immigrant workers' lives across places emerge as a result of long histories of gendered, racialized, nation- and class-based inequalities and forms of exploitation. Distinctive meanings of the "global" take shape in different geo-historical moments and localities, such that, for example, the "global" patterns of Indonesian women's labor rights in Saudi Arabia have both similarities at the level of ideals and differences in practice from the "global" rights claimed by Filipina immigrant women working in Canada. While the UN presents human rights as universal aspirations, or what Spivak has termed that which "we cannot not want," the specific exclusions and expressions of these rights take different forms in different places (Spivak 1999: 110). For migrants, these differences in legal rights across places can mean the difference between working in conditions of slavery or indentured servitude and having a livelihood with dignity and a living wage.

International human rights law was originally based on the United Nations' geographic imaginary that relies on the nation-state as its basic regulatory actor. However, as people have increasingly migrated back and forth between nation-states, international human rights standards have begun to be "expanded to include violations aimed at non-nationals, exploitation of individuals in 'private' places by non-state actors, and forms of abuse that combine multiple forms of discrimination" (Satterthwaite 2005: 66). These directions are hopeful for migrants because as human rights standards are enlarged, they can become more effective in addressing the multiple, intersecting forms of gendered, racialized, and national discrimination that have spread in the context of economic globalization. Given that rights declarations tend to be only as effective as the enforcement mechanisms of the states upholding the declarations, scholars and policy makers can turn to the activism that is organized in the name of low-income migrant domestic workers to draw maps of feminist justice that push beyond the limits of the nation-state and its associated political imaginaries. These emerging maps can contribute to strengthening understandings and enactments of gender justice, as they deepen appreciation of the mutual imbrications of "local" processes of border control with the "global" management of bodies.[7]

Acknowledgments

A warm thank you to Professor Alison Jaggar for organizing and inspiring the workshop on global gender justice in Oslo in May 2008 and for her invaluable feedback on an earlier draft of this chapter. Brooke Ackerly also provided insights that have substantially improved the chapter, and I am very grateful to her. I thank the Centre for the Study of Mind in Nature (CSMN) at the University of Oslo for the generous support of the workshop, and to the director, Christel Fricke, for creating the conditions of possibility for this work. Thanks also to the University of Colorado's Center to Advance Research and Teaching in the Social Sciences (CARTSS) for funding, and director Susan

Clarke for support of this interdisciplinary initiative. Funding for the research was also provided by the University of Toronto's Connaught Faculty Fellowship, and the Social Science Research Council of Canada (SSHRC). That support is greatly appreciated.

Notes

1 Most of the recent international reports on migration as a development issue duly recognize that migrants face specific challenges in terms of rights, but their approach to migration policy is oriented less toward the provision of legal rights protections and more toward encouraging, directing, and planning migration (and non-migration) for poverty alleviation (e.g., UNFPA 2006; World Bank 2007).

2 Canada's immigration policy represents a partial exception to this generalization. That is, in some sectors of the labor market (e.g., live-in domestic service work), it is possible to enter the country as contracted labor, then to work for two years in order to "earn" Canadian citizenship. Once one has become a citizen, family reunification is permitted, and one's family members are eligible for citizenship. Critics of this policy argue that it requires the equivalent of indentured servitude from immigrant workers, and frames citizenship as a gift to be bestowed on the immigrant workers, rather than more fully recognizing the extent of Canadian dependency on their labor (Pratt 2004). The state positions itself as benevolent and the immigrants as recipients of the state's generosity and humanitarian values, whereas many Filipino activists and allied analysts view the policy as a continuation of Canada's long history of discriminatory treatment of non-Anglo residents and citizens, including aboriginal people and non-Anglo immigrants (Razack 1998).

3 As technologies of communication, service, and labor grow increasingly mechanized and transnationalized, the spatiality of reproduction and intimate labor—and the necessity of proximity—is being transformed (Boris and Parreñas 2010).

4 The economic benefits versus the costs to the national economies of the sending economies are a matter of debate. Remittances are indeed very large contributors (US $3 billion reportedly sent home to Indonesia from migrants in 2005) to origin economies (Hugo 2007: 7), but feminist critics (e.g., Herrera 2008) argue that the overall costs and benefits cannot be understood with sole reference to income earned.

5 In practice, of course, some states have more power than others to protect or control their citizens abroad, and the differences in geopolitical influence between nation-states in the transnational arena, as well as the complicated relationships between "nations" and "states," have been a major topic of recent theoretical analysis (Sparke 2005).

6 To be fair to the specific case I am analyzing here, the dedicated human rights activists and researchers at Human Rights Watch (HRW) are not naively attached to serving as saviors of Others, and many of them are descendants of non-European ancestors. Moreover, both the individuals at HRW and HRW as an organization are deeply committed not only to understanding the intersections of multiple inequalities in human rights, but also to staying vigilant about "what human rights [organizations, interventions and discourses] do," in Talal Asad's famous phrasing.

7 Although this chapter paints a generally optimistic picture of the political potential of cross-scale organizing, I must conclude with a cautionary note. A growing body of evidence indicates that global anti-trafficking policies, ostensibly intended to protect women and children from abuses associated with forced migration, have backfired for migrant women in many respects (see especially Parreñas 2011 and Parreñas et al. 2012). There is the danger of such negative effects following from the increasing internationalization of domestic workers' rights, too, particularly given the increased power and responsibility of states in the implementation of rights protections, and the interest of many domestic workers in remaining under the radar of state surveillance and violence. Advocates are aware of these dangers, but they remain convinced that it is better to campaign for formal international conventions, and ratifications by nation-states, than to leave domestic work unregulated or human trafficking ungoverned. Feminist theorists of global justice should approach the emerging global governance norms and laws with as much critical engagement as feminist scholars have granted the politics of the body, the household, and the nation-state.

5

Global Gender Injustice and Mental Disorders

Abigail Gosselin

5.1 Gender and global injustice

5.1.1 Justice

For my analysis of the relationship between structural injustices and the prevalence of some mental disorders among certain groups of women, I use Iris Marion Young's account of structural injustice. According to this account, structures are unjust insofar as they systematically (i.e., regularly and predictably) restrict the ability of certain groups of individuals to realize the conditions necessary for flourishing, or even survival, while enabling other groups of people to prosper (Young 2006: 114). Structural injustice is relational in that the injustice lies in relations of oppression or domination between differently situated groups of people.

Social structures are processes through which individuals interact with each other in spheres of social activity such as politics, economics (e.g., work and consumption), culture, family, and health/well-being (e.g., medicine). Social relations like gender, race, and class position individuals in specific locations within these spheres of activity. Individuals' opportunities for action are enabled and constrained by their social locations; how individuals are situated, therefore, at least partly determines what types and degrees of power and privilege they have (Young 2006: 112–14; 2000: 94–5). Some groups of people are subject to structural harms, in which they are particularly vulnerable to harm based on their social locations (Young 2000: 34; 2006: 112–14). Women, for example, are more vulnerable worldwide to "abuse, exploitation, and material deprivation" (Young 2009: 228) compared to men who are similarly situated, due to gender relations embedded within various social structures. Structural harms constitute structural injustices when certain groups of people experience institutional impediments to flourishing as a result of oppression or domination.

According to Young's conception of justice, which I endorse, structures are unjust insofar as they systematically constrain some groups of people from realizing the two values necessary for a good life, while enabling others to do so. The two values necessary for a good life, according to Young, are self-development, or "developing and exercising one's capacities and expressing one's experience," and self-determination, or "participating in determining one's action and the conditions of one's action" (Young 1990: 37). Institutional barriers to self-development constitute relations of oppression, and they include exploitation, marginalization, powerlessness, cultural imperialism, and violence (Young 1990: 39–65). Institutional constraints on self-determination constitute relations of domination, in which powerful agents reinforce their social positioning by excluding others from enacting power (Young 1990: 31–2).

This chapter examines two forms of structural injustice: socio-economic and hermeneutical. *Socio-economic injustice* occurs when economic and political structures are arranged in ways that create systematic constraints on the ability of certain groups of people to engage in self-development and self-determination. For many women, these constraints arise from carrying an excessive burden of responsibility, especially for caretaking and household duties, which is due at least partly to gendered labor exploitation. *Hermeneutical injustice* occurs when social structures systematically constrain the ability of certain groups of people to participate in processes of knowledge production and meaning-making (Fricker 2007: 152–5). Many women experience epistemic constraints due to narrow and dominant conceptual frameworks which unduly limit their understanding of themselves (as women, persons, and agents), thereby thwarting their self-development and self-determination.

5.1.2 The global order

The structural injustices that are the focus of this chapter are those that result from globalization. The term *globalization* refers to the integration of local and national economies into a single global market (McCarthy 2009: 209; Jaggar 2002a: 238). In the contemporary form of globalization, national economies are merged into a global "free" market which is regulated by the World Trade Organization, established in the 1990s. Global actors and institutions have much greater scope and influence on the everyday lives of people around the world than they ever did in the past, creating new circumstances of justice (Pogge 2010: 14). Most people's social locations now necessarily include a *global economic* aspect, for how individuals are situated within the global economy partly determines the types and degrees of power and privilege they have (or lack). While features of globalization enable the flourishing of some groups of people, they also deeply constrain others, particularly poor and marginalized women (Kang 2008: 360–3). Insofar as global structures constrain the self-development and self-determination of some groups of people, based on their social locations, these structures are unjust.

This chapter analyzes two gender-specific constraints on many women's self-development and self-determination that result from features of contemporary globalization, leading to significant mental distress and high rates of mental disorders among these women. One constraint involves the increased and uncompensated gender-specific responsibilities that many women shoulder, especially poor women, whose labor is easily exploited. The other constraint consists of gendered barriers to hermeneutical participation, which prevent many women from having power over how female identity and agency are conceptualized.

5.1.3 Gender

Gender is a category of "shared conceptions of social identity" through which power operates, and it arises from social structures which perpetuate shared conceptions of what it means to be a certain kind of woman or man (Fricker 2007: 14). Gender intersects with other categories of social identity—including race, class, and sexuality—to position individuals in relation to each other. How one is situated as a white, middle-class American or European woman is different, for example, from how one is situated as a non-white, poor, and/or non-Western woman, and consequently affects one's options for action and participation.[1] Contemporary globalization creates new circumstances of justice in which individuals' social, economic, and political locations are inseparable from claims of justice. Therefore, an analysis of global justice requires accounting for the power relationships that operate through gender and other social categories.

My account will identify two ways in which global structures may be unjust *in gender-specific ways*. First, some aspects of the global order are facially ungendered, but are structured in ways that permit the exploitation of those who are marginalized within the global economy, based on their gendered social locations. The labor of poor and marginalized women, for example, is easily exploited by aspects of economic globalization that burden women with greater responsibilities due to their gendered social location, without adequate (or any) compensation. Second, some aspects of the global order are in fact overtly gendered, with specifically gendered effects. Global structures that perpetuate harmful gender norms and conceptual frameworks about femininity, for example, are explicitly gendered and produce harms specific to women.

My focus in this chapter is on gender-specific constraints and gendered aspects of global structures which harm many groups of women by raising their risk of certain mental disorders. Other gendered analyses may also be given of how global structural injustices toward men contribute to certain mental disorders among men. For example, gendered aspects of the global economic order seem to contribute systematically to the high prevalence of alcoholism in many groups of men, and to the increasing diagnosis of disorders like attention-deficit/ hyperactivity disorder and even autism among some groups of men (Timimi 2008: 174–7; WHO n.d.: 6; WHO 2008: 23). Similarly, hermeneutical injustices may be strong factors in the high prevalence of eating disorders among certain groups of men, such as gay men or men who have been victimized by abuse or violence (Feldman and Meyer 2007a, 2007b). Norms about masculinity, which are supported and perpetuated in part by global economic structures, may create systematic constraints in the ability of many men to understand certain types of experiences, leading to disordered behaviors in response. My chapter is meant to be a starting point for thinking about the relationship between gendered global structural injustices and the high prevalence of mental disorders worldwide.

5.1.4 Causality and risk factors

My claim here is that socio-economic and hermeneutical structural injustices constitute constraints on the self-development and self-determination of certain groups of women, and that these constraints contribute to the high prevalence of certain mental disorders. What I mean in claiming that a structural injustice "contributes" to the prevalence of a disorder is that the injustice is strongly correlated with the disorder, and that the harm caused by the injustice is identified in the scientific literature as a risk factor for the disorder. I began this project by examining the scientific literature on two mental disorders experienced mostly or exclusively by women. From this examination, I identified some of the major risk factors discussed in the literature which seem to be *structural* (and not merely individual) problems. Then I analyzed and assessed the global economic structures that produce many of the harms that constitute these specific risk factors. I do not claim that structural injustices are direct causes of specific incidences of disorder. Rather, my analysis is epidemiological, focusing on structural injustices as likely causal factors that contribute systemically to the prevalence of disorders within certain populations, a claim that is based on the strong correlation between certain disorders and risk factors which seem to constitute structural harms.

My analysis is undertaken in the spirit of what Peg O'Connor calls "attending to the background" of human experience and interaction, by recognizing and questioning structures that are so familiar they usually go unnoticed (2002: 5–7, 45–6). While factors such as individual psychology, family structure, and sometimes cultural norms are typically in the foreground of our understanding of mental health problems, economic and political structures typically exist in the background, taken for granted and not examined as causally relevant. This chapter exposes some of the global economic factors that are part of the "background" of many women's experiences with mental disorders. While firm evidence for specific causal mechanisms of many mental disorders is nearly impossible to acquire, my analysis attempts to bring the structural dimension of mental disorders to the foreground by identifying specific gender-unjust global economic structures that are strongly correlated with the high prevalence of certain mental disorders among some groups of women.

In what follows I offer a normative analysis of how certain global structural injustices contribute in gender-specific ways to mental health problems. For each disorder I discuss, I start with a brief summary of significant non-biological risk factors which arise from social, economic, and political contexts. The summaries are drawn from the relevant scientific literatures. From there I make a normative assessment of how relevant economic, political, and cultural structures are unjust because they unnecessarily generate these non-biological risk factors and thus contribute to the prevalence of disorders.

5.2   Socio-economic injustice and postpartum depression

Women are nearly twice as likely as men to experience common mental disorders such as depression and anxiety.[2] Because these disorders comprise a significant portion of the global burden of disease, a gendered analysis of their causes is important for policy. Depression and anxiety disorders share many of the same risk factors (Lorant et al. 2007; Patel et al. 1999; Patel 2001; Patel and Kleinman 2003), so a gendered analysis of a particular disorder is useful for understanding gendered dimensions of other common mental disorders. The particular disorder I examine here is postpartum depression.

5.2.1   Causal analysis: Prevalence and causes

An analysis of the prevalence of postpartum depression worldwide illustrates the impact of socio-economic injustices on women's mental health. Postpartum depression is characterized by the same criteria as depression, but begins within six months of giving birth. Prevalence rates of postpartum depression vary widely across the world. Most developed countries have rates estimated at 10–15 percent (Halbreich and Karkun 2006: 99). In contrast, many non-Western countries that are undergoing rapid economic transition, and/or have significant populations with entrenched poverty—including Bangladesh, Turkey, India, Vietnam, Taiwan, Pakistan, South Africa, Chile, and Brazil— have rates estimated at 20 percent or higher (Affonso et al. 2000: 211–13; Halbreich and Karkun 2006: 99–106; Husain et al. 2006: 199; Inandi et al. 2005: 726; Nasreen et al. 2011: 6; Yagmur and Ulukoca 2010: 545). Although cultural and psycho-social differences help to explain worldwide rate disparities, socio-economic factors are among the strongest and most consistent factors that account for these disparities.

The most significant non-biological risk factor for postpartum depression is stress. Until recently it was assumed by the Western medical establishment that women in non-Western or developing countries rarely experience postpartum depression because the risk factors that were studied among Western women—stresses that are generally associated with affluence, such as anxiety about meeting idealized standards of "good" motherhood—were not widely experienced in non-Western countries (Hayes et al. 2000: 271–2). Women outside of the United States or Europe, however, experience at least as much stress as Western women, and the degree of their stresses depends in part on how they are socially situated. Poor and marginalized women, in particular, are subject to socio-economic risk factors which are strongly associated with postpartum depression, including low income, low education, illiteracy, living in overcrowded conditions, and lack of access to healthcare (Hartley et al. 2011: 3–5; Inandi et al. 2005: 728; Jadresic et al. 2007: 240–1; Nasreen et al. 2011: 6–7; Ozer et al. 2011: 1566; Yagmur and Ulukoca 2010: 545–6).

5.2.2 Moral analysis: The contributory role of global gender injustice

The strong causal correlation between socio-economic risk factors and postpartum depression suggests that socio-economic structural injustices contribute to postpartum depression by exploiting women's labor, resulting in excessive burdens of responsibility. Economic structures that contribute to this burden oppress women by constraining their self-development and self-determination. As the World Health Organization notes, the stress that results from economic oppression contributes to common mental disorders, including postpartum depression (WHO n.d.: 11–16).

Women carry a tremendous and often disproportionate (compared to similarly situated men) burden of responsibility and workload, which the WHO identifies as the "triple burden of productive, reproductive, and caring work" (WHO n.d.: 12). Women throughout the world increasingly work outside the home, both from financial need and for self-development, even as they maintain the primary and traditionally female domestic responsibilities for caretaking and household labor. While contemporary globalization has benefited some women by increasing their options, allowing them opportunities for power and agency outside the domestic sphere, it has harmed many other women, especially those already poor or otherwise marginalized. The following features of economic globalization directly increase poor women's burden of responsibility, which greatly constrains their capacity for self-development and self-determination, and which therefore likely causes some of the stresses that contribute to postpartum depression:

Privatization decreases formal support for women and increases women's workload: As a result of their gendered responsibilities, women suffer disproportionately from austerity programs that are required as part of the debt restructuring of many countries. Through austerity programs, government-funded social services such as medical, nutrition, and education services are reduced or eliminated, which burdens poor women in at least two ways. Women who are unable to afford these services in the private market, and who can no longer rely on government services, now lack access to resources necessary for the well-being of themselves and their children.[3] The stress of the lack of access to resources that results from cutbacks in social services is a direct causal factor for common mental disorders like depression (WHO n.d.: 15). In addition, as privatization outsources services to the market, women are often obligated to take on additional responsibilities, such as caretaking or accessing safe drinking water, in order to compensate. This especially burdens poor women who are unable to pay others to do this labor and therefore must do it themselves (Chant 2008: 179; Jaggar 2009: 40–1; Sassen 2000: 511–12; Young 2009: 235–6).

Competitive labor markets increase women's workload, subjecting women to difficult labor conditions and decreasing their informal support: While many women in the world benefit from the greater paid work opportunities that contemporary globalization offers them, many other women are harmed by economic factors that require them to work outside the home for their own and their families' survival. The financial need that drives many women into work outside the home is largely a function of globalization, which, through competitive labor and consumer markets, has driven down average wages. At the same time, the competitive global consumer market has increased the price of many basic goods such as food staples. Households that formerly relied on one income now need two to survive. Moreover, whether women choose or are forced to do paid labor, they continue to maintain the primary and traditionally female domestic responsibilities for caretaking and household labor (Chant 2008: 178–82; Elson 2002: 92–5; Young 2009: 235).

While the combination of doing both paid and unpaid labor is a source of great stress for many women, poor women who have little choice in the circumstances of their paid work are especially burdened. These women are more likely to work in low-skill jobs with very long hours, few breaks, no benefits, and no flexibility for conditions like pregnancy. Women who perform paid labor in their homes in order to maintain their domestic responsibilities receive even less pay, while employers are even less accountable for these women's working conditions. Because they are easily replaceable with other women who would be willing to do the same job, women in need of income generally put up with these poor labor conditions. Many women lose their jobs upon becoming pregnant, while those who do not may feel great pressure to return to work immediately (Jaggar 2009: 34–5; Kang 2008: 362; Young 2009: 234–5).

Increasing demands on women's labor are not only a problem with respect to new mothers' own workloads. Extended family members, including mothers and mothers-in-law, also experience increasing workloads, which diminish their ability to help with childcare and household labor.

Mobilization of labor increases women's workload as well as women's isolation: The competitive global labor force requires that people go where the jobs are (Elson 2002: 81). Men may leave their families to find work, leaving women behind to take care of children and household alone. For example, young aboriginal men in Taiwan move to cities to find employment and leave their families behind in the less expensive but remote mountain villages. This relocation destroys traditional tribal communities and severs families. Consequently, women who are to take care of the remaining family and household experience great stress and have a 25 percent prevalence rate of postpartum depression (Wang et al. 2003: 1411; see also Bina 2008: 578–9).

As family members relocate to find paying jobs in the increasingly mobile economy, extended families break apart, and new mothers lose their family support and become increasingly isolated. This isolation is experienced particularly by migrant women, who move for the sake of their own or their husbands' employment and then are isolated by language and culture. For example, Jordanian women who have migrated to Australia experience significant isolation and loneliness separated from their extended families; the stress of this separation is worsened by the central importance of family in traditional Jordanian culture. Without this family support, new mothers have had to forgo meaningful and helpful traditional rituals involving rest and being cared for (Nahas and Amasheh 1999: 43). Isolation and the loss of the support of extended family members, which are typical effects of migration, increase women's responsibility for taking care of children and the home, and, as a result, increase the stress that leads to common mental disorders (see Latzer 2003: 86).

The features of contemporary globalization described here are facially ungendered, but they permit the exploitation of those who are marginalized within the global economy, based on their gendered social locations, while allowing other groups of people to prosper. Poor and marginalized women (including aboriginal women and immigrant women) are particularly harmed by features of globalization that exploit their labor, both paid and unpaid, for the sake of profit and without providing sufficient (or any) compensation.

Global economic structures are unjust insofar as they systematically constrain the self-development and self-determination of certain groups of people while allowing others to prosper. By exploiting the labor of many women and increasing their responsibilities excessively and often disproportionately, oppressive aspects of globalization prevent these women from having the time or resources to develop capacities that would enable them to flourish. These constraints on self-development and self-determination cause high levels of stress and, consequently, likely contribute strongly to common mental disorders such as postpartum depression. In addition, unjust economic structures not only increase poor and marginalized women's vulnerability to mental disorders, but also create institutional barriers to the healthcare access and treatment that might alleviate these women's suffering.

5.3   Hermeneutical injustice and eating disorders

Eating disorders, especially anorexia and bulimia, are strongly gendered mental disorders, both in the sense that women suffer disproportionately from them and in the sense that women suffer from them *on account of* their gender. While statistics on the gender prevalence of these disorders are difficult to find and unreliable, the vast majority of sufferers are women; and, in fact, much of the scientific literature treats these disorders as experienced by women only. This gender disparity is universal across cultures, even though the prevalence of eating disorders varies greatly among cultures. The strongly gendered nature of these disorders makes them particularly suitable for the analysis undertaken here.

5.3.1   Causal analysis: Prevalence and causes

An analysis of eating disorders illustrates the effect of hermeneutical injustice on mental health. Because criteria for clinical eating disorders are controversial, I focus here on eating disordered *behavior*, which includes self-starvation, bingeing, purging, laxative use, and overexercise. When I use the term *eating disorder* I am referring to a set of behaviors and attitudes practiced over time, not to a specific clinical diagnosis. Disordered eating behaviors occur in women throughout the world in nearly all social, racial, and ethnic groups, and prevalence rates have generally increased in response to contemporary globalization. While evidence is contradictory over whether the prevalence of clinical anorexia has increased—partly because conflicts about criteria for anorexia beg the question of how even to measure prevalence (see Becker et al. 2009; Lee 2001)—the prevalence of bulimia worldwide has unquestionably risen dramatically in the past four decades. However, the prevalence of bulimia differs markedly among cultures depending on the degree of modernization and exposure to Western cultural ideals (Keel and Klump 2003: 758, 761).

As with postpartum depression, eating disorders have a variety of complex and interconnected risk factors including neurobiological, psychological, and socio-cultural factors. Some of the most significant non-biological risk factors are created and exacerbated by features of globalization. First, exposure to Western beauty ideals and other gender norms is strongly and consistently associated with increases (sometimes dramatic) in concerns about weight and body size, and in "subclinical" harmful eating (Keel and Klump 2003: 762–4; Njenga and Kangethe 2004: 192; Wildes et al. 2001: 538–9). Several studies interpret these increases as consequences of modernization and the increasing impact of global media and entertainment (Becker 2003: 73–4; Makino et al. 2004: 5–6; Raphael and Lacey 1992; Rathner 2001; Shuriquie 1999: 3; Vander Wal et al. 2008).

Second, the increased prevalence of eating disorders is also strongly associated with cultural conflict or transition. In developing countries, and for migrants of non-Western cultures who now live in Western countries, the *conflict* between traditional gender norms and the modern, Western gender norms that have become the global standard may be more significant than mere exposure to global gender norms (Ali and Maharajh 2004: 4; Miller and Pumariega 2001: 99–104; Nasser 2009: 348–9; Shuriquie 1999: 2–3). Women experiencing cultural conflict may experience a double burden in not only being subject to global gender norms but also having to negotiate between these and traditional feminine values of obedience, deference, adherence to roles and rules, and responsibility toward family, home, and community. This double burden of negotiating between global and traditional gender norms constitutes what Iris Young identifies as the "double consciousness" of being defined by both a dominant and a subordinate culture (1990: 60). For some women, food and weight manipulation may be a way to resolve conflict by enabling them to fit in with global gender norms by means of behavior that is sanctioned or reinforced by traditional gender roles (Catina and Joja 2001; Ruggiero 2001).

5.3.2 Moral analysis: Global gender injustice

Both of these risk factors suggest that some women engage in disordered eating behavior as a response to constraining gender norms, many of which are imposed and reinforced by certain aspects of contemporary globalization. Global structures that systematically perpetuate narrow and harmful conceptions of femininity create epistemic barriers to the self-development and self-determination of many women. Structures that perpetuate cultural narratives and conceptual frameworks that narrowly constrain how certain groups of people understand their own experiences, in ways which prevent them from challenging or transforming these narratives, are hermeneutically unjust (Fricker 2007: 153–5). For some women, disordered eating behaviors may provide a culturally available means to express suffering that they otherwise do not have an ability to communicate—or even understand—and to exercise an agency which is otherwise severely constrained (Katzman 1997; Katzman and Lee 1997: 389–90).

Hermeneutically unjust structures create normalizing epistemic background conditions that limit how women are conceptualized as persons and agents. These background conditions make disordered eating behaviors appear normal and (in many ways) acceptable, obscuring their social and political dimensions. Because relations of marginalization or privilege extend over many spheres of social activity, hermeneutical injustice connects with socio-economic and other forms of structural injustice (Fricker 2007: 155–6). In fact, the hermeneutical marginalization faced by many women results in part from how they are situated within the global economy. Global structures perpetuate norms, cultural meanings, and conceptual frameworks that are highly constraining to women's epistemic self-development and self-determination, thus likely contributing to the prevalence of eating disorders, in the following ways:

Sexualization, objectification, and commodification of women's bodies: Global institutions such as the prostitution and pornography industries blatantly sexualize and commodify women's bodies for economic gain. Less explicitly, global institutions such as the advertising, marketing, media, and entertainment industries also objectify women by using women's bodies as objects of desire to sell products. While the sexualization, objectification, and commodification of women's bodies is nothing new, contemporary globalization increases its scale and scope exponentially. The growth of the global sex and entertainment industries is at least partly a structural feature of economic development and debt servicing, supported by governments eager for tourism revenue (Sassen 2000: 519). The objectification of women's bodies is so pervasive and normalized that it is typically unquestioned and de-politicized. This reductive conception of womanhood has innumerable harms, including the potential for women to internalize this conception and collude in their own objectification.

Promotion of oppressive global beauty norms connecting beauty to privilege: Global institutions such as the advertising, marketing, media, and entertainment industries perpetuate global beauty ideals that embody privilege and that are very difficult if not impossible for most women to attain. Global beauty norms, like other global gender norms, tend to be Western inventions that have spread through processes of globalization to become norms for many women throughout the world. As representations of power and status, global beauty norms reflect categories of global privilege according to race (white), class (middle- or upper-class), and nationality (American or European). Female beauty is typically embodied as tall, thin, shapely, with Anglo features and bone structure (regardless of skin color). Women who are especially vulnerable to internalizing these beauty norms are those who are *members* of privileged social groups (e.g., white and middle- or upper-class) or those who *aspire* to be in these social groups. The aspirational quality of such norms helps to explain why exposure to global beauty norms is a risk factor for women in all social groups. Women who do not naturally have idealized physical features, who do not have the means and economic resources to acquire them (through exercise, plastic surgery, etc.), or who *believe* that they lack these features, are vulnerable to feelings of inadequacy and lack of self-worth. Such women may engage in disordered eating behaviors as a way of addressing feelings of inadequacy, for these behaviors are a means of trying to conform to ideal beauty standards—and, insofar as they are self-harming behaviors, they are also a means of punishing oneself for failing to do so.

Global exploitation of potentially harmful and exploitative local cultural gender norms: In addition to perpetuating global beauty norms associated with privilege, global structures also reinforce more specific cultural gender norms related to the body. For example, the Japanese *shojo*—a teenage, virginal schoolgirl—is a relatively new female role that is an alternative to the traditional dichotomous roles of girlhood and motherhood, the latter of which is seen as overly restrictive. The *shojo* is depicted as physically and sexually undeveloped, innocent, and cute; many Japanese young women who try to emulate this ideal develop eating disordered behaviors in order to appear childlike and dependent (Pike and Borovoy 2004: 494–508). While the *shojo* has a cultural meaning specific to the Japanese, global market forces commodify the image by selling *manga* comics and animated movies to American and European markets, where the cute, innocent girl who is neither child nor woman holds appeal. These markets include not only teenage girls who find the image appealing for reasons similar to those of Japanese teenagers, but also men who fetishize the image and exploit it for pornographic purposes.

Perpetuation of gendered global economic norms that reinforce the connection between female agency and the body: Norms such as autonomy, individualism, productivity, efficiency, and achievement enable those with privilege to succeed in the global marketplace. While these norms are promoted within the global economy as universal and gender-neutral, theoretically enabling anyone to achieve economic success, they are in fact implicitly gendered, raced, and classed. Economic and political barriers systematically prevent some groups of people from embodying these norms, denying them not only the means to attain the kind of economic success enjoyed by many people of privilege, but also the status of appearing to have the *possibility* of attaining this success. For example, the burden of caretaking responsibility shouldered by many women automatically constrains their ability to act in ways that are autonomous, individualist, and "productive" (as measured by accomplishing specific outcomes that have market value). This not only reduces women's ability to achieve significant economic success, it also diminishes women's status as economic and political agents. The fact that this diminished agential status results from an inability to embody certain economic norms is grossly unfair, and puts many women in a bind about how to regard their own agency given the lack of full recognition that is granted to them.

Many women try to resolve the tension between responsibility and autonomy through one of the few resources of agency available to them: their bodies. Cultural messages that largely reduce female identity and agency to the body suggest that body manipulation is a primary way for women to enact power. Moreover, many women, especially those who have or who aspire to relative privilege in the global economy, internalize global economic values. Women who internalize both global beauty norms and global economic values are especially vulnerable to developing eating disorders as ways to try to achieve the ideals of autonomy and achievement so important for success in a global capitalist/consumer economy (King 1993; Meehan and Katzman 2001; Shuriquie 1999: 3).

Spread of knowledge about behaviors and their cultural meanings: Global institutions and technologies easily and quickly expose people to behaviors previously unknown. The internet, of course, makes information accessible to anyone with a computer. Media, advocacy groups, pharmaceutical companies, and medical professionals also spread information about behavior in ways that reiterate and reinforce globally dominant conceptual frameworks. One effect of this accessibility of information is the increased prevalence of certain disorders. For example, consider the significant increase in prevalence of anorexia in Hong Kong since 1994. While previously anorexia was a very rare illness, described by sufferers in somatic terms, the highly publicized death of a 14-year-old girl from anorexia complications in 1994 changed public awareness and perceptions of the illness. As Hong Kong media and newly formed advocacy groups popularized Western conceptions of anorexia in the name of prevention and treatment, the prevalence of anorexia increased dramatically, with sufferers now describing psychological experiences that mirrored Western interpretations of anorexia. This was due at least in part to the cultural availability of expressions of suffering, in which certain behaviors only make sense when they are associated with specific meanings. Highly publicized accounts of self-harming behaviors, such as occurred in Hong Kong, make those behaviors and the meaning attached to them culturally available (Watters 2010: 9–63).

Cultural meanings of disorders are spread not only through media publicity but also through the work of global industries that have vested interests in perpetuating those meanings. Many global industries, for example, reinforce the view that disordered eating behaviors are essentially about food, weight, and the body, because they profit from this belief. Globalized media and entertainment conglomerates, marketing and advertising firms, food and diet industries, and medical and pharmaceutical companies profit directly from having women reduce their feelings of inadequacy and their attempts at success to concerns about food, weight, and body. Many industries also profit indirectly from the reductivist view of eating disorders by obscuring injustices that they are complicit in perpetuating, as I explain below. Insofar as women internalize these reductivist interpretations of their behavior, they do not question—and therefore collude in maintaining—the power of global institutions. When global structures reinforce a narrow conceptual framework that severely limits the meaning given to disordered eating behaviors, thereby obscuring their social and political meanings, they are hermeneutically unjust.

The global structures described here constrain women's hermeneutical participation in gender-specific ways by creating and perpetuating constraining norms about femininity. The aspirational quality of these gender-specific norms helps explain why eating disorders occur in many populations, regardless of women's specific social locations. In addition, the global homogeneity of these norms accounts for the strong correlation between certain features of globalization and eating disordered behaviors. What makes the global structures described here unjust is the way in which they create normalizing hermeneutical background conditions that impede the self-understanding and self-determination of many women, while enabling other agents to profit from these same structures. Pervasive messages that women's bodies are sexual objects, representations of privilege, and the primary means of agency construct a normalizing hermeneutical background in which the connection between woman and body is naturalized. For some women, engaging in disordered eating behaviors may be one of the few ways in which they can enact agency, given these hermeneutical constraints.

5.4 The hermeneutical obscuring of the political context of women's distress

Mental health policies tend not to address gender injustices for at least two reasons. First, gender injustices such as those described in this chapter are often not recognized *as gender injustices* or even *as injustices*. Second, insofar as gender injustices are recognized, their relationship to mental health is typically obscured by existing dominant conceptual frameworks.

Conceptual frameworks that perpetuate and normalize narrow and constraining images of femininity obscure the ways in which women are oppressed and dominated, and thereby obscure gender injustice. Domestic ideals of femininity reinforce beliefs that women are primarily responsible for caretaking and household labor, regardless of their participation in paid employment; these beliefs enable the exploitation of women's labor. Beliefs and norms that connect women to the body by representing the attractive female body as the ultimate object of desire, the embodiment of privilege, and thus the ultimate expression of agency, constrain women's hermeneutical self-development and self-determination. The normalization and internalization of narrow gender norms and beliefs make it difficult for women to conceptualize or articulate alternative understandings of their experience, especially with respect to women's responsibilities and labor, and female identity and agency. Conceptual frameworks that normalize the oppression and domination of many women, while enabling certain agents to prosper, obscure injustice and help to maintain and reinforce the economic status quo.

Existing economic structures are further supported by an additional conceptual framework that medicalizes women's mental distress. Many global industries, including pharmaceutical companies and media conglomerates, systematically reinforce a medical framework for mental disorder that regards mental health problems primarily as biomedical conditions requiring psychotropic medicine for treatment. Regardless of how valid or useful the framework may be, it tends to exclude the social and political dimensions of many mental disorders. This exclusion is not necessarily intentional; medical professionals, for instance, do not generally intend to obscure broader causal factors if they are relevant. However, many agents do gain from this obscuring, and some agents—especially pharmaceutical companies—do intentionally obscure. By minimizing or precluding social and political understandings of mental disorders, the medical framework severs the link between mental health problems and politics as if they belonged to two distinct spheres of human experience. This separation prevents adequate understanding of, and response to, suffering. Moreover, a conceptual framework that ignores the role of power upholds existing economic structures, and therefore contributes to the prevalence of mental disorders insofar as they result from existing structural injustices.

5.5 Conclusion

The above analysis demonstrates that global structural reforms are necessary to address the high and in some cases increasing prevalence of certain mental disorders among many groups of women, and to improve the mental health status of women worldwide. In order to address the gendered aspect of certain mental disorders, structural reforms must take into account specifically gendered injustices. These reforms must account for not only the economic aspects of contemporary globalization, but also its cultural and ideological aspects.

Global gender justice requires eliminating relations of oppression and domination that are embedded within many global structures. To give some examples of the kind of transformations that gender justice requires: In order to ensure that women's labor is not exploited, social services that provide caretaking, educational, nutritional, and health services should be preserved and expanded. Structural barriers that prevent girls from entering primary or secondary education, and that restrict women from typically gendered job opportunities, must be removed. The cessation of labor exploitation requires improving labor conditions for *all* jobs and paying livable wages, and it entails that powerful agents not profit at the expense of those who are most marginalized within the global economy. The need of the very poor to make a living must not be taken advantage of, and the feminine skills and stereotypes that are often targeted for certain types of labor must not be exploited. Additionally, women's bodies must not be exploited. Industries must be strongly encouraged to sell products in ways that do not objectify women or prey on women's dissatisfaction with themselves. Women must be supported in taking more expansive (less reductive) opportunities, roles, and norms in the global economy. Structural reform is necessary in order for global structures to enable women's self-development and self-determination, and, consequently, to be gender-just.

Because structural injustices are typically in the background of public consciousness about mental disorders, it is worth identifying probable causal relations between specific structural injustices and the prevalence of certain disorders among specific groups of people. This chapter has begun this project by analyzing the structural dimensions of some of the risk factors of two different mental disorders, and identifying two specific kinds of gendered structural injustices that likely contribute to these disorders. Moreover, by exposing the causal role of specific gendered injustices, my analysis has pointed to specific structural changes that public health policy must focus on in order to reduce the prevalence of certain disorders among specific populations. In recognizing structural justice as a key factor in how we think about mental disorders, public health policy must explicitly take into account the connections between gendered political realities and women's mental health status.

Acknowledgments

Drafts of this chapter were presented at the 29th International Social Philosophy Conference at Boston University, and at the Center for Values and Social Policy at the University of Colorado at Boulder. I thank participants at both presentations for their helpful feedback. My colleagues in the philosophy department at Regis University provided me with valuable suggestions during a colloquium discussion. I thank Cory Aragon and Karen Adkins for carefully reading and commenting on earlier drafts. Finally, I am most grateful to Alison Jaggar, whose deeply insightful comments and patience throughout the writing process benefited this chapter tremendously.

Notes

1 My use of terms to identify populations and countries, with their norms and conceptual frameworks, follows common usage within the scientific literatures on mental disorders. In much of the paper I use the term *Western* to identify norms and conceptual frameworks that come chiefly from the United States as well as European countries, and which are typically the norms and frameworks spread through processes of globalization. Countries and cultures (along with their norms and conceptual frameworks) which are outside the United States and Europe are *non-Western*. *Traditional* cultures and practices are those that existed before (or outside of) modernization. *Developing* countries are countries in the process of global economic integration and modernization. All of these and related terms are highly problematic geographically, historically, politically, and conceptually. My choice of terms is based on their use in the scientific literature on which my analysis is based.

2 The lifetime prevalence of anxiety disorders for women is estimated at 18.5% compared to 10.4% for men (Somers et al. 2006). The lifetime prevalence of depression is estimated at 21.3% for women compared to 12.7% for men (WHO n.d.: 5–6).

3 See Ozer et al. (2011) on the benefit of macro-level government programs on maternal mental health.

6

Discourses of Sexual Violence in a Global Context

Linda Martín Alcoff

Concepts are determinative over how we name and identify a problem, how we establish legal rights and responsibilities, and how we gather statistical information. And yet the conceptual repertoire any society has at any given time is subject to the arbitrariness of historical accident.

None of the terms we use to describe sexual violence are as straightforward as one might imagine. Today we have concepts of acquaintance rape and marital rape and sexual trafficking; less than 50 years ago none of these terms had entered the English language. The concept of "honor" once used widely in Western discourses in relation to rape is now rarely used except outside the West, and this usage is undergoing a vigorous debate. The concept of statutory rape has an upper age limit that ranges from nine years of age to 18, and sometimes the difference in age of the partner is also taken into account. The concept of "consent" is widely used as the key criterion determining whether a rape has occurred, but the emphasis on that concept may be traceable to a specific cultural history of contract-based social practices. There are significant differences in the way that rape and sexual abuse are defined across countries and even across states and districts within the United States. This variability can make it impossible to gather either national or international information on the scope of the problem.

The concepts we use have formative effects not only on how we identify crimes and culpability but also on our experiences and practices, as Foucault argued. Language makes a difference in not only how an event is statistically tabulated, but also in how it is perceived, judged, and experienced. Words attain their meaning within a context of use, invoking specific connotations and references that may differ a great deal between contexts. If this is true for the object-world (think of the connotations of the English words "gas" and "wind," for example), it is even more obviously true in the realm of human experience, in which the choice of words can elicit different sensations and affective responses. The word "pervert" today can be embedded in a context of use that is normalizing, heteronormative, endearing, or just funny. We cannot assume a given concept has only one true or accurate meaning that is operationalized when it is uttered.

Nor can we assume that our concepts are merely describing or referring; they are also constituting, engendering, and inciting. Efforts to expand the term rape to include anal and oral penetration can change affective and institutional responses. The serious, legal, or activist intent behind the formation of a new concept cannot control all the new meanings, connotations, effects and practices that will be generated. Concepts can give people ideas.

This only makes the debate over concepts that much more difficult, since we must not only argue about their descriptive adequacy and legal utility but also their normative implications for formations of subjectivity and power. Much of the philosophical debate over concepts relevant to sexual violence has focused on the need to specify, clarify, and fine-tune definitions especially for legal purposes. But feminists have also analyzed concepts in light of a larger domain of discourse, asking questions such as: What work is the concept of consent doing when it is used as the all-purpose criterion for sexual crimes? What effects does the term honor have on women's empowerment or on imperialist forms of Western liberalism? What norms of femininity are subtly conveyed by the use of the term victim?

In this chapter I will consider three of the most important and contentious concepts that are widely used in regard to sexual violence: the concepts of consent, victim, and honor.[1] There are feminists who have argued that each of these concepts should simply be abandoned (e.g., Chakravarti 2005; Chamallas 1988; Wolf 1994.) Theorists, social scientists, and activists have debated the scope of the concept of "consent" and the political effects produced by using the term "victim" and the phrase "honor crime" (e.g., Ackerly and Okin 1999; Murray 1998; Ticktin 2008; Appiah 2010). Although a great deal of the debate has been focused on the utility of these concepts—particularly consent— for a legal context intending to establish culpability as well as provide deterrence, I want to shift our attention to a larger public domain of discussion in which they figure in everyday usage. And in particular, I want to consider these three concepts from the point of view of survivors. From this perspective, what are the limits, or disadvantages, of their usage? Can they be refashioned in more useful ways?

The goal of this chapter will be to consider the challenges to global gender justice that are posed by this decentralized, irremediably heterogeneous linguistic and social context that determines the meanings of our political concepts. Feminist solidarity is often strained over our choice of words, but the process of mediating conflicts is not best approached by a majority vote, or even by an acquiescence to accept the terms favored by the least advantaged. Rather, we need an approach that can bring into analysis the diverse normative, political, legal, and social implications of a term. We cannot control the connotations mobilized by a given term, and yet we also cannot ignore what we consider to be mistaken connotations given our goals of social change, of changing minds, attitudes, and practices. Thus, we need an approach to debate that will be attuned to the real world effects of terms in the specific contexts in which they operate. Specifically, we need to keep in mind the global context within which terms may operationalize in radically different ways.

Concepts of sexual violence operate today in a global context. Although legal jurisdictions specify meanings differently, the interpretation of meanings by juries and judges as well as plaintiffs are impacted by transnational domains of connotation and reference, even if latent and unarticulated. It is unwise to assume that a concern restricted to a specific legal context can settle the indeterminacy and fluidity of meanings given the way that any given context will be applied to a polyvocal constituency of diverse communities with pluritopic hermeneutic horizons. Nearly every legal context today, in other words, operates within a multicultural community. This means that the ways concepts are actually understood "on the ground" as they are used in real situations may well be impossible to legislate, contain or control. Meanings we do not intend become the operative understandings in contexts we know little about. Connotations are invoked and images are conveyed that are too varied to pin down. Foucault's own complex and subtle approach to the ways in which terms such as "criminal" or "pervert" accrue meaningfulness is still inadequate to the plurivocal discursive contexts in which most people live today, with access to multiple discursive formations and competing regimes of truth.

While I argue for more realism about the way concepts work, I also understand that there is yet a pressing activism-motivated need to try to contain the multiplicity of terms, definitions, and concepts. Activists, for example, have criticized the recent spread of the term "rape" in video game banter to mean a bland form of generic conquest, robbing it of all serious connotation. And although there is an acknowledged global epidemic of sexual violence, the use of disparate concepts and definitions has made it impossible to gather uniform national or global statistics, and has even created obstacles to the effort to prosecute war crimes.[2] The differences also pose challenges for creating transnational or regional collaborative social movements.

One way to approach the multiplicity of meanings that may slow down the proliferation, or put a brake on the ambiguity, is through a materialist phenomenology that approaches concepts in relation to embodied experience. The term "rape" can be subject to numerous and conflicting representations, but there will be a limit to its ambiguity when applied to experience. It cannot be stretched to include totally inconsequential experiences without deconstructing its forcefulness as the name of a crime. Although it would be wise to acknowledge that our best understandings of sexual experience today may be superseded in the future, we can certainly defend the claim that it is better to say "rape" or "coerce" than to use the common term once used instead: "seduce." After all, the fallibilism of our understandings does not entail that the moon may be made of green cheese, though it should keep us on our toes even about our most confirmed beliefs, and it should motivate us to cultivate an openness to the possibility of learning from others.

Keeping a global context in mind can also assist us in assessing the controversies that erupt over certain concepts. Consider the concerns expressed in some feminist literature in the global North about the use of the term "victim." Could this controversy be the result of a media backlash against feminism, in which feminism is chastised for always focusing on the negative, and for underplaying women's sexual agency? Has the Western focus on agency—and its excessively individualized characterization of agency—produced a context in which to be a victim is to lack dignity? In other words, has personhood been so tied to effective agency that feminists who want to defend women's personhood have felt blocked from being able to name women as victims? Are the intense connotations that swirl around this term peculiarly Western or US-based? It could be helpful to make Western concepts, and our conceptual difficulties with them, "strange" to ourselves. This could shed some light on our debates as well as enhancing the possibilities for dialogue.

A comparative, global analysis is obviously necessary if we are to avoid unreflectively, even unconsciously, universalizing our local frameworks for identifying and analyzing sexual violence. But at the same time that we need to beware of making false analogies across diverse meanings and experiences, we also need to beware of ignoring possible commonalities. As Margo Wilson and Martin Daly argue in their study of patterned differences, men beat their wives in many societies while the reverse happens only rarely, and men are by far the main perpetrators of sexual violence across the globe (Wilson and Daly 1998). The activist and survivor Rachel Lloyd works with sexually trafficked young girls from very diverse backgrounds, yet finds that "our experiences are consistently more similar than different" (2011: 27). Lynn Welchman and Sara Hossain argue that "It is important to identify commonalities as well as differences in the structure of violence." They question the "stereotypical associations of 'honor' with the 'East' and 'passion' with the 'West'," and conclude that overlooking commonalities can assist in cultural imperialism just as surely as overlooking differences can by cordoning off elite societies from cultural interrogation (Welchman and Hossain 2005: 13). Stereotypes of cultural difference continue to attribute rationality, emotionality, sexual intensity, and the fervor of cultural and religious commitments differentially across the globe, and nowhere are the effects of this more obvious than in regard to rape. Sexual violence is variously blamed on an excess of passion in some ethnic groups, an excess of religion in others, and an excess of culture itself in others, while in some societies no uniquely cultural or religious elements are blamed at all and the problem is taken to be rooted in the happenstance of individual pathology or "deviance." In actual fact, however, as Uma Narayan has effectively argued, the so-called "death by culture" women are said to experience in countries such as India is in reality an equal opportunity across the globe (Narayan 1996). All or almost all cultures pose risks for women by having discourses that conceal or excuse the harms against women, that make it difficult to prosecute offenders, and that wildly mischaracterize what has actually occurred.

So we need to watch for universal or commonly shared aspects of the problem of sexual violence. This does not mean that culturally specific elements play no role, or that we can return to a uniform account of an undifferentiated "patriarchy" in the way some feminist theorists did in the past. But perhaps cultural differences operate not as final causes but only as initial causes. In other words, maybe they provide alibis for rape rather than foundational motivations. As the following sections argue, the use of both of the concepts "consent" and "honor," for example, throughout the global North and the global South, may be ultimately about maintaining dominance over women and aiding men to escape culpability.

6.1 "Consent"

The term "consent" resonates with liberal political traditions of contract, in which free agents are imagined to enter into volitional relations that carry obligations and responsibilities. This invites us to wonder whether the overuse we make of the concept of consent, as well as the difficulty we have with the concept of victim, are peculiar to these liberal traditions. Do these concepts harbor individualist metaphysical conceptions of selfhood and agency? If so, what would formulations of sexual violence look like without individualist concepts of the self? How does the concept of consent resonate with experiences of sexual violence and violation?

The debate over the concept of consent has mainly concerned whether it is adequate to describe sexual interactions and what political advantages and disadvantages accrue from its use. Numerous feminists have been wary of the emphasis on consent because it eclipses structural constraints on choice, assuming relations of prior equality between participants (Gauthier 1999; Baker 1999; Pateman and Mills 2007). Some have been concerned that it implicitly positions women on the receiving end of sexual initiation, as if women's only options are to give or withhold consent—to say yea or nay—rather than to initiate themselves (Chamallas 1988). Despite the concept's clear advantages in emphasizing the need for reciprocity and voluntary engagement in sexual activity, the critics have warned that we cannot assume that women even today have attained the status of fully free and equal parties in social interactions. Rather, as Jeffrey Gauthier has effectively argued, women's situation is often more analogous to vulnerable workers in market-based economies whose choices are quite constrained and for whom the discourse of "free choice" is just a subterfuge (Gauthier 1999). Ignoring these contextual realities can completely change the effect of a statute or piece of legislation. "Treating a person whose autonomy lacks social and legal recognition with the 'respect' due a truly autonomous agent will help ensure that her true autonomy remains unrealized" (Gauthier 1999: 75).

This last point demonstrates that there is a way in which the debate over consent mirrors the ideal versus non-ideal political theory debate (see e.g., Pateman and Mills 2007: 94ff). The latter is a meta-level dispute over whether political theory can aim for ideal norms, such as "justice," or whether our best thinking about norms will emerge from considerations of actual non-ideal situations. Ideal-theory proponents maintain that ideal norms have to be established prior to any assessment of a specific institution or policy, because they make it possible to assess specific institutions and policies. Non-ideal-theory proponents argue for a more pragmatist procedure in which norms are defended on the basis of on their likely real world effects given real world conditions. Gauthier's point shows that ideal norms that are constructed for ideal conditions can actually have negative consequences when applied under non-ideal conditions.

Foucault's approach to concepts obviously has much more in common with the non-ideal approach, and this may help to explain why some of his early critics failed to understand the normative thrust of his writings. Foucault is concerned to elaborate the background discursive conditions that give currently used concepts and terms their actual, operative meanings. His argument that rape should be decriminalized, for example, is made within an account of how sexuality came under the domain of legal and normative evaluation, a story that involves the promulgation of certain power/knowledge relations and little concern for ideal justice of any sort. From this point of view, Foucault believed that the actual effect of treating rape as a separate sexual offense within the criminal law is to provide an alibi for the legal regulation of sexual activity of all sorts, since it provides a strong justification for letting the law, with the help of expert discourses such as psychiatry, have a powerful hand in the identification of normatively acceptable sexual conduct.

Foucault was thus introducing a kind of non-ideal consideration into the debates over the discursive place of the concept of rape as this was being redefined by feminist activists. He was hardly taking a pro-rape position. While I disagree with the substance of his position, I agree with the meta-approach he took in assessing terms and concepts. It just makes sense that we should consider all of the sorts of effects the use of a concept may engender, support, or justify, even those quite peripheral to our immediate concerns. There can often be a kind of blowback incurred by the use of concepts meant to address oppression when they work simultaneously to support conservative agendas. The domain of discussion around rape and sexual violence is one of the key arenas where this can happen, given the way that an acknowledgment of the severity of the problem can be used to justify constraints on women's free activity as well as to justify a normalization of correct or legitimate sexual activities, and even motivate unilateral military intervention.

For these reasons it would be wise to consider the concepts we use in terms of their real world effects in the widest possible contexts of use. But I want principally to consider the potential effects on survivors, and in particular, on the capacity of victims to become survivors and to be able to resist, seek help, and speak about their experiences. Let me return to the debates over consent with this idea in mind.

Interestingly, in a recent discussion by Japanese feminists included in Kamala Kempadoo's Collection, *Global Sex Workers*, the real world effects of both the concepts of consent and of victim come up for debate. The conditions of work for many sex workers exist in ambiguous limbo in regard to sexual violence. If they have been coerced into the profession, is every contractual encounter a kind of rape? What if the method of coercion is more economic than it is physical and psychological, involving extremely limited options for making one's livelihood rather than the horror stories of 13-year-old girls getting "seasoned" into the profession, such as the work of Rachel Lloyd and Julian Sher reveals (Lloyd 2011; Sher 2011)? In discussing sex work, Junko Kuninobu expressed wariness of the concept of consent precisely because of the way it can eclipse the real world structural constraints on choice (Group Sisterhood 1998: 91). An encounter with a sex worker may have every overt indication of being consensual, and yet that encounter may have been made possible by extreme conditions of privation, psychological abuse, and the unequal capacity to find wage work. Given the growing epidemic of global sex work under far less than ideal circumstances, the inadequacy of the concept of consent to shed light on workers' real experiences, and even to mask the exchange as legitimate and legal, bodes poorly for the concept.

Brenda M. Baker has offered an amplification of the concept of consent that tries to address just such concerns (Baker 1999). By carefully considering the case of children who appear to consent, Baker's account can address gradations of consent and adverse background conditions that can overdetermine outcomes. Her proposal is to ensure that consent is understood performatively, following Nathan Brett, rather than as a disposition or psychological attitude that can be understood as implicit. In this way, consent avoids being subject to convenient interpretations by interested parties. But just as importantly, Baker differentiates consent from voluntary engagement. The latter is the sort of co-operative action that might be prompted in a child without that child knowing where the activity is leading, or what its full implications are. "Voluntary engagement in sexual activity,"

Baker argues, does not ensure consent because it does not entail the reasoning necessary for consent (1999: 56). If one cannot know the likely results of engaging in an exchange of playful genital touching, one cannot be said to have consented to sex.

However, expanding the concept of consent in this way when it applies to adults may lead to a problematically paternalist diminishment of agency. Building too many strictures into what may count as "real consent" invites third-party interpreters to be the final judge of the nature of the action. But beyond the agency of persons as actors, we need also to attend to the agency of persons as knowers, especially in regard to survivors. In the debate with Kuninobu, Masumi Yoneda argues that focusing on consent provides a way to respect women as knowers by giving epistemic privilege to the first-person point of view on their experience (Group Sisterhood 1998: 92). In regard to both rape and the moral status of prostitution, Yoneda argues that we should start from conferring an initial credibility on the claims of the involved parties. We confer dignity and epistemic credibility on the woman whose consent we take seriously as a decisive way to settle the question of whether she was harmed.

Yet how realistic can such a method of determining harm be, given the constitutive effects of background structural and discursive conditions? In response to Yoneda's argument, Kuninobu wonders whether it makes sense that only "the involved parties" should have the right to speak. If the concept can conceal structural processes that manufacture acquiescence and then name it consent, it may not be a sufficient test for harm.

Thus the feminist debate has ensued.[3] Kuninobu's position is that consent is descriptively inadequate, while Yoneda argues that it has good political effects in respecting survivors. Baker believes that the meaning of consent can be philosophically augmented by a more nuanced and developed account of agential action, while Pateman believes the concept is indelibly marked by its genealogy in liberal individualist ideal theory.

Descriptive concerns such as Pateman and Kuninobu share seem to foreclose the possibility of concepts morphing in unpredictable ways, as if their history fully determines their future. But if we reject the descriptive concerns on the grounds that it is smarter to consider a concept in terms of its possibilities for new iterations, then we may err on the side of indeterminacy, as if the materiality of sexual acts is infinitely plastic. The material reality of sexual encounters, including encounters that may ultimately be classified as rape, may provide the grounds for an approach to the concept and our assessment of its utility as well as its likely effect on the way sexual violence is understood. Thus it is a good idea to begin with looking at how the concept of consent works within a thick, phenomenological description of sexual activity and sexual violence. This can then help us answer the following question: If concepts are constitutive as well as referential, how does consent constitute rape?

Initial thoughts about the issue would indicate that there is a rather wide gulf between contract-based concepts of consent and the phenomenological features of sexual encounters. Recall that the concept of consent is largely derivative upon the discourse of contracts, and is most familiarly used today when we check off the small-print boxes in medical permission forms, privacy agreements, and credit reports—rather alienating and disembodied experiences. Consent is not a concept generally used in intimate or familial settings.

Pateman is right, however, that a great deal of political theory has assumed contractarian relations to be paradigmatic in both private and public social relationships, spanning everything from business to marriage to child custody, and has also assumed that the contract model provides the means for judging whether relationships can be considered just. But much of our lives is not driven by overt contracts, and so the area of tort law has developed as a way to determine what is just in the many sorts of cases where contracts are either nonexistent or implicit. Taking contract models as the paradigm of social relationships in order to settle the non-contract arenas of social life is more than a little bizarre, just as Pateman points out, as if social life is "nothing but contract all the way down." The problem is not just that contract models focus on the explicit terms of agreement and thus generally obscure the sort of structural background conditions that operate silently behind agreements. The problem is also that "the political fiction of property in the person" has conflated personhood with property in its assumption that "there are no limits on the property in the person that can be contracted out" (Pateman 2007: 17–18). The idea here, as the English philosopher John Locke originally argued, is that I can bargain over my own physical personhood in a contractual agreement. Locke differentiated the conditions of "free labor" from slave labor precisely via such an ability to bargain and consent to contracts, in which individuals enter into contracts with one another over the uses to which one's body or labor-power may be put.

But as Pateman points out, "property in the person cannot be contracted out in the absence of the owner." Personhood is not in material fact distinguishable from the body (Pateman and Mills 2007: 17). The capitalist and the laborer are not analogously alien from that which they are contributing to production, in the one case mere money, and in the other case time and labor. This begins to reveal the phenomenological difficulties with the concept of consent.

When issues of sexual violence are assimilated to a contractarian model, women's demands for redress become altered and in some cases distorted to fit a juridical model that requires proof of explicit consent, intent to commit harm, and prior agreements that set the terms for later activities. What clearly motivates this move to use the language of contracts and consent is the need for feminist legal and political activists to make use of existing frameworks and to be able to refer to the history of legal precedent. And theorists like Baker have adeptly made use of the contract concept, suitably filled out, to show how to construct a usefully general legal standard of liability. The concept of consent is also useful beyond the legal arena to mobilize current culturally mediated intuitions about sexual morality for the purposes of persuading the general public. And these domains are highly interdependent: a form of argument that will likely persuade the general public will then be likely to persuade juries and judges.

Despite Pateman's philosophical complaints about the meanings of the concept of consent, it is without question highly useful, explaining why one finds that the ideas of consent, of contracts, and of individuals who "own their own bodies" are widely used in Western feminist argument. Feminists have argued that "having control over this part of ourselves [i.e., how, when, and with whom we express our sexuality] is at the base of all our beliefs about personal rights, individual autonomy, and bodily integrity" (Funk 1993: 10). They have said women have the "right to choose," that we should have "control over our own bodies," that we should be able to do whatever we want as long as it is between "consenting" adults. This phrasing certainly hearkens back to Locke's notion that we can bargain over our physical selves.

When applied to sexual violence, the contractarian tradition defines rape and sexual abuse simply and clearly as sexual contact without a contract, implicit or explicit. The sexual engagement with one's body can legitimately happen only when one has, in effect, contracted it out. But despite the utility (and long history) of this discursive approach, does it carry some effects we are unaware of? Many feminist care ethicists and political scientists have noted that the contractarian model of human relations is applicable only to a small range (see, e.g., Kittay 1999; Pateman 1988, 2002). Relations involving familial bonds, or any bonds of affect and friendship, are not usefully illuminated by the concept of a contract, given that contracts assume relations that are freely chosen and entirely volitional. Familial relations are not generally volitional, nor is the energy expended on children generally given with an expectation of fair compensation, but simply in the joy of the act itself, or out of a sense of duty. There is something phenomenologically inadequate about describing labor in the public sphere as the contracting out of one's body, as if it were a brute machine. Gauthier has tried to make use of this odd analogy between labor and sex by stretching protective legislation for workers to include women under unequal social conditions. He makes a persuasive case for a reform under non-ideal conditions, but is his proposal propping up our willingness to accept such non-ideal conditions? That is, does his proposal help us to find intuitively plausible analogies that we would be better off rejecting?

When contractarian models are applied to human relations that involve sexuality, the dissonance is just as pronounced. The metaphysics implied by a contract model assumes that I can contract out my body and my sexuality, but this splits body and personhood in a way that makes little sense of human experience. If my body is having sex, then I am having sex. One might think that the concept of consent would fare better than the concept of contracts, but it is equally inadequate. The act of choice, implied in legal concepts of consent, implies a decision made prior to an act in which I contract with the other in order to make use of my body and his (or hers) in certain ways. But the nature of human sexuality belies this description. (Let me stress here that in the following analysis I am setting aside questions of moral and legal culpability and responsibility in favor of descriptive adequacy. The issue of culpability is of course crucial, but it too needs to emerge from a descriptively adequate account of sex and sexual violence.)

A phenomenologically apt description of sexuality under its best conditions would reveal, not a desire laying complete before the act, but one evoked, made manifest, in the act itself. In other words, my sexuality emerges in intersubjective interaction, and my intentionality must be understood as both embodied and as having a temporal modality. I know what I want to do fully and with certainty only in the very moment I do it. Moreover, the actions and sensations of the body, the body itself, are coterminous with and thus constitutive of the self, rather than something the self experiences from a distance. This is precisely why rape is so damaging, as Ann Cahill has argued: it is not something separate from my self that has been stolen from me and used against my will (as a contract model might assume), but a piece of myself which has been transformed with lasting effects. Cahill says: "The intersubjectivity of embodiment allows us to understand that the embodied self is significantly affected, even constructed, in relation to others and to the actions of others" (Cahill 2001: 9).

Rape, then, needs to be understood as an event that alters subjectivity or selfhood.[4] Some rape victims are all but lifeless during the violation; but others are forced to perform acts, to play as if they liked it, and some are even made to feel sexual arousal simply through the mechanics of genital stimulation. These acts are no less a violation, but can be even more troubling to the survivor as she later attempts to incorporate the part of herself that was elicited in the experience into a coherent narrative of identity.[5]

A contract approach falsely characterizes the metaphysics of the self by assuming a separation of subjecthood from embodied experience, wherein the consenting "I" operates over and even against the body. It assumes I am freely exchanging that which I have a kind of instrumental control over, that which I can "turn on or off." It also makes a temporality error in assuming that I have a bounded and formed self making decisions that range over later temporal moments, as if I can promise or decisively determine at one period in time what my subjective experiences will be at a later period of time. In reality, I cannot control at one temporal moment the affective responses or desires that may emerge at another moment.

Thus, although the language of contracts and consent works well to make use of existing conceptions of the self in some societies and to mobilize familiar legal strategies in order to protect women from harm and increase our power, it does not accord well with our lived experience of either sex or sexual violence. I want to suggest that this disanalogy between embodiment and contractual relations is one reason why the anti-rape movement has been unable to address effectively many important facets of the problem of sexual violence, such as, for example, the difficulty of getting a successful prosecution for rape of a prostitute. Prostitutes are assumed to have "contracted out" their bodies. They may be able to demand payment but their ability to charge rape is not widely accepted. Contractual thinking also makes it difficult to prosecute rape against both husbands and dates in the context of relations presumed to have set terms decided in advance that predetermine the scope of intimate interaction.

Contract models also create difficulties in regard to rapes that occur after the consensual sexual encounter has begun, in which the woman wants to stop at a certain point in the middle, so to speak, but her partner forces her to continue. In such situations women sometimes acquiesce and continue uncomfortably and only later name the experience a violation. Contractarian approaches provide support for victim-blaming when such women later claim violation because they are castigated as women who want to avoid responsibility for their initial consent. Contract models can also make it difficult to accept a person's reinterpretation of a prior event, in which they re-understand the event in a new light. But isn't the true nature of experience often this way—that is, an unfolding narrative subject to interpretation in light of new experience and new knowledge, as well as simply the time and space to think? I now reinterpret a relationship that I thought at the time to be egalitarian and reciprocal as one based on rigid gender roles and a lack of respect. I see my former partner in a new light. Whether I consented or not to a given act or event is not always decisive in the reassessment of the relation as manipulative, exploitative, perhaps even violent. The full meaning of the events and experiences of our lives are not preset or predetermined by prior consent.

Clearly, the language of consent is motivated by a need to determine culpability in a juridical context. And I would agree that a reinterpretation of an event or a relationship cannot necessarily be used to establish the culpability of one's partner, especially if one at the time expresses a willing desire. But before we jump to the concern with how to establish reasonable culpability, we should endeavor to develop a fuller understanding of sexual experience and sexual violence. Accounts of responsibility should flow *from* a more fully adequate description, rather than constraining our very ability to develop that description. The point of developing the description will not only be to eventually improve legal strategies, but also to create a realistic discourse around sexual violence in which survivors will be able to recognize their experiences. Once one can more ably name one's experiences, one is more likely to break the stigma of silence.

In truth, experiences of sexual violence are often complex, rarely simple, and sometimes ambiguous. When experience must be described and analyzed as if it is simple and unambiguous, with a fixed and stable meaning, victims become motivated to cover up the complexity of their violation. For example, they may be motivated to conceal the fact that they said "no" in the middle of the act, or to hide the part they played or their relationship with the rapist, or worse, they may simply stay silent about the trauma. Such omissions inhibit not only the possibility of prosecution but also the ability of survivors to seek support or counseling.

One of the most difficult and troubling cases for the contract model involves child sexual abuse. In some cases children or young adolescents will apparently participate actively in sexual activity with adults.

They may even elicit, or appear to elicit, the activity. Many countries have dealt with this problem by retreating from the contractarian model in these kinds of cases in favor of statutory categories for determining when rape has occurred, arguing that adult–child sex is a violation by reason of the status of the participants rather than the presence or absence of consent. However, because status-based laws ignore consent, they have been attacked by a new movement of sexual libertarians who argue that adults convicted in such cases have been wronged because children sometimes consent to sex, and consent is sufficient to assess harm. Status-based offenses have also been criticized by proponents who argue that we need to adopt a cultural relativism in order to address, for example, homophobia in teenage culture and other cultural differences concerning the age of (sexual) consent and the widely variant developmental trajectories of adolescents in diverse communities and societies.

Although there can certainly be a strategically targeted use of status offenses to regulate homosexuality or enforce general prohibitions against teenage sex, the concept of the status-based offense provides a helpful check on the hegemony of consent-based approaches, and is sometimes simply an apt description of the nature of the malfeasance. If consent is problematic in some adult cases because of its capacity to conceal manipulation, it is even more so with children. Thus in my view the problem is not with the concept of the status-based offense *per se*, though we may still find cause to critique some forms of its application (this will be discussed further in the next section on honor).

The controversy over the concept of status reveals, I believe, further problems with the contractarian paradigm. If the main way in which a society judges human relationships is in terms of contracts, autonomy, consent, and so on, then it will be put on the defensive when it abrogates this approach and retreats to the paternalism evident in statutory rape laws. Such laws will be vulnerable to contestation, therefore, and will not be very secure. The libertarian critics are right that the continued use of status-based charges produces a slippery slope toward the undermining of consent, but the problem here may be with consent itself.

Children involved in relationships with adults are often "contracting" for something other than sex, such as attention, affection, emotional engagement, and financial support, but they are in such a desperate situation that sex is the only way they can get these other needs met. The sexual libertarian Pat Califia defends sexual relations between adults and children or youth on the grounds that "there is nothing wrong with a more privileged adult offering a young person money, privacy, freedom of movement, new ideas and sexual pleasure" (Califia 1981: 138). The "and" in this list suggests that the first four goods are tied to the last, turning what may appear to be a beneficent relationship into a form of opportunist manipulation. Otherwise, why isn't it sexual pleasure alone that is offered, without the extras? But this is precisely a common scenario of pedophilia, in which there is seduction, manipulation, and a kind of exchange in place of overt violence. The result is that the young person learns to offer sex for attention, companionship, money, and so on. Consent is irrelevant to judging harm in such cases.

A further consideration emerges from the therapeutic literature. Many victims, including both adult women and children, are motivated to protect their assailants. They may feel sympathy with the perpetrator, perhaps due to feminine socialization or from sharing a familial or other form of prior relationship, and they may also be economically or emotionally dependent on the perpetrator. Given such motivations to protect their perpetrator, claiming consent is their best method for doing so in some societies. Status-based criteria for sexual violence remove this option, which can provide a deterrence for men who may otherwise believe that they could garner, in one way or another, a verbal consent.

The question is whether the concept of consent can be adequately revised or expanded so that background structural inequalities can be made relevant, or whether it's simply inapplicable as a descriptive concept in such cases. At the end of this chapter I will discuss how we might answer this question, but first, it will be useful to contrast contract approaches with less individualist approaches that are markedly different at least in some respects from the contract model.

6.2 "Honor" crimes

In feminist debates over the concept of "honor" crimes, considerations arise that provide an interesting contrast to the contract model. As Uma Chakravarti has argued, the concept of honor has tended to exacerbate the problematic tendency of some Western feminist critics to perceive Asian cultures as irrational and pre-Modern, and to operate with a reified East/West binary (Chakravarti 2005: 308). Along with its problematic effects in the global arena of discourse, the concept of honor crime also has problems on the local level: in numerous legal cases honor has been invoked to excuse a crime and mitigate a sentence. Chakravarti's extensive study of honor crimes in northern India leads her to argue that the concept "is essentially a means of maintaining the material structures of 'social' power and social dominance" (Chakravarti 2005: 309).

Yet the fact that this concept has such a discursive utility for these crimes is itself an interesting cultural difference, contrasted with the utility of concepts about "temporary insanity" or "crimes of passion" that are routinely used to mitigate punishment elsewhere (especially throughout north and south America). So the point of contrast I would make here is a discursive one, that is, a contrast in the way violence against women is characterized after the fact. This does not in itself establish a causal or motivational contrast that might *explain* the violence against women—in this case, women in one's family—especially given that such violence is so widespread.

The discursive contrast operating here might be characterized as a contrast between individualized contract-based consent models and communitarian, status-based models. The latter, unlike the former, invoke ideas about inter-subjective obligations, the basic differences between categories of persons, and the ways in which sexual acts and relations affect and even constitute personhood. Status-based concepts assume, for example, that children and adults are not interchangeable, and that there is no equal reciprocity of obligations that obtain across this difference. Adults have certain obligations to children that the presence of consent cannot render null. Though it is often the *victim*'s honor that is purported to be altered in an act of violence, there is also a widespread view that victimizing children or other vulnerable groups is a highly dishonorable way to conduct oneself, that there is something about such crimes that exceeds things like burglary or bank robbing and attaches a moral stigma to the person who engages in it. Putting it in this way indicates a discursive shift from consent-based to virtue-based moral judgments.

The concept of honor invokes another interesting element absent from contract models: that a violation produces effects on other persons besides the immediate victim. Any adequate description of sexual violence would confirm that such effects are universal across cultures, that is, that others are *always* affected. Moreover, we might also affirm that these collateral effects are, in most cases, detrimental. This suggests that sexual crimes against individuals are always also crimes against the others that they are in relation with, such as their families, children, communities.

Still, we should legitimately be concerned if the concept of the "honor crime" de-emphasizes the detrimental effects on the individual victim herself in favour of emphasizing its effects on her family; in fact, in some cases the concept may replace one kind of harm with the other entirely. Yet it is not in error to hold that there will be effects on the family, as well as others. The concept may be wrong in some cases in its description of what those effects are, but there is an indubitable stigma and shame attached to a publicly disclosed humiliation of almost any sort, especially a sexual one. The experience of shame and stigma is not necessarily just the effect of ideology: there is something phenomenologically understandable in feeling shame about being treated with no more respect or dignity than a spittoon.

Another scholar who has analyzed the discourses around "honor crimes," Kalpana Kannabiran, has argued that it is just such communal and shaming effects that motivate rapes of "women of minority groups—religious as well as caste—which signifies the rape of the community to which the woman belongs" (Kannabiran 1996: 33). Kannabiran is thus referring to rapes that cross ethnic, caste, or religious lines, and suggesting that these have as their target whole groups rather than just individuals. I suspect that such motivations are also operating in some cases when rapes cross racial and ethnic lines in Western societies. Certainly the long history of sanctioned sexual violence by whites against African Americans often had communal and not just individual targets. We might criticize such acts on the grounds that they are reducing the victims, in most cases women, to pawns in a communal conflict, or, in other words, that they have stripped away the woman's individuality in order to view them as representatives of a community. But in doing so we risk losing sight of how rape always has communal effects even if it does not always have community-directed motivations. An anti-rape analysis needs to take into account those communal effects rather than exclusively focusing on the individual rights of the victim. It is not disrespectful of victims or belittling of their individual rights to take into account the fact that their lives are intertwined with meaningful relations that will also be affected by their violation.

The concept of status is also invoked in feminist analyses of how "typologies" of women figure in the practices of sexual violence. Rape is used to season girls for prostitution all over the world, and it is used to transform rebellious wives into compliant ones. Rape is also used to stigmatize "good" women as "bad" or as marked forever afterward by a sexual taint. In the West there has been resistance to this last idea on the grounds that the personhood of the woman cannot be altered or morally compromised by an act done to her, without her consent. That is, we have wanted to say that rape shames the rapist, and not the victim. This is clearly true on one level, but if we follow through on the phenomenological description given earlier and the one Cahill develops, we have to allow that personhood, or subjectivity, which is not quite the same, can be altered by non-volitional experiences.[6] The rape of children is sometimes linked to a sharp increase in sexual activity on their part afterward, not turning them "bad" but making them appear bad by most social conventions. Thus, rape might quite effectively be used to alter the subjectivity of persons, of their social and sexual selves, their interrelations with others, and the role they are capable of playing in a family and community. The rape of women used as pawns in a communal fight, then, has the metaphysics of the situation right—given the reverberating effects of the crime on the subjectivity of the victim as well as on many of her relations. This expands rather than mitigates the offensiveness of the crime.

Chakravarti's research reveals another interesting element in the way the concept of honor is used in practice. Although her research on northern India is focused on violence targeted at those who resist arranged marriages, the analysis is relevant here. Daughters who refuse arranged marriages are said to bring dishonor on their family and communities, especially, though not exclusively, when their own choices involve partners of different castes or religions. And in order to bring charges against their daughters, parents and the courts make use of the concept of consent. Was the daughter old enough to make a choice of her own will? Did the man she chose against her parent's wishes coerce her in some way? Courts will overturn marriages if the authenticity of the daughter's consent can be rendered questionable, but the procedure for determining the authenticity of consent is ripe for abuse: parents have altered birth records to change their daughter's age, made false claims about kidnapping, attributed madness, perhaps "hormonal madness," to their daughters, and so on (Chakravarti 2005: 321). Daughters who are returned to their families by the courts on the grounds that their consent was not authentic are then sometimes killed, and their male partners beaten or killed as well. The law's (purported) efforts to protect young women makes use of the concept of consent, but consent turns out to be a highly unreliable concept for protecting women from violence, and in fact can facilitate such violence.

Clearly, the problem here flows from how consent is construed and applied. Consent is construed very narrowly when it applies to the daughters' own choices of partners, and has to meet a high bar. Chakravarti points out that the opposite is the case in rape trials, where consent is used quite liberally:

judges often not only accept but even cast women as consenting partners in cases of rape, dismissing the charges . . . Yet when a woman "elopes" the argument of consent is not accepted. It appears that choice— or desire—as expressed by a woman is somehow intrinsically illicit when it is against parental diktat and caste or community norms, and therefore needs to be disrupted. Thus in situations that could actually be licit sexual relations within marriage, women are not regarded as being able to be consenting partners—or else they must simply be incapable of consenting through their status as minors, intrinsically incapable of discretion on account of their age. It is as if women have no capacity for rational judgment or discretion in any case. (Chakravarti 2005: 321)

Here, one's capacity to consent is based on one's rationality and emotional maturity, traits that have not been strongly associated with women in most cultures. This reveals the weakness of the concept of consent in protecting women from violence, and that in fact consent can be useful in *harming* women.

How then does this discourse of "honor" and "consent" shed light on the usefulness of such concepts for reducing violence against women? One thing it suggests is that what may be different across cultures or societies are discursive constructions of the crime of sexual violence, its motivation or at least the motivation-under-a-description, and some of the specifics of its harm and its effects. Different concepts are useful in different societies for making sense of violence as well as justifying crimes, mitigating sentences, and blaming victims. But these differences at the discursive level coexist with some apparent universals, such as the existence of extra-individual effects and the effect of violence on the subjectivity of the victim.

One can also see more clearly from these cases that, just as honor is invoked to mitigate punishment in some societies, so the focus on consent has a similar motivation. That is, the language of contracts may be largely in place because it promises strong protection for men against unfair accusation. If a man can show he has a "contract" for services, then he can claim good faith on his part, even if the contract is very informal and subject to culturally inflected modes of interpreting communication (such as, in times past, "I paid for her dinner, therefore she owes me sex"). The woman, in contrast, must be able to establish not only that she was harmed but that she did not "sign the contract" even by a gesture (or apparel) that could have been misconstrued. Thus, *her* intent is subordinated to *his*: if she did not intend to have sex, but did not communicate this clearly enough for the courts to recognize, she cannot claim rape. If he "unintentionally" misinterpreted her signals, he is absolved of blame. Her intent establishes nothing; his intent establishes everything. Discursive traditions—whether they involve "honor" or "consent"—are made use of for protecting the perpetrators. Relying on these same traditions to construct anti-rape policies may well be inadequate for reducing the crimes. What is clear is that no tradition of discourse—including consent-based, classical liberal ones—is invulnerable to being used to sanction sexual violence. The solution cannot be simply to replace honor discourse with a consent-based discourse. Both concepts have a partial but limited metaphysical adequacy to describe aspects of sexual violence, but both can be made use of for varied purposes. Societies that focus less on consent than others are not necessarily wrong for that reason, though their discourses may have other, independent problems.

6.3 "Victim"

The association of women with victimization has exacerbated existing gender ideologies about women in many cultures as weak-minded and vulnerable. This in turn has led to the assumption that traumatic experiences have more far-reaching effects on women than they would on men.[7] These problems are aggravated by recent diagnostic concepts such as 'victim personality disorders' that blame victims and essentialize women as having psychological pathologies that invite abuse and assault.[8]

Feminist writer Naomi Wolf's rejection of what she calls "victim feminism" seems to buy into this characterization. Wolf defines victim feminism as "when a woman seeks power through an identity of powerlessness . . . [that] takes our trousseau reflexes and transposes them into a mirror-image set of 'feminist' conventions" (Wolf 1994: 135). Wolf makes references to Adrienne Rich, Catherine MacKinnon, and Andrea Dworkin as examples, even though it is difficult to imagine the late Andrea Dworkin as operating from "trousseau reflexes" in any form. On Wolf's account, any demand for redress of gender-related harms may be taken to be a form of victim feminism, and certainly any account that offers detailed descriptions of such harms. However, though I take Wolf's characterization of victim feminism to be problematic, her arguments are diagnostic of the current discursive arena.

Part of Wolf's concern with the use of the concept "victim" in the context of social movements and social change may be a legitimate concern, and that is whether it has the effect of eclipsing the actual presence of agency. In some instances it may be difficult to judge where agency lies. For example, there is a healthy debate in the feminist literature on global sex workers as to whether the word victim should be used to apply to workers in the industry. This eclipses women's agency in choosing sex work over other options, and can invite paternalistic policies that actually reduce the choices and thus the effective agency of especially immigrant and poor women (Kempadoo 1998).

Moreover, the term victim resonates with stereotypes not just of women in a generic sense (if there is such a sense) but of specific groups of women, with detrimental effects. As Alison Murray explains,

> The anti-trafficking campaigns actually have a detrimental effect on workers and increase discrimination as they perpetuate the stereotype of Asian workers as passive and diseased. Clients are encouraged to think of Asian workers as helpless victims who are unable to resist, so that they may be more likely to violate the rights of these workers. (Murray 1998: 58)

Thus, her concern with the use of the concept of victim is that it may exacerbate exploitation by increasing market value: women who are construed as likely to be passive in the face of unfair treatment have a commodity value higher than non-victims since they can be more thoroughly exploited. This may also generate a higher eroticized effect on desire. What this suggests is that, as we saw with the concepts of honor and consent, the different connotations of the concept "victim" might be mobilized for very different purposes, not all of which have to do with protecting women. An assessment of the term's political effects needs to take specific contexts of use into account.

In the feminist roundtable on prostitution in Japan mentioned earlier, the term "victim" also comes up for debate. Recall that in that discussion, Junko Kuninobu expressed wariness about relying on consent, whereas Masumi Yoneda argued in favor of it insofar as it privileges the first-person point of view. Yoneda's admonishment about giving women epistemic authority over the nature of their experience is probably a response to the way in which women are epistemically disauthorized in nearly every culture. Thus her claim acts as a contextually informed heuristic responding to cross-cultural phenomena of epistemic disempowerment.

There may be further commonalities across cultures concerning women's reluctance to identify as victims. For example, common responses to violation include denial, often as a means for self-protection. Liz Kelly and Jill Radford cite studies that note that "naming and reporting" a rape were seen by some "women as worsening the[ir] situation," not improving it. They also report that "in a U.S. study of 6,159 U.S. college students—when an analytic definition of rape was based on a composite of legal codes, only 27% of women whose experiences fitted the research definition named their own experience as rape" (Kelly and Radford 1998: 61). That study was replicated on a smaller scale in New Zealand with similar findings (Gavey 1991). Kelly and Radford argue that silencing is "still commonplace" in societies where it is comparatively easy to speak about sexual assault. "Choosing to forget or minimize events may transcend culture as a response to the trauma of victimization" (Kelly and Radford 1998: 68). Thus, resistance to the term "victim" may be a widespread psychological defense mechanism and also a defensive strategy against the likely treatment victims receive.

One might wonder whether individualistic societies score worse here. That is, is it harder to admit oneself to be victimized in cultures where individual agency tends to be over-inflated? Certainly in the United States, individuals and groups who claim victimization are routinely accused of political opportunism, self-pity, and the refusal to take responsibility for their own problems (see, e.g., Loury 1995). Thus, ascribing victimhood to oneself makes one vulnerable to such charges. Male victims may be especially disinclined to self-identify as victims because of its dissonance with conventions of masculinity. This indicates that we need to take not only culture but also gender and sexuality into account in assessing discursive practices and their effects.

However, cultures with less individualist proclivities may have their own reasons to eschew the concept of the victim, which is, after all, an attribution about an individual's treatment at the hands of another or group of others. In societies where there is a "corporate sense of identity within an ideal of extreme cohesiveness," that is, in kinship societies, claims of victimization hurt not merely the individual but the group by threatening to sever affective and practical ties (Dobash and Dobash 1998: 12). In cases where the individual's overall quality of life, even indeed her ability to live, are tied to her inclusion within a community, the resistance to the term "victim" may be high. This does not indicate, however, that the term is never apt to describe a given event.

Does the term "victim" also have phenomenological difficulties, as we saw with the concept of consent? It may indeed feel dissonant with the sense of oneself as a survivor. But the term continues to be used in the survivor literature: the term "survivor" does not so much replace the term "victim" as supplement it. And some theorists, such as Kelly,

Burton, and Regan (1996), argue persuasively for the complementarity of these terms: one is a survivor of victimization. Some people report, interestingly, that they are uncomfortable using the designation "survivor" because they feel they don't yet "qualify" (Kelly and Radford 1998: 61).

To the extent that the terms "victim" and "survivor" are taken as stable and fixed identities, they seem to pose problems for a phenomenological account. Further phenomenological considerations concern the actual variability of rape. A wide variation of experiences is recognized by clinicians and therapists, who often discuss with their clients what kind of term (rape, sexual assault, sexual abuse, sexual molestation, for example) is most accurate for what they experienced, a sometimes complicated process. But the variability of the crime is less often discussed within feminist theory, which tends to treat it as a unified concept. In some cases activists assume that challenges to the unity and clear boundaries of the concept of rape, for example, are just attempts to dilute its political importance.[9]

Survivors often have trouble naming their experience as rape or even assault if it does not fit the paradigm of a stranger who uses physical force. But there can be many types of coercion and degrees of coerciveness, and the victim might not have voiced opposition if she was passed out, paralyzed with fear, or just afraid to escalate the violence. Moreover, rape is still sometimes defined exclusively as vaginal penetration, sometimes even requiring ejaculation, which makes no phenomenological sense if the crime is defined in relation to sexual trauma or harm. From the victim's point of view, penetration in any orifice might be equally traumatic, and whether one uses a penis or a broomstick may not make a difference either.[10]

On the one hand, we may be legitimately suspicious that the recalcitrance to name a larger class of cases as rape is the product of legal narrowness, an interest in protecting the accused, etc. On the other hand, we have to be prepared to honor the variety of human experience and give at least initial credibility to the victim's own assessments of their experiences.

The scope of the term rape is subject to ongoing disputation in the courts, among clinicians, and among scholars. Is it rape when a prostitute is forced to have sex with a john she'd rather not service? Is it rape when a partner becomes so excitedly aggressive in the midst of an act that he or she ignores the sudden discomfort of their partner? Is it rape when a 13-year-old says to an adult, "oh, alright"? Some of the discomfort about the word "victim" may well come from persons who are still in the process of narrativizing their experience, or from those who insist on the real complexity of their experience. Such reasons would constitute what I would call phenomenological grounds to decline or at least complicate the attribution of the word "victim."

To summarize this discussion of the controversy over the concept of victim, then, I would suggest the following. There are indeed non-contextual (or non-contingent) reasons to be wary of the term, reasons such as the variability of the experience and the connotations of a stable identity invoked by the noun version of the concept (which might be mitigated by a more dynamic construction like "victimization"). But these reasons apply only against its overuse. There are also non-contextual (or non-contingent) reasons to be skeptical about our wariness of the term: because such wariness may be motivated by common psychological tendencies of self-protection and denial, or because it is motivated by a cultural context that over-inflates individual agency and makes masculinity imaginatively impervious to victimization. Thus, our wariness of the term "victim" should be analyzed and unpacked, and in some cases resisted. If self-protection requires denial of harm, then we need to address the context in which denial is the best option.[11]

And finally, there are specific contextual reasons to be legitimately wary of the term in certain discursive contexts where regressive gender ideologies will be mobilized and perhaps strengthened by its use. These are no doubt Wolf's concerns. However, once again, these contextual considerations do not provide an argument against the adequacy in all cases of the term itself, and thus the better response than a general repudiation of the word "victim" is to address directly the faulty connotations it mobilizes.

6.4 Conclusion

The effort to advance justice for victims of sexual violation needs to become cognizant of the cross-cultural and transnational contexts within which our activist and legal remedies operate. We need to be open to the possibility that we will never be able to gather global statistics because the definitions will continue to vary, and yet the use of wider and looser concepts like "sexual violation" should be able to incorporate multiple kinds of experiences and provide some global picture of the problem. This linguistic pluralism is not mandated by a discursive idealism, but is consistent with an account that places phenomenological limits on how we interpret the nature of embodied harms. Our principal focus should be on making it possible for survivors to come forward, to have the narrative space to develop a sense of what happened to them even when it includes ambiguity and complexity.

Earlier I asked the question whether the concept of consent might be subject to an improved revision, in order to retain its utility while making it more descriptively apt. In conclusion I will address this question to all of the concepts this chapter has discussed.

First, a revision of any concept will need to operate with a two-tiered approach. We want concepts that will be able to accord with more accurate and comprehensively adequate descriptions of the phenomenological experience of the victim's point of view, given that it is this very point of view that has been largely ignored. So this first tier of our approach should be aiming for descriptive adequacy, in which the victim's own experience is at the cornerstone. At another level, however, we should also retain awareness of the contextual variability of concepts and their multiple strategic effects in different contexts. Thus, contexts can determine what the likely legal or political effects of the use of a term will be, and what connotations it will be likely to mobilize. I would argue that both of these levels, or tiers, of analysis should be operational in revisionary work, without one side entirely eclipsing the other.

The history of the concept of consent in its application to sexual violence surely comes out of a classical liberal tradition of contractarian thinking, in which one can contract out one's labor power just as one can contract out the use of one's property. And female sexual body parts—vaginas and wombs in particular—were historically construed as property, with greater or lesser market value depending on whether they were virginal. This property was not owned by the women themselves but by their fathers or husbands, who had rights of exchange, use, and, in some cases, the right to dispose of them in any way they chose. When a woman was raped, it was as if a squatter had illegitimately possessed someone's else's property—thus the crime was against her husband or father, who could legally take violent action against the squatter. Ejaculation made a difference in rape law because then the property being taken was not just the vagina but also, potentially, the womb.

When women began to gain rights, they gained rights along the male model. Thus they gained the right to "own" the property of their own bodies as this "property" was owned by fathers or husbands before. The property could be contracted out, exchanged, even sold, just as before, on the basis of a free consent.

If we now try to alter this discursive approach, putting the experience of victims at the center, we might want to change the legal definition of rape from penetration in the vagina with ejaculation, where such laws are still on the books, to penetration of any orifice with any human body part or physical object. We might also want to replace the concept of consent with the concept of willingness. The concept of consent easily lends itself to what I called the temporal problem, in which we assume an ability to instrumentalize one's body over a temporal range as if we could determine the open flow of our experiences in the future. The concept of willingness, by contrast, does not lend itself so easily to a single moment of time—the moment in which we are said to consent—and can also be more easily accommodated to an embodied notion. To say that I consent invokes images of signed documents or stated vows, whereas the idea of willingness invokes an image of a whole person whose will has been engaged in the event or process.

Work on sexual violence across cultural differences should operate with a two-tiered approach looking for both commonalities and differences. We need to devise categories and conceptualizations for that which is common and widespread as well as that which is more culturally distinct. Eva Lundgren's distinction between the constitutive and the regulative levels of bodily experience nicely organizes such a two-tiered approach without making the more basic level static or outside the realm of the social (Lundgren 1998). Her aim is to capture the phenomenological commonalities of violation without underemphasizing the cultural variation in physical, psychological, and discursive responses.

Resistance to the concept of consent may come from culturally specific ideologies or it may come from a concern for phenomenological accuracy. I am more inclined to be wary of the overuse made of the concept of consent because of its general inadequacy for the very specific nature of human sexual practice and embodied intentionality.

In regard to the term "victim", I believe the problems with the concept are not as indefeasible as the problems with the concept of consent. Connotations that imply stability and reified status are serious problems, but resistance to the term is more about denial and ideology than about its phenomenological and descriptive inadequacy.

I know this short essay has not in any sense fully succeeded at this, but I do believe it has hinted at how an analysis of Western discursive debates over concepts like "consent" and "victim" can benefit from a more global contextualization, to make us strange to ourselves as well as to show how quite common some of our difficulties turn out to be.

It also might provide some theoretical and conceptual resources from the language games played elsewhere that are not simply negative lessons but that hold some quite useful lessons for us all.

Notes

1 In assessing words, obviously language choice is relevant, and the translations of terms may not be exact, although the English words "victim" and "consent" are similar in Spanish and French (*victima* and *victime*, respectively, and *consentir*), two languages used widely in the global South. Yet a similar word may not carry the same history of cultural connotations, philosophical assumptions, and political resonance across different societies. What I am principally after, however, are the *concepts* used to identify and to describe when, and under what conditions, sexual violence has occurred.
2 See, for example, *Prosecutor v. Dragoljub Kunarac, Radomir Kovac and Zoran Vukovic*, Case No. IT-96–23-T & IT-96–23/1-T, Judgment on February 22, 2001.
3 For a related discussion, see Shrage 1994. Shrage stages a debate between Christine Overall and Janet Richards on prostitution, where again the concept of consent is the key term.
4 Susan Brison's work (2002) is useful here in understanding the effect of rape on one's sense of having a continuous self, which is necessary for agency.
5 One of the best narrative accounts of this is in Allison 1993.
6 See, e.g., Hester et al. 1996, a study that looks at the effects of violence on women across differences of identity.
7 Judith Herman's work, among others, shows the falsity of this claim (see Herman 1997).
8 Some feminist psychologists have responded with a list of diagnostic concepts of their own, including such items as "male personality disorder" (see Caplan 1995).
9 For example, at my own institution there was an intense controversy over several months about a proposed change in the name of a campus service provider from the R.A.P.E. Center (standing for Rape Advocacy, Prevention, and Education) to the Sexual Assault Services Center. Clinicians and survivors favored the more expansive term "sexual assault" whereas advocates worried about "diluting" the concept of rape.
10 Again here I am not concerned with issues of culpability or legal action, just with the metaphysics of the event itself.
11 But I would also guard against feminist coerciveness about demanding disclosure.

7

Reforming Our Taxation Arrangements to Promote Global Gender Justice

Gillian Brock

7.1 Introduction

Global gender justice obtains when persons, whatever their gender, (1) are equally enabled to meet their basic needs; (2) have equal protection for their basic liberties; (3) enjoy fair terms of co-operation in collective endeavors; and when (4) social and political arrangements are in place that support 1–3. What is entailed by 1–4 is covered in book-length form elsewhere (Brock 2009). My focus in this chapter concerns creating equitable ways of funding basic elements common to any plausible accounts of global justice and global gender justice. I contend that failure to ensure such equitable arrangements are in place entails that the global basic structure is unjust. Moreover, as I argue, this failure inevitably means that the global basic structure entails gender injustice.

Poverty is one of the most pressing manifestations of global injustice, affecting about half the world's total population.[1] In developing countries the vast majority of women are poor, so adequately addressing global poverty will be especially welcome to women. Furthermore, because adequate funding for public services has special importance for women (for one thing, in the absence of such services, their labor burden can be significantly increased, as I discuss), ensuring the necessary funding is secured to provide these services has gender relevance. The rate at which we are depleting and destroying the global commons is another pressing obstacle to global justice. Failing to protect the global commons has a bearing not only on current and future global poverty but, indeed, on the capacity of the planet to provide a life-sustaining environment, and thus on everyone's ability to meet their basic needs.

The focus for this chapter is taxation and accounting arrangements and how they are part of the problem, but also how they can be transformed to become part of the solution. The structure of the chapter is as follows. In the next section I explore several general problems with our current taxation and accounting arrangements that allow vast amounts of taxable revenue to escape taxation. In the third section I discuss some justifications for levying global taxes and outline several proposals for how these might work. In section four I examine issues of gender justice and taxation. Taxes have important disproportionate effects for women, especially poor women. I review why this is. I also review some recent trends that show that the tax burden is shifting from business owners to workers and also from men to women. In light of the analysis we then return to some of the most plausible contenders for global taxes and discuss their gender implications in section five. The Tobin Tax (a tax on currency conversions) emerges as a promising candidate. However, it is also important to appreciate that the reforms discussed in section two (concerning stemming the flow of tax evasion and avoidance) should be pursued most urgently, as all of these reduce the need to raise further revenue. Eliminating tax havens and blocking avenues that currently provide so much scope for tax escape should be on the agenda to achieve more gender equity. Section six covers some of the ways in which we can enjoy a measure of implementation success given current realities. Section seven concludes. Insofar as we fail to reform our tax arrangements,[2] the basic institutional structure of the global economy will remain unjust, and, as I also explain, involves global gender injustice.

7.2   Some problems with our taxation and accounting arrangements and a few solutions

Tax escape is rampant. It is estimated, for instance, that an amount equivalent to one-third of the total global Gross Domestic Product is held offshore in tax havens, or effectively beyond the reach of taxation (Oxfam 2000; Lopatin 2002).[3] It is further estimated that *about half of all world trade* passes through tax-haven jurisdictions, as profits are shifted to places where tax can be avoided.[4] The policy of "transfer pricing" and other complex financial structures reduce transparency, thus facilitating tax evasion. It is estimated that, through such schemes, developing countries lose revenue amounting to far more than the annual flow of aid (Oxfam 2000: 3; see also Cobham 2005).[5] As one example, consider Ray Baker's (2005) analysis according to which about 3 percent of the 500 to 800 billion dollars of illicit annual financial outflows from developing countries relates to bribery and corruption of public officials. By contrast 60 to 65 percent relates to corporate tax evasion. Consider also that for each dollar of aid that flows into a country, six to seven dollars of corporate tax evasion flows out (Baker 2005). This gives us a sense of the scale of the problems we are facing.

Tax evasion and avoidance threaten both development and democracy, especially in developing countries (Oxfam 2000: 3). Because large corporations and wealthy individuals are effectively escaping taxation, the tax burden is frequently shifted onto ordinary citizens and smaller businesses. Governments often thereby collect much-reduced sums insufficient to achieve minimal goals of social justice, such as providing decent public goods and services, which can also have a dramatic effect on developing or maintaining robust democracies (Christian Aid 2005).[6] Furthermore, because most developing countries are in competition in trying to attract foreign capital, offering tax breaks or tax havens may seem to provide an attractive course. However, as states compete to offer tax exemptions to capital, the number of tax havens increases, thereby making developing countries worse off. Corporations pay much-reduced, if any, taxes, and ordinary citizens have to bear more of the cost of financing the social and public goods necessary for sustaining well-functioning communities (Mitchell and Sikka 2005).

7.2.1   Some problems with transfer pricing schemes, tax havens, and tax evasion

The use of tax havens is an important channel for tax evasion and constitutes a significant reason why many corporations pay little, or even no, income tax. Economic activity is often declared as occurring in places where taxes are low, rather than accurately recording where it actually takes place. "Transfer pricing" is a recognized accounting term for sales and purchases that occur within the same company or group of companies. Because these transactions occur within the company, there is wide scope to trade at arbitrary prices instead of market-attuned ones. Here is a simple example. A multinational company has a factory in one country, F. The factory produces, say, refrigerators for $200, and sells these to a subsidiary in the same group that is based in another country, T, which is a tax haven. The price of the transfer might be defined by the accountants as the cost of production, so in this case as $200. Then the subsidiary in T sells the product to a foreign subsidiary in a further country, S, for (say) $500. If the price of the good to consumers in that third country, S, is $400, the good has then been sold at a loss of $100, technically. This net loss of $100 may be recorded in country S and can be used to reduce taxes to be paid (in country S). Despite a real profit of $200 (the actual sales price less the actual cost of production, so $400 minus $200), the company may declare a net tax loss (of $100). These kinds of accounting schemes, which do not reflect "arm's-length" pricing (i.e., prices the market would use for trade between unrelated parties), and variations on these general themes, are extremely widespread and many of them are perfectly legal.[7] Consider how about 60 percent of all trade takes place within multinational corporations, with approximately 50 percent passing through tax havens.[8] This considerable loss of revenue means less is available to spend on public services.[9]

7.2.2 International double standards: Why we should aim for consistency

In many cases, the revenue that would be derived simply from resource sales, if received and properly spent, would be more than enough to finance the necessary provisions for helping people to meet their needs.[10] This is especially clear if we look at the case of oil and the crippling corruption that sometimes surrounds its sale. As one example, consider how, for instance, more than $4 billion in oil revenue disappeared in Angola between 1997 and 2002, which equals the entire amount the state spent on social programs during the same period (Human Rights Watch 2004c). As the international oil companies refuse to disclose how much they paid for oil in Angola, it is impossible for Angolans to monitor where the money went. More transparency in the payments made to less developed countries would eliminate the ease with which corruption currently flourishes, and could ensure that payments intended to benefit the citizens of a country actually do so. Companies can be made to publish what they pay by various mechanisms; for instance, it could be made a condition for the listing of oil companies on major stock exchanges (such as London or New York) that they adopt the transparency practice.

7.2.3   Solutions to the problems of double standards and tax evasion

It is instructive to look at what proposals are being suggested by agencies mobilizing for changes to international taxation arrangements in the two areas highlighted above. The Tax Justice Network calls for the initiation of a democratic global forum, comprising representatives from citizen groups and governments across the world, to engage in widespread debate on taxation with the possibility of implementing policies such as the following: (1) developing systems of unitary taxation for multinationals to stop the entirely false shifting of profits to countries with low or no taxes; (2) harmonizing tax rates and policy for capital (that is currently highly mobile); and (3) co-operation among states to reduce the destructive effects of tax competition.

Whereas such reforms might have seemed improbable pre-September 2001, since "9/11" there has been considerable interest in phasing out tax havens. Loopholes in international taxation greatly assisted in financing terrorist organizations, which has more recently motivated substantial support for setting international standards for transparency in accounting and for better monitoring all flows of money (Kochan 2005).

7.3   Dues to protect global public goods and tackle global poverty

I have argued at length elsewhere for why taxation on individuals and businesses is justified for the purposes of tackling global poverty (Brock 2009, especially chapters 3 and 9; see also Brock 2008). There I have also explained why no world government would be needed to enact global taxes and that we can coherently and democratically levy such taxes within existing current political arrangements. I cannot possibly rehearse all of those themes here, given the large topics already the target for analysis here. Rather, here I will have space just to outline some of the global tax proposals that have been made in sufficient detail for us to investigate which are likely to promote gender equity. We begin with the two proposals that have enjoyed the most serious consideration so far and have achieved a small measure of implementation success: the carbon tax and the Tobin tax.[11]

The carbon tax: A carbon tax would tax energy sources that emit carbon dioxide. Current trends concerning the release of greenhouse

gases exacerbate climate change, thereby undermining the environment's capacity to continue to be life-sustaining.[12] A carbon tax could
provide incentives to move to more sustainable energy forms. A $200
tax on every ton of carbon is projected to yield a 50 percent decrease
in carbon emissions from current levels, generating at least $630 billion
per year.[13] Such a tax might raise the costs of cooking food or trans-
portation quite significantly for poor people. In order to ensure they
are not disproportionately burdened by this tax, we need to consider
what complementary policies are also needed, perhaps through differential tax rates for different countries or rebates for low-income
households.[14] Carbon taxes could be levied directly at the point of sale
of carbon fuels, just as value-added taxes or sales taxes are currently
levied.[15] Several countries have already enacted a carbon tax, including
Sweden, Finland, Germany, the Netherlands, and Norway, and there
is notable support for the tax in other countries.[16]

The Tobin tax: It is estimated that well over half (on some estimates,
95 percent) of the $1.8 trillion in currency transactions that occur every
day are speculative and as such potentially destabilizing to local economies.[17] Local currencies can devalue rapidly, causing major financial
crises such as occurred in Argentina in 2001, greatly harming millions
of people. In the 1970s, James Tobin suggested a small tax on currency
trades to reduce speculation and promote more long-term investing,
which would prevent such crises (Tobin 1974). The purpose of such a
tax would be to promote more stability and better conditions for
development. The order of magnitude proposed is considerably less
than 1 percent on each trade. The United States, Japan, the European
Union, Switzerland, Hong Kong, and Singapore account for 90 percent
of currency exchange transactions, so the tax could be effectively collected (if, say, imposed at the point of settlement) (see Haq et al. 1996:
109–58; Spahn 2002; Wahl and Waldow 2001). Currency deals already
carry an administrative charge in the main currency exchange countries, so the administrative feasibility of such a tax is already plain. A
tax of just 0.2 percent is predicted to raise about $300 billion annu-
ally.[18] The tax has considerable support not just from NGOs but also
from politicians. More than 800 members of parliament from five
continents signed an international declaration in support of the tax.[19]
Several countries (such as Canada, Belgium, and France) have committed to enacting the tax if there is additional support from the
international community.[20]

Despite the long history of discussion over the carbon and Tobin
taxes, one tax that was proposed only recently has been more successful in terms of widespread implementation, namely the air-ticket tax.

The air-ticket tax: The idea with this tax is that it is a "solidarity contribution" levied on airplane tickets to finance global health programs. An international conference took place in Paris in February 2006 to mobilize support, and 13 governments agreed to introduce it, with further countries subsequently joining, bringing the total to 38 (at the time of writing) (Schroeder 2006: 2). On the current arrangements, in France the tax amounts to one euro per domestic ticket and four euros for an international, economy-class flight, with slightly more charged for business and first-class flights. Other ticket taxes involve similar or smaller amounts (Schroeder 2006: 3). The proceeds are spent on assisting poor countries struggling with malaria, AIDS, and tuberculosis. The WHO operates the fund and (among other things) uses bulk ordering to purchase the necessary drugs at low cost.

The breakthrough of a ticket tax has given momentum to the discussion about finding sources of finance for development in poor countries. However, there are many other proposals that predate this victory, as I now discuss.[21]

The email tax: This tax would aim to raise revenue that could be used to bridge the "digital divide" between rich and poor by improving computer, email, and web access to those in low-income communities. According to one common suggestion, sending 100 emails per day, each with a kilo-byte of data, would incur a tax of 1 cent.[22] Only consumers in the developed world would be charged. In 1996, such a tax would have raised $70 billion and the figure would be much bigger today (UNDP 1999: 66). However, this tax is unlikely to gain widespread approval as the global communication possibilities opened up by email are highly desirable.

Tax on world trade: This tax does not explicitly seek to discourage the activity on which it is imposed. The idea, rather, is that the tax would be a contribution for protecting the underlying conditions necessary to sustain international trade, such as peace and well-being (Evans 1997).

Tax on the international arms trade: Arms imports can constitute a significant obstacle to development. Proposals to implement a tax on the international arms trade have been circulated over a number of years (ICID 1980; Mendez 1992; UNDP 1994; Paul and Wahlberg 2002: 15). The goals of this tax include reducing the level of arms trading, raising funds for development, compensation for victims of wars, and promoting disarmament. About 70 percent of world arms exports come from the United States, France, and the United Kingdom. Some initiatives are already underway that could facilitate collection of this tax, such as the UN register for conventional arms and the

European Code of Conduct on Arms Exports (European Commission 2002: 67).

Aviation fuel taxes: Unlike the air-ticket tax, which aims at fostering development, the target of this tax is to offset harmful carbon emissions. Airplane travel is one of the fastest-growing sources of carbon emissions (ENDS 1999). Increased fuel costs would create good incentives for airlines to use more fuel-efficient aircraft and more efficient air-traffic control systems (IPPC 2001, especially Chapter 10).

Other proposals: Of the many other proposals for global taxes, perhaps a tax on consumption, such as a global sales tax, especially on luxury goods, deserves further thought (Walker 2005: 4–8).

In order to know which of these taxes might be good vehicles for promoting gender justice, we need to analyze some of the gendered effects of taxes, which we do next.

7.4   Gender justice and taxation[23]

About 20 years ago, calls were made to integrate a gender perspective into public budgeting decisions (Barnett and Grown 2004). Indeed, at the United Nations World Conference on Women in Beijing in 1995, governments undertook to do this in an effort to support gender equality. This involves examining both the expenditure and the (more neglected) revenue collection sides of the budget. Taxes are usually governments' main source of revenue.[24] Taxation is an important issue for gender analysis of development policy for a variety of reasons. In the developing world, most people, and the vast majority of women, are poor. Poor people rely more on public services, so ensuring adequate funds are available to support these is important. In their absence, the burdens typically fall on women, so this is a concern with special gender relevance.

Many issues are important for understanding the differential effects of tax on men and women. Here, I will discuss four:

(1) women's labor in the unpaid care economy;
(2) differences in paid employment between men and women;
(3) gender differences within household decision making; and
(4) the fact that women often have relatively little input into tax policy because they are politically underrepresented.

I begin with women's labor in the unpaid care economy.

Women have primary responsibility for the care of children and dependents in every country. Women also do most of the work in the unpaid economy, including the reproductive work (such as managing a household, cleaning, cooking, caring for family members and friends). In developing countries this unpaid work also includes subsistence production and the production of goods (such as food or clothing) for household consumption. Surveys on time-use from around the world demonstrate that women work longer hours than men in almost every country (Barnett and Grown 2004: 3).

Women's paid labor force participation rates are lower than men's (though they have a higher labor burden) and, worldwide, they are clustered in "clerical, sales and service jobs traditionally regarded as 'female' and are under-represented in production, transport, administrative and managerial jobs, in which men predominate" (Barnett and Grown 2004: 4). Although gaps have narrowed in some countries, one of the most persistent forms of inequality between men and women is that in earnings. Men earn more than women, even when we take into account differences in education and other human capital variables. The bulk of new employment in developing countries has been in the informal economy, which is work usually without secure contracts, benefits, or social protection. Women are employed in the informal economy at a higher rate than men (Barnett and Grown 2004: 4–5).

Empirical studies across a wide range of cultures show important gender differentials in consumption (Haddad et al. 1997). Women spend a higher proportion of income that is under their control on goods that enhance children's well-being, such as education, healthcare, and food (Guyer 1988). Price changes on such items can affect women's allocations of time and money. If food prices rise, women may spend more time processing food at home, reduce consumption, or replace more nutritious foods with cheaper, less nutritious ones. Taxation that affects the prices of goods may have an important bearing on women's consumption decisions (Barnett and Grown 2004: 5).

Household decision making is influenced by the relative bargaining power of adults, which in turn depends on both economic factors within the household (e.g., owned assets, education, wages, or kinship) and external factors (such as tax policies or legal systems, including those concerning property rights or divorce laws) (Barnett and Grown 2004: 5). In less developed countries women are often denied crucial opportunities, including those to own or inherit property. Women "rarely represent more than one-quarter of landowners," which can restrict their ability to participate in household and community decision making (Barnett and Grown 2004: 6).

Taxes are the main source of revenue for most countries and the central way of funding public services. Tax policy is frequently at the center of political debate, especially on levels of public provision of goods and services and how the costs of these are to be distributed. Marginalized groups such as women or the poor often do not participate in such debates, indeed, are often excluded from them. Frequently the result is that their interests are not well represented.

At least three general questions concerning taxation usually arise: First, how big should the government budget be? Second, how much should be raised from taxation and how much from alternative sources, such as borrowing? Third, how should the tax burden be distributed? Tax policy can be central to debates concerning the achievement of other desirable goals, such as gender equity or reducing poverty. In general, there is concern about increasing inequality worldwide and "skepticism about the ability of public expenditure to reach the very poor" (Barnett and Grown 2004: 50).

Developing countries also face some particular central challenges. A large percentage of the population is too poor to pay taxes. Many developing countries suffer from weak enforcement and administration. Often tax rates need to be harmonized with neighboring states to avoid competition. There is also a need to harmonize tax, trade, and industrial policies. In such environments, policies must be designed to provide sufficient revenue to support social and economic development without discouraging investment in financial and human capital growth, especially pro-poor growth (Barnett and Grown 2004: 51). Some issues recur that have special gender relevance, such as: How should tax policy deal with low levels of formal employment and relatively large informal sectors (where most women are employed)? How should tax policies deal with low levels of literacy, especially among women? Is there a way to structure family benefits or allowances so that they flow to the mother, since "evidence suggests that a greater family benefit then ensues to the household" (Barnett and Grown 2004: 52)? Also, how should tax systems deal with the value of unpaid caregiving services? Should there be exemptions for spouses or partners who contribute unpaid carework, and if so, what should they be?

Tax analysis aims to identify possible impacts of various tax policy options for stakeholders (such as business owners, consumers, or workers) or policy objectives (such as increasing economic growth). Taxes can be either direct or indirect. Direct taxes include personal income tax and corporate tax. Typical indirect taxes include taxes on consumption (which might take the form of sales taxes or value-added taxes [VAT]), or trade taxes (import or export duties). Each type of tax may involve an explicit or implicit gender bias (Stotsky 1997).

Barnett and Grown's (2004) extensive literature review on gender impacts of taxation yields some interesting results. Throughout the world, personal income taxes are not gender-neutral and several issues remain, even in countries that have attempted to be more gender-equitable. Consider, for instance, how combining all family income and taxing the household (rather than the individual) results in a higher marginal rate, which can deter women from entering the formal labor market or keep them in part-time jobs. (These kinds of results are sometimes referred to as a "marriage penalty.") Also, these wives are taxed at the higher rate of their husbands, so they receive less after-tax income. This provides a disincentive to seek employment and can reinforce gender roles. Countries sometimes levy different tax rates on men and women, and it is not uncommon for a higher rate to apply to married women compared with married men, for instance, as happens in many countries in the Middle East. There are all sorts of biases across codes worldwide; for instance, "in Zimbabwe, married men with non-working wives are entitled to a special credit but there is no such provision for married women with non-working husbands" (Barnett and Grown 2004: 32).

The most commonly endorsed idea of fairness in taxation is that taxes should be progressive—those whose incomes are lower should have a lower share of the tax burden than those whose incomes are higher. When taxes take a greater proportion of income from the poor than from the rich they are regressive. Because the poor spend a higher proportion of their income on consumption than the rich, taxes on consumption are generally regressive. They can be made less regressive through measures such as particular exemptions, lower tax rates for essential goods, or taxing luxury items purchased mostly by affluent consumers (Barnett and Grown 2004: 22).

In recent years, several reforms have taken place in taxation arrangements in developing countries. This reform process has often been driven by agencies such as the World Bank and the IMF aiming to address countries' budget deficits and to enhance their integration into the global economy (Barnett and Grown 2004: 17). Their recommendations have frequently resulted in the following types of reforms:

(i) Simplification and base-broadening (which have entailed the reduction of special credits and exemptions).
(ii) Reducing the top rates of personal income tax and harmonizing these with corporate taxes.

(iii) Introduction of VAT to provide a broad-based consumption tax which can be relatively easily administered.

(iv) Reduction or elimination of various import duties or export tariffs.

(v) Cuts in public spending to achieve fiscal balance and reduce current account deficits.

(vi) Transfer of public services to the private sector on grounds of efficiency.

This has frequently resulted in "user fees" where services were formerly provided without direct payment from the primary beneficiary.

In developing countries, concerns are frequently raised that such reforms have significantly worsened the situation of the poor, in terms of how taxes are both raised and spent. The increased reliance on indirect taxation, such as sales taxes or VAT, is often regressive. The tax burden of the lower-middle and lower-income classes has increased, and there is concern that relative shares of taxes have shifted from corporate to personal income tax. Reductions in tax revenues have frequently resulted in a fiscal squeeze, which can entail "the reduction of needed public services with adverse effects in the short term on the poor and low-income groups and in the long term on overall social and economic development" (Barnett and Grown 2004: 18).

Also, the emphasis on simplification has meant that some deductions and exemptions have been removed or limited, which can have equity implications for both class and gender (for instance, when childcare deductions, exemptions for dependents, or deductions for pension contributions are restricted). Taxes that result in placing a higher tax burden on the poor "will also create higher burdens for women who are disproportionately poor in developed countries, and primarily poor in developing countries" (Barnett and Grown 2004: 18). I say more about this next.

Market liberalization works best in contexts where strong social safety nets are in place to absorb the costs of adjustment. As markets have liberalized, there has been a corresponding higher demand for social protection. However, with less public revenue available, many developing countries have been unable to match the increasing need for services with the social protection resources available to meet these needs. Under trade liberalization, trade taxes have sharply declined. In many low-income countries, this can constitute an important loss of revenue, as such taxes can constitute about a third of government revenue (Grunberg 1998). Moreover, as we have seen, competition

among governments in the quest to attract foreign direct investment
has led to reduction in both corporate and capital gains taxes.
Nilufer Cagaty, a prominent feminist economist, observes that

> the burden of taxation on owners of capital went down. At the same
> time, many countries have introduced export-processing zones where
> businesses are exempt from paying tax. This has meant a shift in the
> burden of taxation from business owners, whose funds are increasingly
> mobile, to workers, who are relatively immobile (except for highly
> skilled people). An implication of these phenomena is that the burden
> of taxation has also been shifting from men to women, since women
> own and control much less property compared to men worldwide.
> (Cagaty 2003: 17)

Privatization and sale of public resources has often simply provided
a further avenue for corruption, as we have already seen in section
two. Over the period there has been no increase in official development
assistance, which for many countries still falls short of the 0.7 percent
of Gross National Product most have pledged. All of the phenomena
documented here have adversely affected developing states' abilities to
promote human development, growth, employment, and social equity
(ECLAC 1998). These moves have had important gender implications,
as I highlight. Social programs can, under the right conditions, ame-
liorate gender inequality and so cutbacks to such programs mean
women and girls suffer disproportionately. As already noted, in most
countries women bear the main responsibility for all unpaid caring
labor, including care of the sick. Cutbacks to state-provided assistance
to care for the sick mean that women and girls often have their labor
burden increased. As a further example, consider also how reductions
to other services can have unequal results. Cutbacks in the provision
of clean water impacts on women and girls more than men. Unclean
water can be a major source of disease in developing countries; if there
is no nearby, accessible, clean water, in many poor countries women
and girls are expected to collect it, which can add hours of work to an
already full day of expected labor.

In developing countries, the fallout from increased economic volatility or other economic crises is often more severe for women for
several reasons, including the following. Women's paid work is disproportionately in the informal sector, which is characterized as work
without formal contracts, benefits, or social protections. When informal sector jobs are lost, women are often placed in a vulnerable position. Social insurance systems are often designed with the assumption
that each household has a male breadwinner in the formal sector who

can provide the necessary social protections (Cagaty and Elson 2000). Furthermore, where social safety nets are weak, women are last-resort providers of social protections. "They buffer their families from the ill-effects of economic crisis by working harder both within and outside the household, to make up for reduced private incomes and reduced public services" (Cagaty 2003: 20). During economic crises, girls (rather than boys) can be taken out of schools to either care for family members or help with domestic labor while their mothers work outside the home to increase household income. There can also be costs in terms of increased violence, especially domestic violence as men seek to regain "a sense of power and agency" (Cagaty 2003: 21). Furthermore, in times of economic volatility, there may be pressure to increase indirect taxes. As already noted, taxes on commodities such as VAT alter the relative prices of goods. Because of women's different consumption patterns, such taxes may result in hidden gender bias, as women bear a larger burden of indirect taxes.

7.5 Global taxes and promoting gender equity: which options are best?

We return now to the catalog of global taxes introduced in section three. Which of the global taxes discussed there should we endorse? Of the positive global taxes discussed, the Tobin tax seems to have one of the strongest cases. Recall that the tax is a tax on currency transactions. A Tobin tax would be progressive because it is very largely higher-income individuals and corporations who would bear the tax. It could be relatively easily implemented and administered, as I discussed in section three. It is likely to promote more long-term investment, thereby resulting in less volatility. The introduction of a Tobin tax would reduce the market volatility caused by large movements in speculative short-term capital flows. Reduced market volatility is to be welcomed in itself. In addition, market volatility has disproportionately negative effects for women. Furthermore, it has also been suggested that a portion of the revenues raised by a Tobin tax could be awarded to governments for the design of gender-equitable social insurance and social protection systems (Cagaty 2003; Barnett and Grown 2004: 44). So a portion of the Tobin tax could be used specifically to promote gender equity. Indeed, Cagaty argues that

> Schemes like the Tobin tax, or the institution of a global taxation authority, need to receive more attention from feminist activists.

> Revenue generated by such taxation could be an important source of universal public provisioning of basic social services, including healthcare, education, nutrition, sanitation and water, and funding to realise country-specific gender equity goals. (Cagaty 2003: 22)

Trade taxes, which include import tariffs and export taxes, can be an important source of revenue for developing countries. As trade liberalization has increased, cuts in trade taxes have ensued. Tariffs affect women in at least three ways: as workers in sectors where goods are traded internationally (such as clothing and agriculture); as traders in such goods; or as consumers of imported goods (Cagaty 2003: 45). So while as workers their interests might sometimes be set back (through, say, loss of jobs), they may gain as consumers (for instance, being able to pay less for imported medicines) or find enhanced trading opportunities. There are trade-offs and each country might find its particular costs and benefits give a different overall result. When tariff reductions lead to job losses this can have far-reaching consequences including economic downturns and cuts in public expenditure (Seguino 2000). Mohan Rao shows that trade taxes have a positive effect on government expenditure and when these decline we see decreased public-sector investment in infrastructure and education, with important negative effects for women in terms of added expense and labor burden (Rao 1999). However, there are also many positive gains that trade liberalization can bring when it creates new market opportunities and therefore jobs. Trade taxes can have fairly mixed results, depending on individual country circumstances, so here I do not argue for any general endorsement or rejection of trade taxes.

Though there is a compelling case for some kind of carbon tax, the details need to be carefully worked out so that the tax does not have regressive or negative gender effects. Being an indirect tax, we already know (from the previous section) that it will have disproportionate effects for women. Skillful design will be needed to avoid this. This is a project which is under construction in collaboration with an economist, so I will not comment further on this tax here.

The air-ticket tax seems worthy of support, especially at its current low level. Similarly, the proposed tax on the international arms trade also appears to bring vastly more benefits than costs and so should be supported. The cases for all the other taxes are more ambiguous and need further study. I have mentioned the fact that the global communication possibilities that email has enabled make taxing emails undesirable. We need to be cautious about consumption taxes, sales taxes, or world trade taxes because, as we have seen, they can be strongly regressive and gender-inequitable, and can lead to undesirable results for particular countries, for instance, when jobs are thereby lost.

It is worth underscoring again that in terms of order of magnitude, most of these global taxes pale into insignificance when we consider the vast amounts of taxable revenue that currently escape taxation through innovative accounting maneuvers, such as the opportunities presented through transfer-pricing schemes discussed in section two. It is important to emphasize that the reforms we outlined there—aimed at prohibiting tax escape and the siphoning of funds paid for natural resources away from the people who own them—could yield vast sums that would considerably reduce the need to find alternative sources of revenue to fund necessary social programs, and indeed could provide all the funds governments need to run their countries reasonably well while promoting desirable social goods such as gender equity.

Recall that in section two I argued against tax arrangements that allow so many to avoid paying tax. It is commonly suggested that since developing countries need to provide tax incentives to attract foreign direct investment (FDI), those countries would be denied important benefits were the reforms discussed above to be enacted. Many developing countries do compete for FDI and do come under pressure to provide tax incentives or exemptions. But the evidence suggests that there are limited, if any, net benefits from such incentives, and that they play little part in investors' decisions, so their use may be futile (Oman 2000).[25] Much more important are fundamental factors such as the quality of institutions, basic infrastructure, stable government, sound fiscal condition, available labor force, respect for the rule of law, good accountability, and so forth (Oman 2000).

7.6   Some issues concerning global taxes for here and now

I have discussed issues of how to implement global taxes effectively elsewhere (Brock 2009: Chapter 5). Here I simply note a few salient issues with a view to blocking the most common objections.

Though universal support is desirable, we do not need it to make progress in the right direction. As the air-ticket tax demonstrates, substantial progress is possible with just a few countries' co-operation. Even when we do not have universal support at first, in due course, non-participating states may eventually join a tax regime for several reasons. Citizens of non-participating states may pressure their governments to join. Non-participating states might lose influence over policies related to the spending revenue raised. Plus, once a successful scheme is in place, there might be pressure from the international community to join as well. Most states have now come to appreciate that it is in their interests to agree on common standards in financial and taxation arrangements. For one thing, opaque tax and financial systems, and lack of co-operation, make it difficult to stop money laundering, the financing of terrorist organizations, and tax evasion (Kochan 2005). Many fora aiming to eliminate harmful tax practices have been put in place, including the forum on harmful tax practices of the OECD and the Financial Action Task Force (European Commission 2002: 33). Since September 11, 2001, action to target terrorist financing has strengthened these initiatives.

Financing global public goods properly will be best promoted by establishing an international tax organization. One major worry concerns the risk that any international tax regime will possess too much power, which it might abuse. Several remarks are worth making in response. First, there has been considerable theorizing on this matter, including work on institutional design and the desiderata for such organizations (see, for instance, Tanzi 1999; Horner 2001). Second, we have recently formed international bodies that have begun the sort of work recommended in section two, notably the OECD Global Forum on Taxation.[26] This body provides a good forum for the exchange of ideas about policy, and with some tangible results, such as the development of proposals for unitary taxation formulae that could be used in devising better arrangements to replace current transfer pricing practices.[27] The OECD body does not, however, have the power to levy taxes directly, nor does any currently existing international tax organization.

However, and third, were an international tax organization empowered to collect revenue, it is not clear why it could not be set up like other international organizations that are adequately held accountable, such as the World Health Organization, or be modeled along similar lines. Decisions might be made by super-majority vote as a way to get high levels of support for decisions. Regular reporting requirements and audits, with full public disclosure of all revenues received plus disbursements, could promote sufficient trust. Clearly specifying the goals of revenue collection and how proceeds will be spent (as is the case with the air-ticket tax) could considerably allay fears about waste or abuse.

Fourth, a further way of encouraging high compliance would be to make membership in other international bodies with high levels of membership (such as the World Trade Organization) conditional on simultaneously being members of an international tax body or on agreeing to be bound by its rules. This could entail accepting annual independent audits (conducted by auditors representing member nations) on global tax matters, thereby ensuring that regular accountability mechanisms are put in place, leading to more accountability than may currently exist in many countries. Under these arrangements, sanctions for non-compliance might also more easily be connected with membership of the World Trade Organization and therefore be easier to monitor and enforce, as they could take the form of penalties that adversely affect trade.

7.7 Summary of main conclusions

In this chapter I have examined how reforming our international tax regime could be an important vehicle for realizing key aspects of global gender justice. Ensuring that all, including and especially multinationals, pay their fair share of taxes is crucial to ensuring that all countries, especially developing countries, are able to fund education, job training, infrastructural development, programs that promote gender equity, and so forth, thereby enabling all countries to help themselves better. I also discussed various positive proposals for levying global taxes, reviewing why overtly gender-neutral taxes can sometimes have unintended gendered consequences, disproportionately burdening or benefiting individuals according to their gender. Any endorsement of global taxes must take this concern into account. Fortunately there is a good fit between the rationale for the Tobin tax and the way in which it can be harnessed to promote gender equity; so, of the taxes discussed here, it emerges as one of the most promising.

However, it is worth underscoring that eliminating tax havens and blocking avenues that currently facilitate tax escape must also be part of the agenda to promote gender equity, given the vast amounts of revenue that currently escape taxation. In the context of globalization, fiscal policies cannot achieve equity (including gender equity) at national levels alone. Many concerns, such as clamping down on tax evasion and harmonizing corporate tax rates, can only effectively be tackled at a global level. As I have also discussed, feasible arrangements for tackling such issues are available, as are mechanisms for collecting and disbursing funds in ways that promote accountability and compliance. Failing to reform our tax arrangements means that the basic institutional structure of the global economy is unjust and also involves gender injustice. Here is one instance where gender consciousness is indispensable for developing an adequate account of taxation justice and therefore a global institutional structure that is gender-just.

Acknowledgments

For very helpful comments and advice about this chapter, I am deeply grateful to John Christensen, Alex Cobham, Caren Grown, Alison Jaggar, and all the participants at the Global Gender Justice conference which took place in Oslo, May 29–31, 2008. I am very grateful to the Centre for the Study of Mind in Nature (hosted by the University of Oslo) for financial support to attend this conference; to Alison Jaggar for organizing the workshop and inviting me; and to all the participants who made the conference such a stimulating and successful event.

Notes

1 About 2.8 billion people live on less than US $2 per day (see European Commission 2002: 40). Though deprivation with respect to income is a crude and imperfect measure of poverty, it is widely used as at least a rough indicator of the condition of interest.
2 By "we" in such contexts I refer to the collection of typical citizens of affluent, developed countries and, especially, to the agents well positioned to act on their behalf—the governments appointed by such citizens.
3 For a greater estimate see Tax Justice Network, "The Price of Offshore" (2005), http://www.taxjustice.net/cms/upload/pdf/Price_of_Offshore.pdf (accessed May 13, 2013). Thirty percent of the holdings of the world's richest individuals are currently held in offshore tax havens, according to estimates from Christian Aid (2005). These estimates are based on studies done by the Boston Consulting Group as published in the report "Winning in a Challenging Market: Global Wealth 2003," www.go-fi.com/infos_studiedetail.php4?ref=1-35P-488.
4 French finance minister Dominique Strauss-Kahn speaking to the Paris Group of Experts in March 1999 as discussed in Christensen and Hampton 1999: 14–17.
5 Locating holdings in tax havens and taxing them at very low levels (such as 0.5 percent) could greatly contribute to eliminating global poverty (Christian Aid 2005: 11).

6 See also Tax Justice Network, "Tax Us If You Can," http://www.taxjustice.net/cms/upload/pdf/tuiyc_-_eng_-_web_file.pdf (accessed May 13, 2013), and Vigueras 2005.

7 Though many of these schemes are currently classed as (legitimate) tax avoidance, they should be reclassified as (illegitimate) tax evasion. As I argue, they resemble practices of tax evasion that are illegal.

8 See Tax Justice Network, September Newsletter (2003), p. 11, http://www.taxjustice.net/cms/upload/pdf/e_ns_0903.pdf (accessed May 7, 2013), For similar claims, see Neighbour 2002. See also, "Offshore Watch," http://visar.csustan.edu/aaba/aaba.htm (accessed May 7, 2013).

9 See the Center on Budget and Policy Priorities at www.cbpp.org for information on this connection (e.g., Furman 2006).

10 "Oil and Corruption," *New Zealand Herald*, editorial, April 9, 2002, p. 10.

11 All these proposals are discussed in more detail in Brock 2008.

12 For regularly updated information, see the Intergovernmental Panel on Climate Change's website at www.ipcc.ch.

13 As with any revenue projections, assumptions must be made, notably concerning demand elasticity and salient effects on economic activity. For more on why these assumptions are reasonable, see Paul and Wahlberg 2002 and Cooper 1998, 2002.

14 For more on how to ensure a carbon tax is not regressive, see the Carbon Tax Center website on "Managing Impacts," http://www.carbontax.org/issues/softening-the-impact-of-carbon-taxes (accessed January 11, 2008). Since taxes on fuels are typically highly regressive, poor, developing countries might be exempt from paying a 1 percent tax, at least if usage is under a threshold thought to be a reasonable allocation based on individual use.

15 For more on these and other suggestions, see Baumert 1998.

16 For instance, see the Carbon Tax Centre (www.carbontax.org), which provides a forum for Americans to discuss carbon taxes.

17 See Tobin Tax websites, such as www.tobintax.org and www.ceedweb.org, for regularly updated information. See also Wahl and Waldow 2001.

18 The most common tax proposals are for considerably less than 0.2 percent, so are more likely to yield amounts of between $16 and $60 billion. See, for instance, UNDESA 2005: 137.

19 For more on support for the tax, see Tobin Tax websites such as www.tobintax.org.

20 See Global Policy Forum, "Currency Transaction Taxes," http://www.globalpolicy.org/socecon/glotax/curtax/index.htm for the Belgian and French bills.

21 For more details on all of these, see, for instance, Baumert 1998; Walker 2005; and Paul and Wahlberg 2002: 13–16.

22 http://www.caslon.com.au/taxationguide2.htm (accessed 2008).

23 I am very much indebted to the outstanding research conducted by Kathleen Barnett and Caren Grown (2004).

24 Taxes in developing countries range between about 10 and 40 percent of a country's GDP (Barnett and Grown 2004: 1).

25 See the McKinsey report, http://www.taxjustice.net/cms/upload/pdf/
McKinsey_Report_summary.pdf (accessed 2008).

26 There is also the UN Committee on Taxation, which has become part of
the Financing for Development Process. However, I believe the OECD
body is currently more effective.

27 "Transfer Pricing Guidelines for Multinational Enterprises and Tax
Administrations" (OECD Publishing, 2001), http://www.oecd-ilibrary.
org/taxation/transfer-pricing-guidelines-for-multinational-enterprises-
and-tax-administrations_9789264192218-en (accessed May 13, 2013).

8

Gender Injustice and the Resource Curse: Feminist Assessment and Reform

Scott Wisor

8.1 The resource curse

Every day, consumers purchase and use products that contain natural resources from other parts of the world, or were produced using energy derived from these natural resources. If you have a phone or a computer, drive a car or heat your home, you almost certainly consume natural resources from across the globe. Many of these resources come from countries that are beset by widespread violations of human rights including, as we will see later, women's rights. In the last decade, philosophers have turned their attention to the causal role that this trade in natural resources plays in harming the citizens of resource-exporting states. Most notably, Thomas Pogge (2002, 2010) and Leif Wenar (2008, 2011) have argued that wealthy consumers, corporations, and the governments that represent them are morally responsible for at least some of the harms that befall citizens in resource-exporting states. In this chapter I will build from this previous work to provide a feminist normative and empirical assessment of the resource curse, and I will suggest how proposed reforms to the resource curse can be made gender-sensitive.

8.1.1 The standard description

Thomas Pogge describes the international resource privilege as follows:

Any group controlling a preponderance of the means of coercion within a country is internationally recognized as the legitimate government of

> this country's territory and people—regardless of how this group came to power, of how it exercises power, and of the extent to which it may be supported or opposed by the population it rules . . . we accept this group's right to act for the people it rules and, in particular, confer upon it the privileges to freely borrow in its name (international borrowing privilege) and freely to dispose of the country's natural resources (international resource privilege). (Pogge 2002: 113)

By conferring the international resource privilege (among other international privileges)[1] upon groups who take or hold power over a given territory, states, international institutions, corporations, and consumers incentivize a variety of harmful activities in resource-exporting countries. In the empirical literature on the resource curse, there are three commonly recognized classes of harm that are correlated with natural resource exports.

8.1.2 Conflict

First, there is a *conflict resource curse*: the international resource privilege incentivizes civil conflict, including civil war, insurgencies, and coups.[2] Since would-be rebel groups know that, if they take power, they will be authorized to sell and profit from natural resource exports, they have a greater reason to attempt to do so.[3] They are also more likely to secure financial support for their insurgencies from those who anticipate that any loans can be repaid by future resource revenues and/or favorable rates on future concessions in the extractive sector.[4] Once in power, governments rely on resource revenue to arm themselves, guard against potential coups or insurgents, and buy off potential spoilers. The conflict resource curse may affect the likelihood of conflict, the length of conflict, the intensity of conflict, the nature of the conflict, and the likelihood of resolution.[5]

8.1.3 Governance

Second, there is a *political resource curse*: the resource privilege deters democratic governance.[6] Resource-dependent authoritarian governments use resource rents to strengthen their hold on power to suppress civil and military opposition, while also using resource rents to buy the support of would-be opponents. Some authoritarian states also quiet citizen opposition through resource rent redistribution, rather than enacting genuine social policy (Ross 2011).[7] Because authoritarian states can rely on natural resource revenue, they do not need to govern on behalf of citizens and their interests, since the financial support of these citizens is not needed for continued government expenditure.[8]

8.1.4 Economics

Third, there is an *economic resource curse*: the resource privilege incentivizes economic mismanagement and prevents the economic diversification needed for stable growth characterized by low unemployment. By providing states with large revenues in fungible resources, particularly revenues that have not been collected through taxes on citizens, rulers are often able to extract large sums of money for their personal gain. The list of wealthy dictators in resource-rich states is not short.[9] Furthermore, resource-exporting states are prone to a variety of other macro-economic ills. They may suffer from Dutch disease, whereby the value of the domestic currency rises as a result of natural resource exports, thus making other exports less competitive, diminishing economic diversification. This lack of diversification, exacerbated by the attraction of financial and human capital to extractives sectors, becomes a great vulnerability given the high volatility of commodity prices and the subsequent boom-and-bust cycle of resource-dependent economies.

Though widely acknowledged, each of these three theses about the resource curse is disputed. Many thinkers deny that such a curse exists, and in fact assert that resource-dependent states are better off than their peers who have not been blessed by abundant natural resources. However, critics who reject the idea of a resource curse are often making one of three mistakes. First, they fail to recognize that the resource curse should be understood as a conditional thesis: if a country has not yet developed good institutions (the rule of law, government accountability, checks and balances, and so on), and it becomes dependent on natural resources, it will then be harder to transition to good institutions. Countries that established good institutions before becoming resource-dependent are not affected by the resource curse (though they too must manage volatility in commodity prices and inflationary pressures on domestic currency, which can inhibit the export of other goods and services).[10] Second, critics mistakenly assume that the resource curse, if it exists, must persist over long periods of time. Michael Ross has rightly pointed out that the resource curse became most profound following the end of the Cold War. During the Cold War, states attempting democratic transformation or an end to civil conflict were plagued by the competing interests of the US, the Soviet Union, and their respective allies, but in the last 20 years states should have seen more success in making democratic transitions. However, states dependent on natural resource exports have been less successful in moving to democratic governance than their non-resource-dependent peers.[11] Third, identification of a resource curse is highly dependent on the nature of the resources in question.[12] Fourth, everything else being equal, one would expect countries with greater natural resources to be better off than their peers. In fact, this was widely accepted among economists until the 1980s (see Rosser 2006: 7). Prior to empirical investigation, one would expect that, absent a resource curse, countries with valuable resources would be able to grow faster, better provide public services, and thus govern better than their resource-scarce peers. Moreover, even if one remains skeptical that a correlation exists between the presence of natural resources or dependence on natural resource exports, and a country's prospects for peace, democratic governance, and shared growth, it may still be true that some countries are plagued by a resource curse. As Leif Wenar argues, alcohol may, across a population, be overall good for health, but nonetheless be very bad for alcoholics.[13] A careful examination of the histories of specific countries like Sudan, Burma, and the Democratic Republic of Congo reveals that natural resources have played a significant role in civil conflict, authoritarianism, and squandered opportunities for growth.[14]

8.2   Feminist revision

There is much to commend in the standard account of the resource curse. However, the standard account has hitherto largely ignored problems pertaining to gender.[15] As evidence: Paul Collier's books, *The Plundered Planet* and *The Bottom Billion*, which both systematically address the resource curse, make no mention of women or gender. In *Escaping the Resource Curse*, edited by leading economists Jeffrey Sachs, Joseph Stiglitz, and Marcatan Humphries, there is only one author who mentions women, on a single page. Women are similarly absent in the leading philosophical analyses of the resource curse (Pogge 2002; Wenar 2008; Nili 2011). Gender has also been overlooked in work that is critical of the resource curse thesis (Brunnschweiler and Bulte 2008; Pineda and Rodriguez 2010). Furthermore, concerns about gender inequities are also absent from proposed reforms intended to address the resource curse.

A feminist analysis of the resource curse reveals at both the macro and micro levels gendered injustices in the distribution of benefits and burdens that result from the international resource trade, and in the distribution of the authority to oversee and authorize resource trades. Failure to take account of the gendered dimensions of the resource privilege results in gender-blind normative assessment and proposed reform, to the detriment of women, and to a lesser extent men, who are harmed by the resource curse in gender-specific ways.

8.2.1 Gender inequality

There are two general ways in which the international resource privilege exacerbates gender inequality in resource-exporting states. First, there is a recently discovered *gender inequality resource curse*: dependence on oil exports is statistically correlated with higher levels of gender inequality. Work by Michael Ross, arguably the leading authority on the resource curse, highlights a causal relationship between oil exports and gender inequality. He argues that

> Oil production affects gender relations by reducing the presence of women in the labor force. The failure of women to join the nonagricultural labor force has profound social consequences: it leads to higher fertility rates, less education for girls, and less female influence within the family. It also has far-reaching political consequences: when fewer women work outside the home, they are less likely to exchange information and overcome collective action problems; less likely to mobilize politically, and to lobby for expanded rights; and less likely to gain representation in government. This leaves oil-producing states with atypically strong patriarchal cultures and political institutions. (Ross 2008: 207)

To understand how oil production deters the development of employment-intensive manufacturing and service sectors, especially those in sectors that tend to employ large numbers of women, we must focus on the economic and political consequences of the resource trade. Economically, high dependence on natural resource exports leads to large volumes of foreign currency entering the exporting state—this makes other exports, such as manufactured goods or services, more expensive and thus less competitive. Furthermore, political elites, entrepreneurs, and many educated citizens are drawn to resource-exporting industries, to the detriment of manufacturing and service sectors. Thus employment-intensive industries, especially those in which women are most likely to be employed, are weakened, while extractive industries, characterized by lower levels of overall employment and higher proportions of male employees, become dominant.[16]

Second, each of the harms described above—authoritarianism, civil conflict, and economic mismanagement—has gendered aspects, and men and women are likely to suffer in different ways, and to different degrees, as a result.

8.2.2 Women and authoritarianism

Authoritarianism is not gender-neutral. Nearly all dictators are men. The status of most women in authoritarian regimes is systematically low as compared to men, though high status may be accorded to a few women in elite families. Importantly, authoritarian governments are less likely to permit the formation and growth of women's rights movements. Authoritarianism is particularly detrimental to the presence of women in government, which in turn has well-recognized impacts on the welfare of women and children (World Bank 2011: 48). Politically, if governments become dependent on natural resource rents, and are corrupted by that dependence, they are typically less likely to deliver good social policies in areas including health, education, sanitation and water. This has two disproportionately harmful impacts on women. First, women lose opportunities for employment because they are more likely than men to be employed in industries providing public services, including health and education. Second, women, who through their socially prescribed roles bear primary responsibility for childcare, housework, and healthcare, are disproportionately burdened when the state fails to provide these services.

8.2.3 Women and conflict

Civil conflict and war are also deeply gendered, and have gender-specific differential impacts on men and women. This is not to deny that war can be very harmful for men. It is simply to note that gender shapes the distribution of harms in conflict. In war, women suffer a variety of gender-specific harms. First, while women are less likely than men to be combatants, women are more likely to be among the civilian victims of war and to suffer gender-specific attacks. The use of sexual violence as a weapon of war in recent resource wars, including in the Democratic Republic of Congo, Burma, and Sudan, highlights the gendered vulnerabilities that are present during wartime. Second, when warfare destroys or disrupts the provision of public services, including health, education, sanitation, and access to drinking water and cooking fuel, women are systematically disadvantaged because they are obligated as primary caretakers to become the *de facto* providers of these services to their children and families.

8.2.4 Women and the economy

Economic mismanagement and corruption also have gender-specific impacts. The beneficiaries of corruption, and those who are most corrupt, are often men. Increased gender equity may account for higher growth rates and less corruption, and greater government spending on social protection (see, for example, World Bank 2011: 48). There is considerable debate in feminist circles about the fact that women tend to be less corrupt than men.[17] A plausible interpretation of this empirical evidence is that women's lower rates of corruption are a result both of social norms governing the conduct of men and women and of the lower exposure that women have to corruptible offices. It may be that over time the entrance of women into corruptible offices will lead to higher rates of corruption among women. But it is of course equally plausible that gender equity in positions that are susceptible to corruption would result in lower corruption. Regardless, there are stand-alone reasons to endorse a gender-equitable representation in the management of natural resources, independent of whether such a distributional change results in lower corruption.

My focus on natural resources and gender inequality does not entail either a deterministic or a reductionist account of the relationship between natural resources and gender equity. The international resource privilege is only part of the story in explaining civil conflict, authoritarianism, economic mismanagement or gender inequality. First, dependence on natural resource exports is neither necessary nor sufficient for explaining high levels of gender inequality. States with very high levels of gender inequality may have very little or no natural resource trade. Similarly, some states with very high dependence on natural resource exports may be more gender-equitable. Second, natural resource dependence will never be a complete explanation of gender inequality or other harms. A variety of other contextual factors jointly determine progress towards gender justice.

8.3   Normative assessment of the resource curse

Thus far I have argued that a morally adequate description of the resource curse must attend to the gendered distribution of benefits and burdens that often result from dependence on natural resource exports. I now show that feminist insights into the resource trade also call for revisions to extant normative assessments of participation in that trade. Existing normative assessment provides two broad justifications for the moral obligations of resource importers to compensate for the harms created by the purchase of natural resources and/or to stop participating in this harmful trade. Resource importers are morally responsible because either (1) they are participating in illegitimate trade tantamount to theft, or (2) they are at least partially causally responsible for harms to innocent civilians in resource-exporting states, and a change in their behavior would result in fewer harms, as long as the importers can foresee the harms they are causing and have feasible alternatives.

8.3.1   The legitimate ownership view

On the *legitimate ownership view*, the international resource privilege and complicit participation by consumers, corporations, and governments in the resource trade is morally wrong because of the theft that occurs when resources are extracted and sold without the proper consent of their owners. In the words of Leif Wenar:

> The natural resources of a country belong to the citizens of that country, and no one may sell off this property without some sort of authorization. A thief who steals your watch from your nightstand cannot legally sell your watch to anyone else, for neither you nor anything else in the law has empowered the thief to sell your watch. The thief may have

taken possession of your watch and then transferred possession to someone else, but no valid transfer of the title to your watch has taken place. The watch is still your property, and the thief and his transferee have merely handled stolen goods. (Wenar 2008: 12)

On Wenar's account, the theft of the watch and its subsequent sale are just like the purchase of natural resources from regimes which fail to protect minimal civil and political rights. On his view, it is morally wrong to participate knowingly in the trade of natural resources if citizens, the owners of those resources, have not properly authorized their sale.

8.3.2 Types of legitimate ownership

In my view, the legitimacy perspective requires two levels of assessment, at the national and subnational levels.[18] At the *national level*, legitimate ownership requires adequate guarantee of everyone's civil and political rights in a country. Can it be said that the people authorize natural resource sales given background institutional and social conditions? Could citizens plausibly be said to have consented to the existing management of natural resources, or could they reasonably undertake to change that management if unsatisfied with current arrangements?

There are also relevant considerations regarding the internal procedures for managing a given resource sale. Whatever the civil and political conditions in a country, that country will almost certainly have set some procedures for determining how to authorize the extraction and sale of natural resources. Whether or not these procedures are independently justifiable and subsequently adhered to also confers a degree of legitimacy. For example, one could plausibly argue that the Democratic Republic of Congo does not currently have external legitimacy to authorize the sale of resources, due to the absence of meaningful protections of civil and political rights. Nonetheless, it has formal government arrangements for authorizing resource sales, and has been active in promoting the sale and development of mining concessions. The legitimacy of a resource trade can thus be judged (in part) by evaluating both a) the independent legitimacy of those procedures and b) the degree to which the procedures are appropriately followed. For example, if the Congolese government has outlawed the bribery of domestic officials, and it is later discovered that a mining company has bribed a public official to win a mining concession, this is reason to doubt the legitimacy of the concession, and of subsequent trades emanating from that concession.

Finally, at the national level, there is a third perspective from which to evaluate a given resource regime. Is the population harmed by the trade in natural resources, and does the trading regime in place justly distribute the benefits and burdens of the resource trade among the population? While it is controversial that beneficial consequences can confer legitimacy (see Wellman 1996 in defense of this view), it is difficult to deny that harmful consequences for the majority of the people are a mark against the legitimacy of a particular resource regime. When assessing the legitimacy of the oil trade in Nigeria, for example, it is very difficult to deny the relevance of oil spills and environmental degradation, or the incentivizing of civil conflict, in assessing the legitimacy of the overall resource regime.[19]

There is a second level of *subnational legitimacy* that deserves consideration. Consider a resource-exporting state in which civil and political rights are not minimally protected. Further, suppose that much resource extraction is not merely profitable for multinational corporations and foreign employees, but an important livelihood source for local populations. Given these subnational conditions, two distinct considerations come into play. The first is whether any particular person or group can be said to have proper authority to extract and sell natural resources in the absence of proper national-level authorization. Can they give sharable reasons to their compatriots as to why they should be authorized to sell natural resources?[20] Do small-scale artisan miners in the eastern provinces of the Democratic Republic of Congo have the proper authority to exploit natural resources? That is, internal to the dynamics of the resource trade, can groups involved in the trade justify a claim to be participants? Once an individual or group, absent national-level authorization, has undertaken to extract and sell natural resources, there is a second subnational consideration of legitimacy: namely, does the group conduct itself in such a way as to justify the authority it has usurped? This second kind of subnational legitimacy is concerned with the consequences of the exercise of power over natural resources—are the benefits and burdens of resource extraction distributed in such a way that the subnational assertion of authority is justified?

This leaves a rather complicated picture of the legitimacy of the resource trade. Legitimacy is a scalar concept, and the degree to which a particular regime of resource trades is deemed legitimate must take account of the following considerations:

Level of Legitimacy	Criterion	Standard of Assessment
National	Civil and Political Rights	Do background conditions for consent exist? Absent conditions of consent, can democratic consent nonetheless be inferred?
National	Procedural Justice	Are the procedures for managing and trading natural resources justifiable? Have the pre-specified procedures for exploiting and selling natural resources been followed?
National	Benefits and Burdens	Does the resulting national-level distribution of benefits and burdens from resource management confer a degree of legitimacy?
Subnational	Just Claim (representation, association, etc.)	Does the group that subnationally claims authority over natural resources have sharable reasons for making that claim?
Subnational	Procedural Justice	Does the group that subnationally manages resources follow transparent, morally justifiable procedures for its management?
Subnational	Benefits and Burdens	Does the subnational distribution of benefits and burdens confer some degree of legitimacy?

8.3.3   Contribution to injustice

There is an alternative normative perspective from which to evaluate the trade in natural resources. The international resource privilege, and complicit participation by consumers and governments, is morally wrong not only because resources are being stolen, but because of the foreseeable and avoidable *injustice* that many people suffer as a result of resource trades.[21] When authoritarians use oil money to imprison opponents or crush dissent, to limit free speech or to personally profit at the expense of poor people, consumers bear responsibility as they have foreseeably contributed to that harm through the provision of revenue and could have done otherwise.[22] If there is a feasible alternative scenario under which the modified conduct of resource importers and consumers would bring about less harm and more benefit, then they bear responsibility for at least the difference between actual outcomes and feasible counterfactual outcomes.[23]

On this perspective, important normative facts about natural resource trade with China, for example, include not only whether Chinese citizens have legitimately authorized resource extraction and sale, but also whether that sale confers a reasonably just distribution of benefits or burdens on Chinese citizens, and whether feasible alternative schemes of resource trades exist that would confer fewer harms and more benefits on more Chinese citizens. Arguably, an assessment of the contribution to harm could extend beyond the Chinese state—a more cosmopolitan assessment would examine all of the benefits and burdens, to those both within China and outside it, from the trade in China's resources.

8.4   Feminist normative assessment

By attending to the feminist redescription of the resource curse above, we are well positioned to revise existing normative assessments of the natural resource trade.

8.4.1   Feminist legitimacy

On my account, legitimacy can be assessed at both the national and subnational levels. National-level legitimacy is about the government's power to rule being authorized in some way by the governed. On the standard account, the legitimacy of a government (and thus its ability to authorize the extraction and sale of natural resources, and the distribution of the resulting benefits and burdens) is to be assessed primarily with regard to the degree to which the government is democratically authorized by its citizens. For Wenar, adequately protecting civil and political rights is necessary to authorize natural resource sales. I accept Wenar's view that natural resources are owned by the people of a country.[24] Taking gender seriously, one must assess not just the degree to which the people in general, as an undifferentiated mass, can be said to have properly authorized the sale of natural resources, but should focus (among other things) on the degree to which women can be said to have properly authorized that sale. What Wenar and others object to in states where citizens have not consented to the sale of natural resources is the dismissal of ownership claims. If natural resources are owned by the citizens, then all citizens, men and women, ought to be able to exercise ownership control. Therefore, one must benchmark assessments of legitimacy not just to democratic participation in general but to the status of women as resource owners—that is, one must examine the degree to which women can be said to have authorized national governance in general, and natural resource management in particular.

Consider the case of Papua New Guinea (PNG).[25] Though a very faulty democracy, PNG is formally democratic. However, there are only three female parliamentarians out of 111 in PNG. The country also has one of the highest rates of violence against women in the world (AusAID 2008). These high rates of violence, among other things, may deter women from politically organizing to formally participate in governance. PNG also has a large extractives sector and, as of 2012, is experiencing a commodity boom.

While concessions are granted through formal bureaucratic processes overseen by the democratic government, to what extent have the women of PNG consented to current natural resource management? Whatever else one is inclined to say regarding the normative assessment of resource trades with this government, surely the fact that women are not adequately represented in national-level governance of natural resources is a mark against the legitimacy of any resource trades with PNG. If proper authority requires, in part, channels for consent, when these channels are effectively (if not formally) closed off to half of the population, we must assess the legitimacy of these trades as being lower than those where women are equally participating in the governance and management of natural resources.

8.4.2   Feminist assessment of contribution to injustice

Evaluating whether the natural resource trade contributes to injustice requires a gender-sensitive accounting of the distribution of benefits and burdens of the domestic extractive industry. Taking gender seriously in the evaluation of the harms of natural resource trade should imply three reforms in evaluation.

First, the assessment of the impact of overall benefits and burdens must move beyond average outcomes—for example, overall impact on average incomes, or average changes in human development—and instead disaggregate the results by gender (and likely other social categories as well). After this disaggregation occurs, moral evaluation or assessment ought arguably to "penalize" countries for inequities between men and women.[26]

Second, the space of evaluation should take account of the broad range of dimensions in which gender injustice can emerge. Rather than simply focusing on consumption or income, evaluation can take account of a range of other material needs, including health, education, shelter, sanitation, and access to running water, and various dimensions related to social relations and agency, such as time-use, voice in the community, control over decision making, freedom from violence, and so on. Therefore, if an increase in natural resource extraction improves overall incomes (of those who are employed, presumably men), but also increases violence against women and reduces their control over decision making in the family, the net evaluation may well be that the counterfactual scenario of no increase in natural resource extraction is preferable, despite the fact that average incomes have risen.[27]

Third, an adequate assessment of the distribution of benefits and burdens must be sensitive to differential needs, conversion factors, and social locations. That is, rather than merely assessing the goods individuals have at a given time and place, it should assess the genuine opportunities they have, which requires sensitivity to their unique personal needs but also to their ability to convert resources into achievements.[28]

8.4.3 Composite feminist normative assessment

We've now reached a point where we can provide a composite framework for the normative assessment of a resource-exporting state, and thus a normative assessment of the participation in the resource trade by resource importers (consumers, corporations, and the governments that represent them). A suitable approach to assessing the trade in natural resources will be pluralist, taking account both of the legitimacy of the overall regime of resource management and of particular resource trades, while also assessing the degree to which a particular trade or trading regime contributes to injustice. And it will be feminist, making gender central to the assessment of justice by considering whether and to what extent the benefits and burdens of existing (and possible alternative candidate) resource regimes are distributed among men and women.

Level	Criterion	Standard of Assessment	Feminist Revision
National	Civil and Political Rights	Do background conditions for consent exist? Absent conditions for consent, can consent nonetheless be inferred?	Do conditions exist for women to consent? Can most women's consent be inferred?
National	Procedural Justice	Are the procedures for managing and trading natural resources justifiable? Have the pre-specified procedures for exploiting and selling natural resources been followed?	Are women involved in the national procedures for managing resources? Are women's interests represented?
National	Benefits and Burdens	Does the resulting national-level distribution of benefits and burdens from resource management confer a degree of legitimacy?	On the whole, is the status of women in the society improved or undermined by the resource trade?
Subnational	Procedural Justice	Does the group that subnationally manages resources follow transparent, morally justifiable procedures for its management?	Are women involved in the subnational procedures for managing resources? Are their interests represented?
Subnational	Just Claim (representation, association, etc.)	Does the group that subnationally claims authority over natural resources have sharable reasons for making that claim?	Are women represented? Are their interests?
Subnational	Benefits and Burdens	Does the subnational distribution of benefits and burdens confer some legitimacy?	Do particular resource sales improve or undermine women's status?

8.5   Feminist reform

Feminist revisions to the standard description and normative assessment of the resource privilege now leave us well placed to reconsider various prescriptions to eliminate or mitigate the gender injustices associated with natural resource exports. Proposed reforms adopt one (or more) of three strategies. Some reforms attempt *to block* the causal link between natural resource dependence and its associated gender injustices. Other reforms aim at providing *countervailing pressures* that would weaken these causal links or reduce the likelihood of gender injustices associated with natural resource dependence. Finally, some reforms simply aim *to mitigate* the attendant injustices of natural resource dependence. The gendered nature of the extractives industry and its governance provides reasons to feminize natural resource management. The gendered distribution of benefits and burdens from natural resource exports provides a reason to make gender-sensitive prescriptions to mitigate the resultant injustices of the international resource privilege.

There are many proposals to address the resource curse. I'll focus here on four sets of approaches. No single approach will be the decisive way to lift the curse. Rather, a range of measures, taken by different actors, are needed to combat the resource curse and its attendant harms. My aim is to show how feminist analysis can improve these recommendations.

8.5.1   Norms, transparency, and audits

Several efforts seek to establish global norms regarding the management of natural resources, to recommend best practices to states and corporations, and to see these norms eventually codified into recognized domestic and international law. Through regulation and voluntary effort, civil society and to a lesser extent governments have promoted transparency regarding the allocation of resource rights and the management of resource revenues. The Natural Resource Charter[29] contains 12 precepts that are meant to guide domestic resource management in a way that produces the most social benefits and mitigates risks and injustices associated with natural resource extraction. The Extractive Industries Transparency Initiative (EITI)[30] seeks to ensure transparency and accountability regarding payments and revenues related to natural resource extraction. EITI requires member countries to publish revenues and payments from companies to governments, and conduct independent audits of these payments, to be reconciled by an independent administrator. Civil society is to be involved in the monitoring and evaluation of these efforts, and the rules apply to state-owned companies as well as other firms.

Like other efforts to address the resource curse, these proposals make no mention of gender or women. The Natural Resource Charter could easily be modified to recognize the risks of exacerbated gender inequality arising from a heavy dependence on natural resource exports, and to identify the equitable sharing of the benefits and burdens between the genders as a norm that should be adopted by resource-exporting states. Furthermore, a gender-sensitive EITI, or a new initiative, could include not only auditing of payments and revenues, but gender-responsive audits of both the operations of companies in extractive sectors and the spending of resource revenues. For over a decade gender-responsive budgeting has been used to analyze, and subsequently reform, the spending of governments and donors. There is no principled reason that this cannot be applied to the extractives sector, and be supported or even required by resource importers.

8.5.2 Cash transfers

A number of thinkers argue that resource rents should be distributed directly to citizens.[31] Just as the state of Alaska distributes oil rents directly to Alaskans, so too might South Sudan and Iraq make cash payments directly to South Sudanese and Iraqi citizens. The idea of "Oil to Cash" schemes is attractive and, if the political difficulties can be surmounted, it offers a promising avenue to reduce the risk of economic mismanagement and to counteract the incentives towards authoritarianism and conflict. States that seek to spend resource revenues on public goods must raise those revenues through individual taxation, thus increasing their accountability to citizens who can help to ensure the public services actually be delivered.

Gender-sensitive analyses can improve the distribution of these funds so as to create larger welfare benefits for both direct recipients and their families, and to ensure that the distribution of resources leads to women's empowerment and counteracts the gender-inequality resource curse. First, consideration must be made by the distributing state regarding *to whom* cash payments should be made. Should similarly situated men and women receive equal shares of resource rents? Or might women be provided a higher share, perhaps proportional to the number of the children in their families plus themselves?[32] Second, consideration should be given to *how* cash payments are made. Several recent innovations in development thinking and policy may offer guidance here. The success of conditional cash transfers in advancing human development suggests that some conditionality on payments may achieve important human development outcomes, including combating gender inequality. However, this may require some institutional capacity that is often lacking in resource-cursed states, and raises risks of corruption in the transfer process. Cash payments may also focus on the importance of building up the assets of recipients rather than simply providing an additional flow of income. For example, payments might be made into accounts that recipients could not access immediately. As cash accrues in the account, and if it can be accessed from anywhere after an initial period of restricted access, this might enhance the bargaining power and exit options of women in violent or exploitative relationships. Recent research suggests that women who own assets are much less likely to be victims of long-term violence.[33] Therefore, it may be that using cash payments to build assets rather than provide income might best improve the status of women in resource-cursed countries.

8.5.3 Sanctions

In some cases, resource management is so bad, and the resulting harms so significant, that "the international community" is morally justified in imposing sanctions on these sectors, and/or the individuals involved in them, so as to prevent further harm and to protect citizens from ongoing harm. For example, when the Libyan regime of Muammar Gaddafi turned its guns on Libyan citizens in 2011, sanctions imposed by the European Union were intended to curtail the economic viability of the regime.[34]

Taking gender seriously in addressing resource-related sanctions might lead to two related reforms. First, sanctions may be benchmarked to violations of women's rights. Whereas sanctions are commonly imposed for (real or perceived) threats to international security, or for (real or perceived) serious crimes against citizens in resource-exporting countries, I propose that one criterion for evaluating whether sanctions should be imposed is whether women's rights are being systematically violated. This criterion could be included in a rule-based system for the imposition of sanctions. For example, Wenar (2008, 2011) proposes that a club of like-minded countries could agree to impose sanctions on exports from "worst of the worst" countries as measured by Freedom House's index of civil and political rights. Such a rule-based sanction mechanism could take effect not simply on a gender-insensitive assessment of civil and political rights, but with a particular eye toward the status of women. Similarly, Pogge's (2002) proposed Democracy Panel would authorize sanctions when democracies turn autocratic, if the country in question had adopted a constitutional amendment barring the sale of its natural resources just in the case that the country reverts away from democratic governance. This procedurally grounded sanctioning mechanism could also be based not simply on whether the Democracy Panel determines that democratic governance has slipped away, but also on whether women's formal right to govern or substantive opportunity to govern had been protected.

Likewise, if sanctions are not imposed according to a rule-based mechanism[35] but are instead imposed ad hoc in reaction to changing circumstances, one relevant piece of evidence for imposing sanctions should be the status of women, and one benchmark for having sanctions lifted should be efforts to promote the status of women. For example, a range of sanctions by the United States, the European Union, and a select set of other countries have been imposed against Burma and Sudan for their human rights records.[36] On my account, one reason for imposing sanctions can include the low status of women, and one reason for lifting sanctions can be efforts to improve the status of women.

However, sanctions are often harmful and fail to bring about the objective for which they were initially designed. Most famously, comprehensive sanctions on Iraq significantly harmed civilian populations but did little to weaken the regime of Saddam Hussein (Gordon 2010). Just as gender-sensitive analysis might favor the imposition of sanctions, it may also weigh against imposing sanctions if the foreseeable harms to civilian populations, including women, are too great.

8.5.4 Development policy

Finally, development policy, whether that of international institutions, donor governments, or NGOs and civil society, should be sensitive to the role of natural resources in causing gender inequality. Development policy in resource-exporting states should focus on policies that empower women, especially though not exclusively through the creation of high-quality employment opportunities. Common approaches to women's empowerment focus on funding for civil society organizations, or creating access to finance or job training for women. While these micro-level efforts may do some good, if my argument is correct, then one promising strategy for promoting women's rights in resource-rich countries will be creating formal employment opportunities outside the home. This requires not merely micro-finance to jump-start small businesses (which are often informal and secondary in nature), but more sustained efforts to develop employment-intensive industries in which women will find formal employment. For example, just as the reduction of trade barriers is used to incentivize the development of certain sectors in poor countries, both tariff and non-tariff trade barriers could be reduced for countries that employ an adequate number of women. In a wealthy country like Saudi Arabia, such trading benefits may be inconsequential, and thus unlikely to advance women's rights in the country. But in other states where the development of nascent manufacturing sectors is both possible and economically profitable for would-be entrepreneurs, such measures may be able to induce greater female labor force participation.

8.6 Conclusion

There is reason to expect the resource curse to continue. Not only is there a considerable boom in most commodity prices, but economic growth in resource-hungry countries including Brazil, India, and China can be expected to maintain high commodity prices in the future. Furthermore, improvements in resource extraction technologies have increased the scope of exploration and production—only five out of 55 African states are neither exploring for nor producing oil (*The Economist* 2012). Furthermore, growing resource demand and increasing resource scarcity may mean even higher prices in the future (Evans 2011). It is therefore imperative that solutions to the resource curse be found.

In the limited space here I have been able only to suggest why those concerned with global gender justice should take seriously how natural resource exports and the international resource privilege undermine struggles for women's rights. Much work remains to be done on this topic. The extant academic research on gender and the resource curse is limited, and more practical learning is needed on how the resource curse can be overcome and how women's rights can be secured in resource-rich states. This chapter aims to move the issue of the natural resource trade from the margins to the center of the struggle to secure women's rights, and to move women from the margin to the center of research and advocacy aimed at combating the resource curse.

Acknowledgments

I began thinking about this chapter after a workshop at Australian National University on the resource curse. I am grateful to comments then and after from, among others, Leif Wenar, Thomas Pogge, Christian Barry, and David Wiens. I am grateful to subsequent audiences at the Centre for Ethics at the University of Toronto and the Australian Agency for International Development. Excellent written comments were provided by Alison Jaggar and Eamon Aloyo. All errors remain my own.

Notes

1 In addition to the resource privilege and borrowing privilege (the ability to borrow on citizens' behalf), Pogge identifies the arms privilege (the ability legally to procure arms) and the treaty privilege (the ability to negotiate and affirm international treaties) as four privileges that the international order confers on groups who take power. See Pogge 2010: 18–21.
2 Studies confirming the conflict resource curse include Collier and Hoeffler 1998, 2005, and Ross 2012.
3 This is the "greed" thesis. There is a competing grievance thesis—that natural resources raise inequalities, and thus give would-be rebels suitable grievances to undertake rebellion. See Rosser (2006: 18) for further exploration. To my eye, both explanations are compatible in explaining some or all resource rebellions.
4 One notable recent effort to finance a coup involved Simon Mann and Mark Thatcher, son of Margaret Thatcher. The pair were arrested for attempting to overthrow the government of Equatorial Guinea, a highly endowed oil exporter. Mann later testified that Thatcher had personally invested $350,000 in the effort. For one account of the coup, see Roberts 2006.
5 For a review of these theses, see Rosser 2006.
6 Studies confirming the political resource curse include Ross 2001, Jenson and Wantchekon 2004, and Wiens et al. forthcoming.
7 Ross suggests that countries with large financial reserves from oil, including Algeria, Saudi Arabia, and Kuwait, have been able to provide generous benefits to their citizens in an effort to avoid citizen uprising, while countries with less or no oil, like Egypt, Tunisia, and Yemen, were not

able to make equivalently large payments, and thus faced stronger citizen opposition.

8 Wiens et al. (forthcoming) argue that dependence on natural resource revenue extends the survival of authoritarian regimes, but has no impact on the survival of democratic governments.

9 At the time of his death, Muammar Gaddafi was rumored to possess $40 billion.

10 I am grateful to David Wiens for highlighting this point for me.

11 See Ross 2012 for elaboration. He argues that following the end of the Cold War, countries without plentiful natural resources were three times more likely to transition to democracy than those without.

12 See Le Billon 2001 and Snyder and Bhavnani 2005 for further elaboration. Point-source resources are those that can only be captured in a particular area, as opposed to alluvial diamonds, for example, which can be gathered anywhere along the river in which they are found. Lootable resources are those that could be stolen. Some resources, such as mined diamonds, are much more lootable than, say, natural gas deposits. Whether a resource can be easily stolen, and whether it is concentrated in a particular location, can inform both how the resource may incentivize conflict, and how it may be used to finance conflict.

13 See Wenar's forthcoming book on the resource curse.

14 For Sudan, see Johnson 2003; for the DRC see Prunier 2009 and Stearns 2011.

15 There are a variety of micro-level impacts—such as oil extraction or mining directly impacting gender relations in the place of extraction, rather than more causally distant impacts on economic opportunity and thus on gender relations. These micro-level impacts are covered much more thoroughly in the academic literature and popular press, so I'll just briefly mention a few here. Extractive industry employment, unlike some manufacturing or service industries, is dominated by men. Male employees often travel away from home to work in mining and oil, leaving behind families. Higher salaries associated with extractive industries frequently lead to widespread prostitution in areas of mining. Of course male employees in mines also suffer gender-specific harms—mining in particular is highly dangerous, brings great health risks, and is often characterized by weak labor standards. Environmental damage often associated with extractive industries, and the drain on public resources to support them, can harm women in particular who bear responsibility for carework in the household, and thus face additional burdens when clean water is harder to access, or other public goods are damaged. These micro-level harms are important and gender-specific, but they are not my focus here. Rather, I will draw attention to the longer causal chain between natural resource extraction and systemic gender inequality.

16 This area of academic inquiry is relatively recent and deserves further exploration. While Ross's initial article has received significant academic attention, much more work should be done to determine the impact of the

natural resource trade on gender equity. Ross uses representation in government and labor force participation to assess the correlation between dependence on oil exports and women's status. Future work on the macro-level impacts of natural resources on gender equity should move in several directions. First, researchers should seek to confirm Ross's finding by determining whether similar correlations exist between natural resource exports and other indicators of gender equality— including voice in the household, time-use, freedom from violence, and composite metrics of gender equity. These indicators can focus on institutions, such as the OECD's Social Institutions Gender Index, or on outcomes, such as the World Economic Forum's Global Gender Gap Index. Though data is still sparse, more gendered statistics are coming online and this may allow for more sophisticated analysis. Second, future work should investigate whether different resources, particularly oil and mining, vary in their impact on gender equity. Third, this research should examine "natural" experiments—namely, when a country discovers natural resources and their extraction begins, what impact does this have on gender equity? Alternatively, when a country is already dependent on natural resource exports, do shifts in the value of these exports (and thus underlying changes in economic activity) correspond to shifting levels of gender inequality?

17 See Dollar et al. 2001 on cross-country evidence of a correlation between gender equity and lower corruption. See Goetz 2007 questioning the narrative of women as less corruptible.

18 I have addressed this at more length in Wisor 2012, and "The Resource 'Curse': Rethinking Moral Assessment and Reform" (manuscript).

19 This does not commit me to the view that despots are politically legitimate if they rule benevolently. It only commits me to the view that they are more legitimate than their despotic counterparts who rule in ways that harm the population. Sudan and China may be equally formally undemocratic, but Sudan's government is less legitimate than China's, because of the harms it inflicts on most of its citizens.

20 The reader will note that this is a weaker requirement than that which is posed at the national level. Whereas national-level assessments examine civil and political rights and the possibility for consent, at the subnational level groups may simply not be capable of securing those rights, nor can they be required to. A group of miners cannot ensure everyone in a province has a right to vote. They can, however, provide reasons (which may or may not be sharable) as to why they have a moral right to extract resources.

21 Thomas Pogge uses the international resource privilege to substantiate his view that wealthy societies are complicit in imposing harms that contribute to the persistence of severe poverty. Though Pogge is also concerned about the legitimacy of the seller, I take it that he is primarily concerned with the resource trade's contribution to unjust harm. He emphasizes his concern with deontological rather than utilitarian considerations.

22 The defender of this view may strengthen her moral complaint against participation in the resource trade by noting not only that it causes harm, but that consumers and corporations benefit from that harm, by enjoying the products that are derived from natural resources, or by receiving profits or revenue as investors in or employees of corporations that use them.

23 Note that this is one of two ways to understand moral responsibility for global justice. Either individuals and their institutions are morally responsible just insofar as they foreseeably contribute to harm, or individuals and institutions are morally responsible because they foreseeably contribute to harm and had feasible alternatives whereby they could have been in less harmful or unharmful relationships. This latter reading is how I understand Pogge's broad project.

24 This is contested in recent philosophical literature by cosmopolitans. I agree with Wenar that we can appeal to international law, which grants the ownership of natural resources to peoples. Margaret Moore (2012) gives a strong defense of national control over natural resources grounded in collective self-determination, while maintaining that wealthy states may have obligations to distribute wealth beyond their borders so as to meet basic needs.

25 PNG receives scores of 4 for political rights and 3 for civil liberties on the Freedom House Index, and is categorized as an electoral democracy.

26 It is common practice in composite indices of, for example, human development to penalize countries for either vertical inequality (between those at the top of the distribution and those at the bottom) or horizontal inequality (between groups, such as between men and women). Assessing distributive outcomes based in part on the distributive shares that are held by members of different social groups requires denying what is often known as the anonymity condition. On this see Pogge 2007: 52–3.

27 I am fortunate to be involved in a resource project that is developing a gender-sensitive measure of poverty by engaging in critical discussion with poor men and women who live with deprivation on a daily basis. For our answers to the selection of dimensions, see www.genderpovertymeasure. org.

28 Here I broadly follow Sen's (2009) capability approach, which is particularly well suited to identifying different biological and social needs that correspond to one's gender, and to highlighting the relational and social features of an individual's life that allow her to convert resources into achievements.

29 http://naturalresourcecharter.org.

30 http://eiti.org.

31 The idea has been most thoroughly developed at the Center for Global Development, a think-tank based in Washington DC. See their collective work at http://www.cgdev.org/section/initiatives/_active/ revenues_distribution.

32 The possible benefits of such a scheme have to be weighed against the fact
    that higher levels of unearned female income may deter women's entrance
    into the formal labor force. If this is correct, then an assessment of such
    schemes must assess whether the benefits of higher female income exceed
    the costs of lower rates of female labor force participation.
33 For example, Agarwal and Panda (2007) find that the ownership of land
    is a critical determinant in whether women are free from violence in India.
34 Of course the question of who has the right authority to impose sanctions
    is important. Feminist assessment of the right-authority question requires
    sensitivity to the representation of women and their interests in the pro-
    cedures for issuing sanctions determinations. Similarly it is a separate
    question whether some form of military intervention was justified in the
    case of Libya.
35 A rule-based mechanism for imposing sanctions would require a sanction-
    ing body to enact sanctions whenever a country met a pre-specified set
    of conditions, such as that a genocide or crimes against humanity are
    occurring.
36 In the case of Sudan, sanctions were imposed initially and nominally for
    state support of terrorism—but now for the human rights record of
    the government. At the time of writing, sanctions against Burma are being
    lifted because of movements towards democratic governance in the
    country.

Bibliography

Ackerly, Brooke and Susan Moller Okin (1999) "Feminist Social Criticism and the International Movement for Women's Rights as Human Rights," in Ian Shapiro and Casiano Hacker-Cordón (eds.) *Democracy's Edges*, Cambridge: Cambridge University Press, pp. 134–62.

Affonso, Dyanne D. et al. (2000) "An International Study Exploring Levels of Postpartum Depressive Symptomatology," *Journal of Psychosomatic Research* 49: 207–16.

Agarwal, B. and P. Panda (2007) "Toward Freedom from Domestic Violence: The Neglected Obvious," *Journal of Human Development and Capabilities* 8(3): 359–88.

Ali, Akleema and Hari D. Maharajh (2004) "Anorexia Nervosa and Religious Ambivalence in a Developing Country," *Internet Journal of Mental Health* 2(1): 1–5, http://archive.ispub.com/journal/the-internet-journal-of-mental-health/volume-2-number-1/anorexia-nervosa-and-religious-ambivalence-in-a-developing-country.html#sthash.ZkFm5oiv.dpbs (accessed May 13, 2013).

Allison, Dorothy (1993) *Bastard Out of Carolina*, New York: Penguin Books.

Ambrose, Soren (2001) "Congress Takes Action Against IMF/World Bank User Fees," in Kevin Danaher (ed.) *Democratizing the Global Economy: The Battle Against the World Bank and the IMF*, Monroe ME: Common Courage Press.

Amott, Teresa L. and Julie Matthaei (1991) *Race, Gender, and Work: A Multi-Cultural History of Women in the United States*, Boston MA: South End Press.

Anderson, Bridget (2000) *Doing the Dirty Work? The Global Politics of Domestic Labour*, London and New York: Zed Books.

Appiah, Kwame Anthony (2010) *Honor Code: How Moral Revolutions Happen*, New York: W.W. Norton.

Arat-Koc, S. (2006) "Whose Social Reproduction? Transnational Mother-hood and Challenges to Neoliberalism," in K. Bezanson and M. Luxton (eds.) *Social Reproduction: Feminist Challenges to Neoliberalism*, Montreal and Kingston: McGill/Queens University Press, pp. 75–92.

Asad, T. (2002) "What do Human Rights Do? An Anthropological Enquiry," *Theory and Event* 4: 5–25.

AusAID (2008) *Violence Against Women in Melanesia and East Timor: A Review of International Lessons*, Canberra: Office of Development Effectiveness.

Bagchi, A. (2008) "Immigrants, Morality and Neoliberalism," *Development and Change* 39: 197–218.

Baker, Brenda M. (1999) "Understanding Consent in Sexual Assault," in Keith Burgess-Jackson (ed.) *A Most Detestable Crime: New Philosophical Essays on Rape*, Oxford: Oxford University Press, pp. 49–70.

Baker, Raymond W. (2005) *Capitalism's Achilles Heel: Dirty Money and How to Renew the Free-Market System*, Hoboken NJ: John Wiley and Sons.

Bakker, I. (2007) "Social Reproduction and the Constitution of a Gendered Political Economy," *New Political Economy* 12: 541–56.

Barnett, Kathleen and Caren Grown (2004), *Gender Impacts of Government Revenue Collection: The Case of Taxation*, London: Commonwealth Secretariat.

Barry, Brian (1998) "International Society from a Cosmopolitan Perspective," in David R. Mapel and Terry Nardin (eds.) *International Society: Diverse Ethical Perspectives*, Princeton NJ: Princeton University Press, pp. 144–63.

Baumert, Kevin (1998) "Global Taxes and Fees: Recent Developments and Overcoming Obstacles," http://www.globalpolicy.org/socecon/glotax/baumert.htm (accessed August 3, 2004).

Becker, Anne E. (2003) "Eating Disorders and Social Transition," *Primary Psychiatry* 10(6): 71–5.

Becker, Anne E., Jennifer J. Thomas, and Kathleen M. Pike (2009) "Should Non-Fat-Phobic Anorexia Nervosa be Included in DSM-V?," *International Journal of Eating Disorders* 42(7): 620–35.

Beitz, Charles (1979) *Political Theory and International Relations*, Princeton NJ: Princeton University Press.

Beitz, Charles (1994) "Cosmopolitan Liberalism and the States System," in Chris Brown (ed.) *Political Restructuring in Europe: Ethical Perspectives*, London: Routledge.

Beitz, Charles (2001) "Does Global Inequality Matter?" *Metaphilosophy* 32: 95–112.

Beneria, Lourdes (2003) *Gender, Development, and Globalization: Economics as if All People Mattered*, New York: Routledge.

Benston, Margaret (1969) "The Political Economy of Women's Liberation," *Monthly Review*, September 13–25.

Bettio, Francesca, Annamaria Simonazzi, and Paola Villa (2006) "Change in Care Regimes and Female Migration: The 'Care Drain' in the Mediterra-nean," *Journal of European Social Policy* 16(3): 271–85.

Bhagwati, Jagdish (2004) *In Defense of Globalization*, Oxford: Oxford University Press.

Bina, Rena (2008) "The Impact of Cultural Factors Upon Postpartum Depression: A Literature Review," *Health Care for Women International* 29: 568–92.

BNP2TKI (Badan Nasional Penempatan dan Perlingdungan Tenaga Kerja Indonesia, National Body for the Placement and Protection of the Indonesian Work Force) (2012) "Penempatan Berdasarkan Jenis Kelamin. Placements Based on Gender, 2006–2012," http://www.bnp2tki.go.id (accessed May 11, 2013).

Boris, E. and R. S. Parreñas (2010) *Intimate Labors: Cultures, Technologies, and the Politics of Care*, Stanford CA: Stanford University Press.

Boserup, Ester (1970) *Women's Role in Economic Development*, New York: Saint Martin's Press.

Brison, Susan (2002) *Aftermath: Violence and the Remaking of the Self*, Princeton NJ: Princeton University Press.

Brock, Gillian (2008) "Taxation and Global Justice: Closing the Gap Between Theory and Practice," *Journal of Social Philosophy* 39: 161–84.

Brock, Gillian (2009) *Global Justice: A Cosmopolitan Account*, Oxford: Oxford University Press.

Brunnschweiler, C. and E. Bulte (2008) "Linking Natural Resources to Slow Growth and More Conflict," *Science* 320: 616–17.

Bubeck, Diemut (1995) *Care, Gender, and Justice*, Oxford: Clarendon Press.

Cagaty, Nilufer (2003) "Gender Budgets and Beyond: Feminist Fiscal Policy in the Context of Globalization," *Gender and Development* 11(1): 15–24.

Cahill, Ann J. (2001) *Rethinking Rape*, Ithaca NY: Cornell University Press.

Califia, Pat (1981) "Man/Boy Love and the Lesbian/Gay Movement," in Daniel Tsang (ed.) *The Age Taboo: Gay Male Sexuality, Power and Consent*, London and Boston MA: Gay Men's Press and Alyson Publications.

Caplan, Paula J. (1995) *They Say You're Crazy: How the World's Most Powerful Psychiatrists Decide Who's Normal*, New York: Perseus Books.

Carmichael, Stokely and Charles V. Hamilton (1967) *Black Power: The Politics of Liberation in America*, New York: Random House.

Catina, Ana and Oltea Joja (2001) "Emerging Markets: Submerging Women," in Mervat Nasser, Melanie A. Katzman, and Richard A. Gordon (eds.) *Eating Disorders and Cultures in Transition*, Hove, East Sussex and New York: Brunner-Routledge, pp. 111–19.

Chakravarti, Uma (2005) "From Fathers to Husbands: Of Love, Death, and Marriage in Northern India," in Lynn Welchman and Sara Hossain (eds.) *"Honour": Crimes, Paradigms, and Violence Against Women*, London: Zed Books, pp. 308–31.

Chamallas, Martha (1988) "Consent, Equality, and the Legal Control of Sexual Conduct," *Southern California Law Review* 61: 777–862.

Chang, Grace (2000) *Disposable Domestics: Immigrant Women Workers in the Global Economy*, Boston MA: South End Press.

Chant, Sylvia (2008) "The 'Feminisation of Poverty' and the 'Feminisation' of Anti-Poverty Programmes: Room for Revision?" *Journal of Development Studies* 44(2): 165–97.

Cholewinski, R. (1997) *Migrant Workers in International Human Rights Law: Their Protection in Countries of Employment*, Oxford: Clarendon Press.

Chomsky, N. (2002) "Clash of Civilizations?" http://www.india-seminar.com/2002/509/509%20noam%20chomsky.htm.

Chowdhry, G. and S. Nair (eds.) (2002) *Power, Postcolonialism, and International Relations: Reading Race, Gender, and Class*, New York: Routledge.

Christensen, John and M. P. Hampton (1999) "All Good Things Come to an End," *The World Today* 55 (8/9): 14–17.

Christian Aid (2005) "The Shirts Off Their Backs: How Tax Policies Fleece the Poor," http://www.christianaid.org.uk/images/the_shirts_off_their_backs.pdf (accessed May 13, 2013).

Cobham, Alex (2005) "Tax Evasion, Tax Avoidance and Development Finance," *Queen Elizabeth House Working Paper* 129, http://www3.qeh.ox.ac.uk/pdf/qehwp/qehwps129.pdf (accessed May 13, 2013).

Collier, Paul (2007) *The Bottom Billion: Why the Poorest Countries Are Failing and What Can Be Done About It*, Oxford: Oxford University Press.

Collier, P. and A. Hoeffler (1998) "On Economic Causes of Civil War," *Oxford Economic Papers* 50: 563–73.

Collier, P. and A. Hoeffler (2005) "Resource Rents, Governance, and Conflict," *Journal of Conflict Resolution* 49(4): 625–33.

Collins, Patricia Hill (1990) *Black Feminist Thought: Knowledge, Consciousness, and the Politics of Empowerment*, Boston MA: Unwin Hyman.

Cooper, Richard (1998) "Toward a Real Global Warming Treaty: The Case for a Carbon Tax," *Foreign Affairs* (March/April): 66–79.

Cooper, Richard (2002) "The Double-Dividend of Emissions Taxes: Greenhouse Gas Reduction and Revenue," Background Paper, Dinner Meeting on Financing Global Public Goods, Office of Development Studies, UNDP, January 15.

Darwall, Stephen (2002) *Welfare and Rational Care*, Princeton NJ: Princeton University Press.

Dobash, Rebecca Emerson and Russell P. Dobash (1998) "Cross-Border Encounters: Challenges and Opportunities," in R. Emerson Dobash and Russell P. Dobash (eds.) *Rethinking Violence Against Women*, London: Sage, pp. 1–22.

Dollar, D., R. Fisman, and R. Gatti (2001) "Are Women Really the 'Fairer' Sex? Corruption and Women in Government," *Journal of Economic Behavior and Organization* 46: 423–9.

Dugger, Celia W. (2006) "US Plan to Lure Nurses May Hurt Poor Nations," *New York Times*, May 24, http://www.nytimes.com/2006/05/24/world/americas/24nurses.html?pagewanted=all&_r=0 (accessed April 30, 2013).

Dwyer, Daisy and Judith Bruce (eds.) (1988) *A Home Divided: Women and Income in the Third World*, Stanford CA: Stanford University Press.

Eckenwiler, Lisa (2009) "Health Worker Migration and Transnational Justice," *International Journal of Feminist Bioethics* 4(2): 1–31.

ECLAC (1998) *The Fiscal Covenant: Strengths, Weaknesses, Challenges*, Santiago: ECLAC, http://archivo.cepal.org/pdfs/1998/S9800024.pdf (accessed May 7, 2013).

Economist (2012) "Show Us the Money: Africans Need More Transparency to Benefit from their Resource Wealth," September 1, http://www.economist.com/node/21561886 (accessed September 9, 2012).

Ehrenreich, Barbara and Arlie Russell Hochschild (eds.) (2002) *Global Woman: Nannies, Maids, and Sex Workers in the New Economy*, New York: Henry Holt.

Elson, Diane (2002) "Gender Justice, Human Rights, and Neo-liberal Economic Policies," in Maxine Molyneaux and Shahra Razavi (eds.) *Gender Justice, Development, and Rights*, Oxford and New York: Oxford University Press, pp. 78–114.

Elson, D. and N. Cagaty (2000) "The Social Content of Macroeconomic Policies," *World Development* 28(7): 1347–64.

ENDS Environmental Daily (1999) "Aviation Climate Effect 'Could Grow Four-Fold'", June 3.

Enloe, C. (1989) *Bananas, Beaches and Bases: Making Feminist Sense of International Politics*, Berkeley: University of California Press.

Enloe, C. (2000) *Maneuvers: International Politics of Militarizing Women's Lives*. Berkeley: University of California Press.

European Commission (2002) "Responses to the Challenges of Globalization: A Study on the International Monetary and Financial System and on Financing for Development," http://www.globalpolicy.org/component/content/article/213-financing-for-development/45756.html (accessed May 7, 2013).

Evans, A. (2011) "Resource Scarcity, Fair Shares and Development," WWF-UK/Oxfam Discussion Paper.

Evans, William (1997) "To Help the UN, A Tax on Trade," *New York Times*, July 6.

Fausto-Sterling, Anne (1985/1992) *Myths of Gender: Biological Theories About Women and Men*, New York: Basic Books.

Fausto-Sterling, Anne (1999) *Sexing the Body*, New York: Basic Books.

Feldman, Matthew B. and Ilan H. Meyer (2007a) "Eating Disorders in Diverse Lesbian, Gay, and Bisexual Populations," *International Journal of Eating Disorders* 40(3): 218–26.

Feldman, Matthew B. and Ilan H. Meyer (2007b) "Childhood Abuse and Eating Disorders in Gay and Bisexual Men," *International Journal of Eating Disorders* 40(5): 418–23.

Fineman, Martha Albertson (1995) *The Neutered Mother, the Sexual Family and Other Twentieth-Century Tragedies*, New York: Routledge.

Fischer, Bernice and Joan Tronto (1990) "Towards a Feminist Theory of Caring," in Emily K. Abel and Margaret K. Nelson (eds.) *Circles of Care*, Albany: SUNY, pp. 35–62.

Folbre, Nancy (1994) *Who Pays for the Kids? Gender and the Structures of Constraint*, New York: Routledge.

Folbre, Nancy (2002) *The Invisible Heart: Economics and Family Values*, New York: New Press.

Folbre, Nancy (2003) "Caring Labor: Transcription of a video by Oliver Ressler," http://www.republicart.net/disc/aeas/folbre01_en.htm (accessed May 13, 2013).

Ford, M. (2004) "Organizing the Unorganizable: Unions, NGOs, and Indonesian Migrant Labour," *International Migration* 42: 99–119.

Fraser, Nancy (1997) "From Redistribution to Recognition? Dilemmas of Justice in a 'Postsocialist' Age," in *Justice Interruptus: Critical Reflections on the "Postsocialist" Condition*, New York and London: Routledge, pp. 11–39.

Fraser, Nancy (2008) "Abnormal Justice," *Critical Inquiry* 34(3): 393–422.

Fricker, Miranda (2007) *Epistemic Injustice: Power and the Ethics of Knowing*, Oxford and New York: Oxford University Press.

Funk, Rus Ervin (1993) *Stopping Rape: A Challenge for Men*, Philadelphia: New Society Publishers.

Furman, Jason (2006) "Closing the Tax Gap," Center on Budget and Policy Priorities, http://www.cbpp.org/4-10-06tax3.htm (accessed May 7, 2013).

Gauthier, Jeffrey A. (1999) "Consent, Coercion, and Sexual Autonomy," in Keith Burgess-Jackson (ed.) *A Most Detestable Crime: New Philosophical Essays on Rape*, Oxford: Oxford University Press, pp. 71–91.

Gavey, Nicola J. (1991) "Sexual Victimization among Auckland University Students: How Much and Who Does it?," *New England Journal of Psychology* 20(2): 63–70.

Goetz, A. (2007) "Political Cleaners: Women as the New Anti-Corruption Force," *Development and Change* 38: 87–105.

Goodin, Robert E. (1985) *Protecting the Vulnerable: A Reanalysis of our Social Responsibilities*, Chicago: University of Chicago Press.

Gordon, J. (2010) *Invisible War: The United States and the Iraq Sanctions*, Cambridge MA: Harvard University Press.

Grewal, Inderpal and Caren Kaplan (1994) *Scattered Hegemonies: Postmodernity and Transnational Feminist Practices*, Minneapolis: University of Minnesota Press.

Group Sisterhood: Junko Kuninobu, Rie Okamura, Natsumi Takeuchi, Mari Yamamoto, Masumi Yoneda, and Midori Wada (1998) "Prostitution, Stigma, and the Law in Japan: A Feminist Roundtable Discussion," in Kamala Kempadoo and Jo Doezema (eds.) *Global Sex Workers: Rights, Resistance and Redefinition*, New York: Routledge, pp. 87–97.

Grunberg, Isabelle (1998) "Double Jeopardy: Globalization, Liberalization and the Fiscal Squeeze," *World Development* 26(4): 591–605.

Guyer, Jane (1988) "Dynamic Approaches to Domestic Budgeting: Cases and Methods from Africa," in Daisy Dwyer and Judith Bruce (eds.), *A Home Divided: Women and Income in the Third World*, Stanford CA: Stanford University Press.

Haddad, Lawrence, J. Hoddinott, and H. Alderman (eds.) (1997) *Intrahouse-hold Resource Allocation in Developing Countries: Methods, Models, and Policy*, Baltimore MD: Johns Hopkins University Press.

Halbreich, Uriel and Sandhya Karkun (2006) "Cross-Cultural and Social Diversity of Prevalence of Postpartum Depression and Depressive Symptoms," *Journal of Affective Disorders* 91: 97–111.

Haq, Mahbub ul, Inge Kaul, and Isabelle Grunberg (1996) *The Tobin Tax: Coping with Financial Volatility*, Oxford: Oxford University Press.

Hartley, Mary et al. (2011) "Depressed Mood in Pregnancy: Prevalence and Correlates in Two Cape Town Peri-Urban Settlements," *Reproductive Health* 8(9): 1–7, http://www.reproductive-health-journal.com/content/8/1/9 (accessed April 20, 2012).

Hayden, Tom and Charles Kernaghan (2002) "Pennies an Hour, and No Way Up," *New York Times*, July 6, http://www.nytimes.com/2002/07/06/opinion/pennies-an-hour-and-no-way-up.html (accessed May 13, 2013).

Hayes, M. J., S. Roberts, and A. Davare (2000) "Transactional Conflict Between Psychobiology and Culture in the Etiology of Postpartum Depression," *Medical Hypotheses* 55(3): 266–76.

Heng, Geraldine (1997) "'A Great Way to Fly': Nationalism, the State and the Varieties of Third-World Feminism," in Chandra Talpade Mohanty and M. Jacqui Alexander (eds.) *Feminist Genealogies, Colonial Legacies, Democratic Futures*, New York and London: Routledge, pp. 30–45.

Herman, Judith (1997) *Trauma and Recovery*, New York: Basic Books.

Herrera, G. (2008) "States, Work and Social Reproduction Through the Lens of Migrant Experience: Ecuadorian Domestic Workers in Madrid," in I. Bakker and R. Silvey (eds.) *Beyond States and Markets: The Challenges of Social Reproduction*, New York: Routledge, pp. 93–107.

Hester, Marianne, Liz Kelly, and Jill Radford (1996) *Women, Violence and Male Power: Feminist Activism, Research, and Practice*, Buckingham UK: Open University Press.

Hochschild, Arlie Russell and Barbara Ehrenreich (2002) *Global Woman: Nannies, Maids, and Sex Workers in the New Economy*, New York: Henry Holt and Company.

Hondagneu-Sotelo, P. (2001) *Doméstica: Immigrant Workers Cleaning and Caring in the Shadows of Affluence*, Berkeley: University of California Press.

Hondagneu-Sotelo, Pierrette and Ernestine Avila (2006) "'I'm Here, but I'm There': The Meanings of Latina Transnational Motherhood," in Mary K. Zimmerman, Jacqueline S. Litt, and Christine E. Bose (eds.) *Global Dimensions of Gender and Carework*, Stanford CA: Stanford University Press, pp. 254–65.

Horner, Frances (2001) "Do We Need an International Tax Organisation?," *Tax Notes International* (October 8): 1–16.

Huang, S. and B. S. Yeoh (1996) "Ties That Bind: State Policy and Migrant Female Domestic Helpers in Singapore," *Geoforum* 27: 479–93.

Hughes, Donna M. (2000) "The 'Natasha' Trade: The Transnational Shadow Market of Trafficking in Women," *Journal of International Affairs* 53(2): 625–51.

Hughes, Donna M. (2004) "The Role of 'Marriage Agencies' in the Sexual Exploitation and Trafficking of Women from the Former Soviet Union," *International Review of Victimology* 11: 49–71.

Hugo, G. (1995) "Labour Export from Indonesia: An Overview," *ASEAN Economic Bulletin* 12: 275–98.

Hugo, G. (2007) "Indonesia's Labor Looks Abroad," http://www.migrationin formation.org/Feature/print.cfm?ID=594 (accessed October 15, 2008).

Huh, Ra-Keum (2008) "The Politics of Meaning: Care Work and Migrant Women," *Asian Journal of Women's Studies* 13(3): 37–60.

Human Rights Watch (2004a) "Help Wanted: Abuse Against Female Migrant Domestic Workers in Indonesia and Malaysia," *Human Rights Watch* 16, 9(B): 1–91.

Human Rights Watch (2004b) "Bad Dreams: Exploitation and Abuse of Migrant Workers in Saudi Arabia," *Human Rights Watch* 16, 5(E).

Human Rights Watch (2004c) "Angola: Account for Missing Oil Revenues," *Human Rights Watch*, January 12, http://www.hrw.org/english/docs/2004/ 01/12/angola6925.htm (accessed May 7, 2013).

Human Rights Watch (2010) "Slow Reform: Protection of Migrant Domestic Workers in Asia and the Middle East," http://www.hrw.org/reports/ 2010/04/28/slow-reform-0 (accessed December 31, 2012).

Human Rights Watch (2011) "ILO: New Landmark Treaty to Protect Domestic Workers," http://www.hrw.org/news/2011/06/16/ilo-new-landmark-treaty-protect-domestic-workers (accessed December 31, 2012).

Human Rights Watch (2012) "Anis Hidayah, Indonesia," http://www.hrw .org/news/2012/08/13/anis-hidayah-indonesia (accessed December 31, 2012).

Hune, S. (1991) "Migrant Women in the Context of the International Convention on the Protection of the Rights of all Migrant Workers and Members of their Families," *International Migration Review* 25: 800–17.

Husain, N. et al. 2006. "Prevalence and Social Correlates of Postnatal Depression in a Low Income Country," *Archives of Women's Mental Health* 9: 197–202.

Hyndman, J. and M. Walton-Roberts (2000) "Interrogating Borders: A Transnational Approach to Refugee Research in Vancouver," *Canadian Geographer* 44: 244–58.

ICID (Independent Commission on International Development) (1980) *North-South: A Programme for Survival, Report of the Independent Commission*, London: Pan.

Inandi, Tacettin et al. (2005) "Risk Factors for Depression in the First Postnatal Year," *Social Psychiatry and Psychiatric Epidemiology* 40: 725–30.

Ingeborg Wick (2010) *Women Working in the Shadows: The Informal Economy and Export Processing Zones*, Südwind Institut für Ökonomie und Ökumene, Siegburg, http://labordoc.ilo.org/record/431871?ln=en (accessed April 30, 2013).

INSTRAW (2008) "Laboral Insert," in *Gender and Migration*, United Nations INSTRAW, http://www.un-instraw.org/en/grd/in-numbers/women-migrants-laboral-insertion-in-numbers-3.html (accessed December 2008).

International Confederation of Free Trade Unions (2004) "Export Processing Zones—Symbols of Exploitation and a Development Dead-End," http://www.newunionism.nets/library/intenationalism/ICFTU%20-%Export%20Processing%20Zeues%20-%202003.pdf.

International Labour Organization (ILO) (1998) "Labour and Social Issues Relating to Export Processing Zones," http://www.ilo.org/actrav/what/pubs/WCMS_114918/lang–en/index.htm (accessed September 1, 2012).

International Labour Organization (ILO) (1999) "Decent Work: Report of the Director-General," International Labor Conference, 87th Session, Geneva, http://www.ilo.org/public/english/standards/relm/ilc/ilc87/rep-i.htm (accessed April 30, 2013).

International Labour Organization (ILO) (2000) "Making the Best of Globalization: Migrant worker remittances and micro-finance," http://www.ilo.org/public/english/employment/finance/download/remitt.pdf (accessed October 27, 2008).

International Labour Organization (ILO) (2004a) "Organizing for Social Justice: Global Report under the Follow-up to the ILO Declaration on Fundamental Principles and Rights at Work," http://www.ilo.org/global/publications/ilo-bookstore/order-online/books/WCMS_PUBL_9221130304_EN/lang–en/index.htm (accessed April 30, 2013).

International Labour Organization (ILO) (2004b) "Global Employment Trends For Women, 2004," http://www.ilo.org/empelm/pubs/WCMS_114325/lang–en/index.htm (accessed August 6, 2006).

International Labour Organization (ILO) (2008) "Economic Development and Working Conditions in Export Processing Zones: A Survey of Trends," http://ilo.org/public/french/dialogue/download/wp3englishfinal.pdf (accessed September 1, 2012).

International Labor Organization (ILO) (2012) "Achieving Decent Work for Domestic Workers: An Organizer's Manual to Promote ILO Convention no. 189 and Build Domestic Workers' Power," http://www.ilo.org/public/libdoc/ilo/2012/112B07_75_engl.pdf.

International Monetary Fund (2012) "IMF Executive Directors and Voting Power" (updated September 22, 2012), http://www.imf.org/external/np/sec/memdir/eds.htm (accessed December 10, 2012).

IPCC (Intergovernmental Panel on Climate Change) (2001), "Aviation and the Global Atmosphere," http://www.grida.no/climate/ipcc/aviation/index.htm (accessed January 15, 2008).

Jackson, Cecile (1998) "Rescuing Gender from the Poverty Trap," in Cecile Jackson and Ruth Pearson (eds.) *Feminist Visions of Development: Gender Analysis and Policy*, London and New York: Routledge.

Jadresic, E., D. N. Nguyen, and U. Halbreich (2007) "What Does Chilean Research Tell Us About Postpartum Depression?" *Journal of Affective Disorders* 102(1–3): 237–43.

Jaggar, Alison M. (1987) "Sex Inequality and Bias in Sex Difference Research," *Canadian Journal of Philosophy*, Supplementary Volume 13: 25–39.

Jaggar, Alison M. (1995) "Toward a Feminist Conception of Moral Reasoning," in James P. Sterba, Milton Fisk, William A. Galston, Carol C. Gould, Alison M. Jaggar, Tibor Machan, and Robert Solomon, *Morality and Social Justice: Point Counterpoint*, Lanham MD and London: Rowman and Littlefield.

Jaggar, Alison M. (1998) "Globalizing Feminist Ethics," *Hypatia* 13(2): 7–31.

Jaggar, Alison M. (2001) "Is Globalization Good for Women?" *Comparative Literature* 53(4): 298–314.

Jaggar, Alison M. (2002a) "Challenging Women's Global Inequalities: Some Priorities for Western Philosophers," *Philosophical Topics* 30(2) (Fall): 229–52.

Jaggar, Alison M. (2002b) "A Feminist Critique of the Alleged Southern Debt," *Hypatia* 17(4): 119–42.

Jaggar, Alison M. (2005a) "'Saving Amina': Global Justice for Women and Intercultural Dialogue," *Ethics and International Affairs* 19(3) (Fall): 85–105.

Jaggar, A. (2005b) "Western Feminism and Global Responsibility," in Barbara S. Andre, J. Keller, and L. Schwartzman (eds.) *Feminist Interventions in Ethics and Politics*, Lanham MD: Rowman and Littlefield, pp. 185–200.

Jaggar, Alison (2009) "Transnational Cycles of Gendered Vulnerability," *Philosophical Topics* 37(2) (Fall): 33–52.

Jaggar, Alison M. (2013) "Does Poverty Wear a Woman's Face? Some Moral Dimensions of a Transnational Research Project," *Hypatia* 28(2): 1–18.

Jenson, N. and L. Wantchekon (2004) "Resource Wealth and Political Regimes in Africa," *Comparative Political Studies* 37: 816–41.

Johnson, D. (2003) *The Root Causes of Sudan's Civil Wars*, Bloomington: Indiana University Press.

Jones, Charles (1999) *Global Justice: Defending Cosmopolitanism*, Oxford: Oxford University Press.

Judd, Dennis and Susan Fainstein (1999) *The Tourist City*, New Haven CT: Yale University Press.

Kang, Hye-Ryoung (2008) "Transnational Women's Collectivities and Global Justice," *Journal of Social Philosophy* 39(3) (Fall): 359–77.

Kannabiran, Kalpana (1996) "Rape and the Construction of Communal Identity," in Kumari Jayarwadena and Malathi de Alwis (eds.) *Embodied Violence: Communalising Women's Sexuality in South Asia*, New Delhi: Kali for Women, pp. 32–41.

Kaplan, Caren (1994) "The Politics of Location as Transnational Feminist Critical Practice," in Inderpal Grewal and Caren Kaplan (eds.) *Scattered Hegemonies: Postmodernity and Transnational Feminist Practices*, Minneapolis: University of Minnesota Press.

Katz, C. (2001a) "On the Grounds of Globalization: A Topography for Feminist Political Engagement," *Signs* 26: 1213–34.

Katz, C. (2001b) "Vagabond Capitalism and the Necessity of Social Reproduction," *Antipode* 33: 709–28.

Katzman, Melanie A. (1997) "Getting the Difference Right: It's Power not
Gender that Matters," *European Eating Disorders Review* 5(2): 71–4.

Katzman, Melanie A. and Sing Lee (1997) "Beyond Body Image: The Integration of Feminist and Transcultural Theories in the Understanding
of Self Starvation," *International Journal of Eating Disorders* 22(4):
385–94.

Keel, Pamela A. and Kelly L. Klump (2003) "Are Eating Disorders Culture-
Bound Syndromes? Implications for Conceptualizing their Etiology," *Psychological Bulletin* 129(5): 747–69.

Kelly, L., S. Burton, and L. Regan (1996) "Beyond Victim and Survivor:
Sexual Violence, Identity, Feminist Theory, and Practice," in L. Adkins and
V. Merchant (eds.) *Sexualizing the Social: The Social Organization of
Power*, London: Macmillan, pp. 77–101.

Kelly, Liz and Jill Radford (1998) "Sexual Violence Against Women and
Girls: An Approach to an International Overview," in R. Emerson Dobash
and Russell P. Dobash (eds.) *Rethinking Violence Against Women*, London:
Sage, pp. 53–76.

Kempadoo, Kamala (1998) "Introduction," in Kamala Kempadoo and Jo
Doezema (eds.) *Global Sex Workers: Rights, Resistance and Redefinition*,
New York: Routledge, pp. 1–28.

Kempadoo, Kamala (2005) "Sex Workers' Rights Organizations and Anti-
Trafficking Campaigns," in Kamala Kempadoo (ed.) *Trafficking and Prosti-
tution Reconsidered: New Perspectives on Migration, Sex Work, and Human
Rights*, Boulder CO and London: Paradigm, pp. 149–55.

Khader, Serene (2008) "Judging Others' Deprivation: Adaptive Preferences,
Moral Pluralism, and the Good," PhD thesis, Stony Brook University.

King, Michael B. (1993) "Cultural Aspects of Eating Disorders," *International
Review of Psychiatry* 5: 205–16.

Kittay, Eva (1999) *Love's Labor: Essays on Women, Equality and Dependency*,
New York: Routledge.

Kittay, Eva Feder (with Bruce Jennings and Angela Wasunna) (2005) "Dependency, Difference, and Global Ethic of Longterm Care," *Journal of Political
Philosophy* 13: 443–69.

Kittay, Eva Feder (2008) "The Global Heart Transplant and Caring across
National Boundaries," *Southern Journal of Philosophy* 46, Summer Supplement: 135–65.

Kochan, Nick (2005) *The Washing Machine: How Money Laundering and
Terrorist Financing Soil Us*, Mason OH: Thomson.

Kymlicka, Will (1991) "Rethinking the Family," *Philosophy and Public Affairs*
20(2) (Spring): 77–97.

Laslett, Peter (1956) *Philosophy, Politics and Society*, Oxford: Blackwell.

Latzer, Yael (2003) "Traditional versus Western Perceptions of Mental Illness:
Women of Moroccan Origin Treated in an Israeli Mental Health Center,"
Journal of Social Work Practice 17(1): 77–94.

204   Bibliography

Lawson, V. (1998) "Hierarchical Households and Gendered Migration in Latin America: Feminist Extensions to Migration Research," *Progress in Human Geography* 22: 39–53.

Le Billon, P. (2001) "The Political Ecology of War: Natural Resources and Armed Conflict," *Political Geography* 20: 561–84.

Lee, Sing (2001) "Fat Phobia in Anorexia Nervosa: Whose Obsession Is It?," in Mervat Nasser, Melanie A. Katzman, and Richard A. Gordon (eds.) *Eating Disorders and Cultures in Transition*, Hove, East Sussex and New York: Brunner-Routledge, pp. 40–54.

Lloyd, Rachel (2011) *Girls Like Us*, New York: HarperCollins.

Lopatin, Marc (2002) "Tax Avoiders Rob Wealth of Nations," *Observer*, November 17.

Lorant, Vincent et al. (2007) "Depression and Socio-economic Risk Factors: 7-Year Longitudinal Population Study," *British Journal of Psychiatry* 190: 293–8.

Louie, Miriam Ching Yoon (2001) *Sweatshop Warriors: Immigrant Women Workers Take on the Global Factory*, Cambridge MA: South End Press.

Loury, Glenn (1995) *One by One from the Inside Out: Race and Responsibility in America*, New York: Free Press.

Lowe, Lisa (1996) *Immigrant Acts: On Asian American Cultural Politics*, Durham NC: Duke University Press.

Lundgren, Eva (1998) "The Hand That Strikes and Comforts: Gender Construction and the Tension Between Body and Social," in R. Emerson Dobash and Russell P. Dobash (eds.) *Rethinking Violence Against Women*, London: Sage, pp. 169–98.

Lutz, H. (2002) "At Your Service Madam! The Globalization of Domestic Service," *Feminist Review* 70: 89–103.

McCarthy, Thomas (2009) *Race, Empire, and the Idea of Human Development*, Cambridge and New York: Cambridge University Press.

MacKinnon, Catharine A. (1987) *Feminism Unmodified: Discourses on Life and Law*, Cambridge MA: Harvard University Press.

Makino, Maria, Koji Tsuboi, and Lorraine Dennerstein (2004) "Prevalence of Eating Disorders: A Comparison of Western and Non-Western Countries," *Medscape General Medicine* 6(3): 1–15, http://www.ncbi.nih.gov/pmc/articles/PMC1435625/?report=printable (accessed May 4, 2012).

Marchand, M. and A. S. Runyan (2011) *Gender and Global Restructuring: Sightings, Sites and Resistances*, London and New York: Routledge.

Marston, S. (2000) "The Social Construction of Scale," *Progress in Human Geography* 24: 219–42.

Massey, D. (1993) "Power-Geometry and a Progressive Sense of Place," in J. Bird, B. Curtis, and T. Putnam (eds.) *Mapping the Future: Local Culture, Global Change*, London: Routledge, pp. 59–69.

Mattingly, D. (2001) "The Home and the World: Domestic Service and International Networks of Caring Labor," *Annals of the Association of American Geographers* 91: 370–86.

Meehan, Oscar L. and Melanie A. Katzman (2001) "Argentina: The Social Body at Risk," in Mervat Nasser, Melanie A. Katzman, and Richard A. Gordon (eds.) *Eating Disorders and Cultures in Transition*, Hove, East Sussex and New York: Brunner-Routledge, pp. 148–62.

Mendez, Jennifer Bickham (2002) "Creating Alternatives from a Gender Perspective: Transnational Organizing for Maquila Workers' Rights in Central America," in Nancy A. Naples and Manisha Desai (eds.) *Women's Activism and Globalization: Linking Local Struggles and Transitional Politics*, New York and London: Routledge, pp. 121–41.

Mendez, Ruben (1992) *International Public Finance*, Oxford: Oxford University Press.

Miller, David (1995) *On Nationality*, Oxford and New York: Clarendon Press.

Miller, David (1998) "Limits of Cosmopolitan Justice," in David R. Mapel and Terry Nardin (eds.) *International Society: Diverse Ethical Perspectives*, Princeton NJ: Princeton University Press, pp. 164–81.

Miller, David (1999) *Principles of Social Justice*, Cambridge MA: Harvard University Press.

Miller, David (2006) *Nationalism*, Oxford and New York: Oxford University Press.

Miller, Merry N. and Andres J. Pumariega (2001) "Culture and Eating Disorders: A Historical and Cross-Cultural Review," *Psychiatry* 64(2) (Summer): 93–110.

Mitchell, Austin and Prem Sikka (2005) *Taming the Corporations*, Basildon, Essex: Association for Accountancy and Business Affairs.

Moeller-Leimkuhler, Anna Maria (2003) "The Gender Gap in Suicide and Premature Death: Or, Why are Men so Vulnerable?" *European Archives of Psychiatry and Clinical Neuroscience* 252(1): 1–8.

Moghadam, M. Valentine (2005) *Globalizing Women: Transnational Feminist Networks*, Baltimore MD and London: Johns Hopkins University Press.

Mohanty, Chandra Talpade (1991) "Cartographies of Struggle: Third World Women and the Politics of Feminism," in Chandra Talpade Mohanty, Ann Russo, and Lourdes Torres (eds.) *Third World Women and the Politics of Feminism*, Bloomington: Indiana University Press.

Mohanty, Chandra Talpade (1997) "Women Workers and Capitalist Scripts: Ideologies of Domination, Common Interests, and the Politics of Solidarity," in Chandra Talpade Mohanty and M. Jacqui Alexander (eds.) *Feminist Genealogies, Colonial Legacies, Democratic Futures*, New York and London: Routledge, pp. 3–29.

Monzini, Paola (2005) *Sex Traffic: Prostitution, Crime, and Exploitation*, London: Zed Books.

Moore, M. (2012) "Natural Resources, Territorial Rights, and Global Distributive Justice," *Political Theory* 40(1): 84–107.

Mountz, A. and J. Hyndman (2006) "Feminist Approaches to the Global Intimate," *Women's Studies Quarterly* 34: 446–63.

Murray, Alison (1998) "Debt-bondage and Trafficking: Don't Believe the Hype," in Kamala Kempadoo and Jo Doezema (eds.) *Global Sex Workers: Rights, Resistance and Redefinition*, New York: Routledge, pp. 51–64.

Nahas, Violeta and Nawal Amasheh (1999) "Culture Care Meanings and Experiences of Postpartum Depression among Jordanian Australian Women: A Transcultural Study," *Journal of Transcultural Nursing* 10(37): 37–45.

Nam, Jeong-Lim (2002) "Women's Labor Movement, State Suppression, and Democratization in South Korea," *Asian Journal of Women's Studies* 8(1): 71–95.

Narayan, Uma (1996) "Contesting Cultures: 'Westernization,' Respect for Cultures, and Third-World Feminists," in Linda Nicholson (ed.) *The Second Wave: A Reader in Feminist Theory*, New York and London: Routledge, pp. 396–414.

Nasreen, Hashima E. et al. (2011) "Prevalence and Associated Factors of Depressive and Anxiety Symptoms During Pregnancy: A Population Based Study in Rural Bangladesh," *BMC Women's Health* 11(22): 1–9, http://www.biomedcentral.com/1472-6874/11/22 (accessed April 20, 2012).

Nasser, Mervat (2009) "Eating Disorders Across Cultures," *Psychiatry* 8(9): 347–50.

Neighbour, John (2002) "Transfer Pricing: Keeping it at Arm's Length," *OECD Observer* (April).

Nelson, L. and J. Seager (2005) *A Companion to Feminist Geography*, Oxford: Blackwell.

NGO Committee on Migration (2008) "Statement for the 2008 Global Forum on Migration and Development: A Call for a Human Rights-Based Approach to Migration and Development," in *Seventh Coordination Meeting on International Migration*, New York: Population Division, Department of Economic and Social Affairs, United Nations Secretariat.

Nili, Shmuel (2011) "Conceptualizing the Resource Curse: Two Views on our Responsibility for the Resource Curse," *Ethics and Global Politics* 4(2): 103–24.

Njenga, F. G. and R. N. Kangethe (2004) "Anorexia Nervosa in Kenya," *East African Medical Journal* 81(4): 188–93.

Nussbaum, Martha C. (1995) "Human Capabilities, Female Human Beings," in Martha Nussbaum and Jonathan Glover (eds.) *Women, Culture and Development: A Study of Human Capabilities*, Oxford: Oxford University Press.

Nussbaum, Martha C. (1996) "Patriotism and Cosmopolitanism," in Joshua Cohen (ed.) *For Love of Country: Debating the Limits of Patriotism*, Boston: Beacon Press.

Nussbaum, Martha C. (2000) *Women and Human Development: The Capabilities Approach*, Cambridge: Cambridge University Press.

O'Connor, Peg (2002) *Oppression and Responsibility: A Wittgensteinian Approach to Social Practices and Moral Theory*, University Park: Pennsylvania State University Press.

OECD (2004) "Migration, Remittances and Development," http://www.oecd.org/document/34/0,3343,en_2649_33931_35744418_1_1_1_37415,00.html (accessed July 1, 2008).

Okin, Susan Moller (1989) *Justice, Gender, and the Family*, New York: Basic Books.

Okin, Susan Moller (1994) "Gender Inequality and Cultural Differences," *Political Theory* 22(1): 5–24.

Oman, Charles (2000) *Policy Competition for Foreign Direct Investment: A Study of Competition among Governments to Attract FDI*, OECD Development Centre, http://www.oecd.org/mena/investment/35275189.pdf (accessed May 7, 2013).

Oxfam (2000) *Tax Havens: Releasing the Hidden Billions for Poverty Eradication*, http://policy-practice.oxfam.org.uk/publications/tax-havens-releasing-the-hidden-billions-for-poverty-exadication-114611.

Oxfam (2002) *Rigged Rules and Double Standards: Trade, Globalisation and the Fight Against Poverty*, http://policy-practice.oxfam.org.uk/publications/rigged-rules-and-double-standards-trade-globalisation-and-the-fight-against-pov-112391 (accessed April 30, 2013).

Oxfam (2004) *Trading Away Our Rights: Women Working in Global Supply Chains*, available at http://www.oxfam.org/en/policy/report-042008-labor (accessed April 30, 2013).

Özden, Çağlar and Maurice Schiff (2007) *International Migration, Economic Development, and Policy*, New York: Palgrave Macmillan; "Overview," http://siteresources.worldbank.org/INTINTERNATIONAL/Resources/1572846-1182276832896/Book_Overview.pdf (accessed May 13, 2013).

Ozer, Emily J. et al. (2011) "Does Alleviating Poverty Affect Mothers' Depressive Symptoms? A Quasi-Experimental Investigation of Mexico's *Oportunidades* Programme," *International Journal of Epidemiology* 40: 1565–76.

Parreñas, Rhacel Salazar (2001) *Servants of Globalization: Women, Migration, and Domestic Work*, Stanford CA: Stanford University Press.

Parreñas, Rhacel Salazar (2002) "The Care Crisis in the Philippines: Children and Transnational Families in the New Global Economy," in Barbara Ehrenreich and Arlie Russell Hochschild (eds.) *Global Woman: Nannies, Maids, and Sex Workers in the New Economy*, New York: Henry Holt.

Parreñas, R. (2005) *Children of Global Migration: Transnational Families and Gendered Woes*, Stanford CA: Stanford University Press.

Parreñas, R. (2011) *Illicit Flirtations: Labor, Migration and Sex Trafficking in Tokyo*, Stanford CA: Stanford University Press.

Parreñas, R. S., M. C. Hwang, and H. R. Lee (2012) "What is Human Trafficking? A Review Essay," *Signs* 37: 1015–29.

Patel, Vikram (2001) "Cultural Factors and International Epidemiology," *British Medical Bulletin* 57: 33–45.

Patel, Vikram et al. (1999) "Women, Poverty and Common Mental Disorders in Four Restructuring Societies," *Social Science and Medicine* 49: 1461–71.

Patel, Vikram and Arthur Kleinman (2003) "Poverty and Common Mental Disorders in Developing Countries," *Bulletin of the World Health Organization* 81(8): 609–15.

Pateman, Carole (1988) *The Sexual Contract*, Stanford CA: Stanford University Press.

Pateman, Carole (2002) "Self-Ownership and Property in the Person: Democratization and a Tale of two Concepts," *Journal of Political Philosophy* 10(1): 20–53.

Pateman, Carole and Charles W. Mills (2007) *Contract and Domination*, Cambridge and Malden, MA: Polity.

Paul, J. and K. Wahlberg (2002) "Global Taxes for Global Priorities," http://www.globalpolicy.org/socecon/glotax/general/glotaxpaper.htm (accessed May 13, 2013).

Penson, Cesar Nicolas (2007) "Gender, Remittances and Development Global Care Chains," Working Paper 2: A Strategic Instantiation of the Migration-Development Link: Global Care Chains. United Nations International Research and Training Institute for the Advancement of Women.

Phillips, Joan L. (1999) "Tourist-Oriented Prostitution in Barbados: The Case of the Beach Boy and the White Female Tourist," in Kamala Kempadoo (ed.) *Sun, Sex, and Gold: Tourism and Sex Work in the Caribbean*, Lanham MD: Rowman and Littlefield.

Pike, Kathleen and Amy Borovoy (2004) "The Rise of Eating Disorders in Japan: Issues of Culture and Limitations of the Model of 'Westernization,'" *Culture, Medicine and Psychiatry* 28: 493–531.

Pineda, J. and F. Rodriguez (2010) "Curse or Blessing? Natural Resource and Human Development," UNDP Human Development Research Paper, http://hdr.undp.org/en/reports/global/hdr2010/papers/HDRP_2010_04.pdf.

Piper, N. (2004) "Rights of Foreign Workers and the Politics of Migration in South-East and East Asia," *International Migration* 42: 71–97.

Piper, N. (2005) "Gender and Migration," paper prepared for the Policy Analysis and Research Programme of the Global Commission on International Migration, http://www.iom.int/jahia/webdav/site/myjahiasite/shared/shared/mainsite/policy_and_research/gcim/tp/TP10.pdf.

Piper, N. (ed.) (2008) *New Perspectives on Gender and Migration: Livelihood, Rights and Entitlements*, New York: Routledge.

Pogge, Thomas W. (1992) "Cosmopolitanism and Sovereignty," *Ethics* 103(1): 48–75.

Pogge, Thomas W. (2002) *World Poverty and Human Rights*, Cambridge: Polity.

Pogge, Thomas W. (2004) "'Assisting' the Global Poor," in Deen K. Chatterjee (ed.) *Ethics of Assistance: Morality and the Distant Needy*, Cambridge: Cambridge University Press, pp. 260–88.

Pogge, Thomas W. (2007) *John Rawls: His Life and Theory of Justice*, Oxford: Oxford University Press.

Pogge, Thomas W. (2010) *Politics as Usual: What Lies Behind the Pro-Poor Rhetoric*, Cambridge and Malden MA: Polity.

Pratt, G. (2004) *Working Feminism*, Philadelphia: Temple University Press.

Pratt, G. (2012) *Families Apart: Migrant Mothers and the Conflicts of Labor and Love*, Minneapolis: University of Minnesota Press.

Pratt, G. and B. Yeoh (2003) "Transnational (Counter) Topographies," *Gender, Place and Culture* 10: 159–66.

Prunier, G. (2009) *Africa's World War: Congo, the Rwandan Genocide, and the Making of a Continental Catastrophe*, Oxford: Oxford University Press.

Rao, Mohan (1999) "Globalization and the Fiscal Autonomy of the State," *Human Development Background Papers 1999*, New York: UNDP.

Raphael, Frances J. and J. Hubert Lacey (1992) "Sociocultural Aspects of Eating Disorders," *Annals of Medicine* 24: 293–6.

Rathner, Gunther (2001) "Post-communism and the Marketing of the Thin Ideal," in Mervat Nasser, Melanie A. Katzman, and Richard A. Gordon (eds.) *Eating Disorders and Cultures in Transition*, Hove, East Sussex and New York: Brunner-Routledge, pp. 93–104.

Rawls, John (1971) *A Theory of Justice*, Cambridge MA: Belknap Press of Harvard University Press.

Rawls, John (1999) *The Law of Peoples, with "The Idea of Public Reason Revisited,"* Cambridge MA: Harvard University Press.

Rawls, John (2001a) *Justice as Fairness: A Restatement*, Cambridge MA: Harvard University Press.

Rawls, John (2001b) *The Law of Peoples*, Cambridge MA: Harvard University Press.

Razack, S. (1998) *Looking White People in the Eye: Gender, Race, and Culture in Courtrooms and Classrooms*, Toronto: University of Toronto Press.

Risse, T. and S. Ropp (eds.) (1999) *The Power of Human Rights: International Norms and Domestic Change*, Cambridge: Cambridge University Press.

Roberts, A. (2006) *The Wonga Coup: Guns, Thugs, and a Ruthless Determination to Create Mayhem in an Oil-Rich Corner of Africa*, New York: Public Affairs.

Robinson, K. (1991) "Housemaids: The Effects of Gender and Culture in the Internal and International Migration of Indonesian Women," in G. Bottomley, M. Lepervanche, and J. Martin (eds.) *Intersexions: Gender, Class, Culture, Ethnicity*, Sydney: Allen and Unwin, pp. 33–51.

Robinson, K. (2000) "Gender, Islam, and Nationality: Indonesian Domestic Servants in the Middle East," in K. Adams and S. Dickey (eds.) *Home and Hegemony: Domestic Service and Identity Politics in South and Southeast Asia*, Ann Arbor: University of Michigan Press, pp. 249–82.

Robinson, K. and S. Bessell (2002) "Introduction to the Issues," in K. Robinson and S. Bessell (eds.) *Women in Indonesia: Gender, Equity, and Development*, Singapore: Institute of Southeast Asian Studies, pp. 1–12.

Rollins, Judith (1987) *Between Women: Domestics and Their Employers*, Philadelphia: Temple University Press.

Ross, M. (2001) "Does Oil Hinder Democracy?," *World Politics* 53: 297–322.

Ross, M. (2008) "Oil, Islam, and Women," *American Political Science Review* 102: 107–23.

Ross, M. (2011) "Will Oil Drown the Arab Spring?," *Harper's*, November, pp. 17–21.

Ross, M. (2012) *The Oil Curse: How Petroleum Wealth Shapes the Development of Nations*, Princeton NJ: Princeton University Press.

Rosser, A. (2006) "The Political Economy of the Resource Curse: A Literature Survey," Institute of Development Studies, Working Paper 268.

Ruggiero, Giovanni (2001) "One Country, Two Cultures," in Mervat Nasser, Melanie A. Katzman, and Richard A. Gordon (eds.) *Eating Disorders and Cultures in Transition*, Hove, East Sussex and New York: Brunner-Routledge, pp. 127–36.

Sassen, Saskia (2000) "Women's Burden: Counter-geographies of Globalization and the Feminization of Survival," *Journal of International Affairs* 53(2) (Spring): 503–24.

Sassen, Saskia (2002) "Women's Burden: Counter-Geographies of Globalization and the Feminization of Survival," *Nordic Journal of International Law* 71: 255–74.

Satterthwaite, M. (2005) "Crossing Borders, Claiming Rights: Using Human Rights Law to Empower Women Migrant Workers," *Yale Human Rights and Development Law Journal* 8: 1–66.

Schroeder, Frank (2006) "Innovative Sources of Finance After the Paris Conference," Friedrich Ebert Foundation/Stiftung (FES) Briefing Paper, April.

Schutte, Ofelia (2002) "Dependency Work, Women, and the Global Economy," in Eva Feder Kittay and Ellen K. Feder (eds.) *The Subject of Care: Feminist Perspectives on Dependency*, Lanham MD: Rowman and Littlefield, pp. 138–59.

Seguino, Stephanie (2000) "Accounting for Asian Economic Growth: Adding Gender to the Equation," *Feminist Economics* 6(3): 22–58.

Sen, Amartya (1990) "Millions of Women are Missing," *New York Review of Books*, December 20.

Sen, Amartya (2009) *The Idea of Justice*, Cambridge MA: Harvard University Press.

Sher, Julian (2011) *Somebody's Daughter: The Hidden Story of America's Prostituted Children and the Battle to Save Them*, Chicago: Chicago Review Press.

Shrage, Laurie (1994) *Moral Dilemmas of Feminism: Prostitution, Adultery, and Abortion*, New York: Routledge.

Shuriquie, N. (1999) "Eating Disorders: A Transcultural Perspective," *Eastern Mediterranean Health Journal* 5(2): 354–60.

Silvey, R. (2009). "Development and Geography: Anxious Times, Anemic Geographies, and Migration," *Progress in Human Geography* 33: 507–15.

Singer, Peter (1972) "Famine, Affluence, and Morality," *Philosophy and Public Affairs* 1(1): 229–43.

Singer, Peter (2002) *One World: The Ethics of Globalization*, New Haven CT and London: Yale University Press.

Somers, J. M., E. M. Goldner, P. Waraich, and L. Hsu (2006) "Prevalence and Incidence Studies of Anxiety Disorders: A Systematic Review of the Literature," *Canadian Journal of Psychiatry* 51(2): 100–13.

Spahn, Paul (2002) *On the Feasibility of a Tax on Foreign Exchange Transactions*, Report to the German Federal Ministry for Economic Cooperation and Development, http://www.wiwi.uni-frankfurt.de/profs/spahn/tobintax/ Tobintax.pdf (accessed May 7, 2013).

Sparke, M. (2005) *In the Space of Theory: Postfoundational Geographies of the Nation-State*, Minneapolis: University of Minnesota Press.

Spivak, G. C. (1999) *A Critique of Postcolonial Reason: Toward a History of the Vanishing Present*, Cambridge MA: Harvard University Press.

Standing, Guy (1999) "Global Feminization Through Flexible Labor: A Theme Revisited," *World Development* 27(3): 583–602.

Stearns, J. (2011) *Dancing in the Glory of Monsters: The Collapse of the Congo and the Great War of Africa*, New York: Public Affairs.

Stilwell, Barbara et al. (2003) "Developing Evidence-based Ethical Policies on the Migration of Health Workers: Conceptual and Practical Challenges," *Human Resources for Health* 1(1): 8.

Stotsky, Janet (1997) "Gender Bias in Tax Systems," *Tax Notes International* (June 9): 1913–23.

Strasser, Susan (1982) *Never Done: A History of American Housework*, New York: Pantheon Books.

Swarr, A. and R. Nagar (eds.) (2010) *Critical Transnational Feminist Praxis*, New York: SUNY Press.

Synder, A. and R. Bhavnani (2005) "Diamonds, Blood, and Taxes: A Revenue-Centered Framework for Explaining Political Order," *Journal of Conflict Resolution* 49(4): 563–97.

Tagaroa, R. and E. Sofia (2002) *Buruh Migran Indonesia: Mencari Keadilan (Indonesian Migrant Workers: Searching for Justice)*, Lembaga Advokasi Buruh Migran—Solidaritas Perempuan (Migrant Workers Advocacy Institute—Women's Solidarity), Bekasi.

Tanzi, Vito (1999) "Is There a Need for a World Tax Organization?," in Assaf Razin and Efraim Sadka (eds.) *The Economics of Globalization: Policy Perspectives from Public Economics*, Cambridge: Cambridge University Press, pp. 173–86.

Taran, P. (2000) "Human Rights of Migrants: Challenges of the New Decade," *International Migration* 38: 7–51.

Ticktin, Miriam (2008) "Sexual Violence as the Language of Border Control: Where French Feminist and Anti-immigrant Rhetoric Meet," *Signs* 33(4): 863–89.

Timimi, Sami (2008) "Children's Mental Health and the Global Market: An Ecological Analysis," in Carl I. Cohen and Sami Timimi (eds.) *Liberatory Psychiatry: Philosophy, Politics, and Mental Health*, Cambridge and New York: Cambridge University Press, pp. 163–82.

Tobin, James (1974) *The New Economics, One Decade Older. The Eliot Janeway Lectures on Historical Economics in Honor of Joseph Schumpeter, 1972*, Princeton NJ: Princeton University Press.

Tronto, Joan C. (2002) "The 'Nanny Question' in Feminism," *Hypatia* 17(2): 34–51.

UNDESA (United Nations Department for Economic and Social Affairs) (2005) *World Economic and Social Survey 2005: Financing for Development*, http://www.un.org/esa/desa/ousg/statements/2005/20051010_wess2005.pdf (accessed May 7, 2013).

UNDP (United Nations Development Programme) (1994) *Human Development Report 1994*, New York: Oxford University Press.

UNDP (United Nations Development Programme) (1999), *Human Development Report 1999*, New York: Oxford University Press.

UNFPA (United Nations Population Fund) (2006) *State of the World Population 2006. A Passage to Hope: Women and International Migration*, http://www.unfpa.org/webdav/site/global/shared/documents/publications/2006/sowp06-en.pdf (accessed December 29, 2012).

UNHCR (United Nations High Commission on Refugees) (1990) *International Convention on the Protection of the Rights of All Migrant Workers and Members of Their Families*. Adopted by General Assembly Resolution 45/158 of December 18, 1990, http://www.unhcr.org/496323780.pdf.

United Nations (1948) The Universal Declaration of Human Rights, December 10.

United Nations (1959) Declaration of the Rights of the Child, November 20.

United Nations (1999) *1999 World Survey on the Role of Women in Development: Globalization, Gender and Work*, New York: United Nations.

United Nations Development Fund for Women (2002) "Women Challenging Globalization: A Gender Perspective on the United Nations International Conference on Financing for Development, March 18–22, Monterrey, Mexico," http://www.wedo.org/wp-content/uploads/ffdreport_eng.pdf (accessed April 30, 2013).

UNSRHRM (United Nations Special Rapporteur on the Human Rights of Migrants) (2001) "Visit to Canada," UN Economic and Social Council, E/CN. 4/2001/83/Add. 1, http://daccess-dds-ny.un.org/doc/UNDOC/GEN/G01/100/61/PDF/G0110061.pdf (accessed December 29, 2012).

Vander Wal, Jillon S., Judith L. Gibbons, and Maria del Pilar Grazioso (2008) "The Sociocultural Model of Eating Disorder Development: Application to a Guatemalan Sample," *Eating Behaviors* 9: 277–84.

Vigueras, Juan Hernández (2005) *Tax Havens: How Offshore Centres Undermine Democracy*, Madrid: Akal.

Wahl, Peter and Peter Waldow (2001) *Currency Transaction Tax—A Concept with a Future: Chances and Limits of Stabilising Financial Markets Through the Tobin Tax*, Bonn: WEED.

Walker, James (2005) "Alternative Financing for the United Nations," http://www.globalpolicy.org/finance/alternat/currtax/walker.htm (accessed in 2008 from the Global Policy Forum website).

Walzer, Michael (1983) *Spheres of Justice: A Defense of Pluralism and Equality*, New York: Basic Books.

Walzer, Michael (1994) *Thick and Thin: Moral Argument at Home and Abroad*, Notre Dame IN: University of Notre Dame Press.

Wang, Shing-Yaw et al. (2003) "A Comparative Study of Postnatal Depression and Its Predictors in Taiwan and Mainland China," *American Journal of Obstetrics and Gynecology* 189(5): 1407–12.

Waring, Marilyn (1988) *Counting for Nothing: What Men Value and What Women are Worth*, Wellington, New Zealand: Allen and Unwin.

Watters, Ethan (2010) *Crazy Like Us: The Globalization of the American Psyche*, New York: Free Press.

Weir, Allison (2008) "Global Care Chains: Freedom, Responsibility, and Solidarity," *Southern Journal of Philosophy* 46, Summer Supplement: 166–75.

Welchman, Lynn and Sara Hossain (2005) "Introduction: 'Honour,' Rights and Wrongs," in Lynn Welchman and Sara Hossain (eds.) *"Honour": Crimes, Paradigms and Violence Against Women*, London: Zed Books, pp. 1–21.

Wellman, C. (1996) "Liberalism, Samaritanism, and Political Legitimacy," *Philosophy and Public Affairs* 25: 211–37.

Wenar, L. (2008) "Property Rights and the Resource Curse," *Philosophy and Public Affairs* 36: 2–32.

Wenar, L. (2011) "Clean Trade in Natural Resources," *Ethics and International Affairs* 25(1): 27–39.

West, Robin (2002) "A Right to Care," in Eva Feder Kittay and Ellen K. Feder (eds.) *The Subject of Care: Feminist Perspectives on Dependency*, Lanham MD: Rowman and Littlefield, pp. 14–39.

Wiens, D. et al. (forthcoming; manuscript on file with author) "Is there a Political Resource Curse? A Theoretical and Empirical Re-evaluation."

Wildes, Jennifer E., Robert E. Emery, and Anne D. Simons (2001) "The Role of Ethnicity and Culture in the Development of Eating Disturbance and Body Dissatisfaction: A Meta-Analytic Review," *Clinical Psychology Review* 21(4): 521–51.

Wilson, Margo and Martin Daly (1998) "Lethal and Nonlethal Violence Against Wives and the Evolutionary Psychology of Male Sexual Proprietariness," in R. Emerson Dobash and Russell P. Dobash (eds.) *Rethinking Violence Against Women*, London: Sage, pp. 199–230.

Wisor, Scott (2012) "Property Rights and the Resource Curse: A Reply to Wenar," *Journal of Philosophical Research* 37: 185–204.

Wolf, Naomi (1994) *Fire with Fire: The New Female Power and How to Use It*, New York: Ballantine Books.

Woolf, Virginia (1938) *Three Guineas*, San Diego, New York and London: Harcourt, Brace.

World Bank (2005) *Global Economics Prospect 2006: International Remittances and Migration*, Washington DC: World Bank.

World Bank (2007) *World Development Report 2008: Agriculture for Development*, http://siteresources.worldbank.org/INTWDR2008/Resources/WDR_00_book.pdf (accessed December 29, 2012).

World Bank (2011) *World Development Report 2012: Gender Equality and Development*, Washington DC: World Bank.

World Health Organization (WHO) Department of Mental Health and Substance Dependence (n.d.) "Gender Disparities in Mental Health," http://www.who.int/mental_health/media/en/242.pdf (accessed June 7, 2012).

World Health Organization (WHO) and World Organization of Family Doctors (Wonca) (2008) "Integrating Mental Health into Primary Care: A Global Perspective," http://www.who.int/mental_health/policy/services/mentalhealthintoprimarycare/en (accessed May 13, 2013).

Wright, M. (2006) *Disposable Women and Other Myths of Global Capitalism*, New York: Routledge.

Yağmur, Yurdagul and Nese Ulukoca (2010) "Social Support and Postpartum Depression in Low-Socioeconomic Level Postpartum Women in Eastern Turkey," *International Journal of Public Health* 55: 543–9.

Yeoh, B. S. A. and S. Huang (1999) "Spaces at the Margins: Migrant Domestic Workers and the Development of Civil Society in Singapore," *Environment and Planning A* 31: 1149–67.

Young, Iris Marion (1990) *Justice and the Politics of Difference*, Princeton NJ: Princeton University Press.

Young, Iris Marion (2000) *Inclusion and Democracy*, Oxford and New York: Oxford University Press.

Young, Iris M. (2006) "Responsibility and Global Justice: A Social Connection Model," *Social Philosophy and Policy* 23(1): 102–30.

Young, Iris Marion (2009) "The Gendered Cycle of Vulnerability in the Less Developed World," in Debra Satz and Ron Reich (eds.) *Toward a Humanist Justice: The Political Philosophy of Susan Moller Okin*, Oxford and New York: Oxford University Press, pp. 223–37.

Yuval-Davis, N. (1997a) "Women, Citizenship and Difference," *Feminist Review* 57: 4–27.

Yuval-Davis, Nira (1997b) *Gender and Nation*, London, Thousand Oaks and New Delhi: Sage Publications.

Zarembka, Joy M. (2002) "America's Dirty Work: Migrant Maids and Modern Day Slavery," in Barbara Ehrenreich and Arlie Russell Hochschild (eds.) *Global Woman: Nannies, Maids, and Sex Workers in the New Economy*, New York: Henry Holt, pp. 143–53.

Index

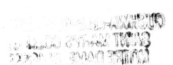

CPSIA information can be obtained
at www.ICGtesting.com
Printed in the USA
FSOW04n1731010817
37103FS

9 780745 663777